Western Painting

Portrait Miniatures

Works of Art and

Manuscripts on Paper

Photographs

Books

Textiles

Archaeological Objects

Ethnographic Objects

Metals

Ceramic and Glass Objects

Stone Objects and

Sculpture

Outdoor Sculpture

Furniture and

Wooden Objects

Frames

Plastics

Home Movies,

Videotape and

Audiotape

Conservation Resources for Art and Antiques

Second Edition

First Washington Conservation Guild edition 2001

Printed in the United States of America

Washington Conservation Guild
Conservation Resources for Art and Antiques / Washington Conservation Guild
Includes index.
ISBN 0-9706385-1-5
Library of Congress Control Number: 2004106777

Cover and interior design by Sims Design Co. LLC

Cover Photo Credits

Photo of Man: from Kyser-Hollingsworth
Lion Sculpture: after Antonino Canova, *Lions,* 19th century Bronze
In the Collection of the Corcoran Gallery of Art, Washington, D.C.,
Museum Purchase 88.10.1 and 88.10.2
Chinese Die Proof: National Postal Museum, Linda Edquist
Conservator: from Martin Kotler
Keys: from Kathleen Sims
Photo of two women: from Kathleen Sims
Woman with hat: from Linda Edquist

Contents

Acknowledgments

Editorial Committee
Christine Smith,
  Chair 1st edition
Mary Ballard
Melissa Heaver
Helen Ingalls
Emily KlaymanJacobson,
  Chair 2nd edition

Submissions Committee
Dare M. Hartwell,
  Chair
Marisa Keller,
  Processor

Publication Committee
Linda S. Edquist,
  Co-chair
Sarah Stauderman,
  Co-chair
Fern Bleckner
Alexandra Dennis-Tice
Davida Kovner

Fulfillment Committee
Quentin Rankin,
  Co-chair
Rachel-Ray Cleveland,
  Co-chair
Ed McManus
Lisa Young

Authors
Carol Aiken
Sylvia Albro
Mary Ballard
Harriet Beaubien
Ron Blank
Fern Bleckner
Terry Boone
Katherine Eirk
Janice S. Ellis
Rosemary Fallon
Lizou Fenyvesi
Alec Graham
Carol Grissom
Stephanie Hornbeck
Helen Ingalls
Timothy Killalea
Davida Kovner
William Lewin
Catherine Magee
Edward McManus
Stephen Mellor
Catherine Metzger
Dana Moffett
Yoshi Nishio
Ryo Nishiumi
Michele Pagan
Arthur Page
Brian Ramer
R. Quentin Rankin
Andrew Robb

Bruce Schuettinger
Kate Singley
Sarah Stauderman
Donna Strahan
Stephen Wilcox
Sidney Williston
Mary Wootton
Lisa Young

Contributors
Eileen Blankenbaker
W. Thomas Chase
Alexandra Dennis-Tice
Valerie Gouet
Xiangmei Gu
Dare M. Hartwell
Emily Klayman Jacobson
Paul Jett
Catherine Maynor
Catherine Nicholson
Mark Rabinowitz
Gail Singer
Martha Smith
Hanna Szczepanowska
Nicholas Veloz

Preface

In 1998, the Washington Conservation Guild undertook the publication of the first edition of this resource guide as part of our public education program. Since *Conservation Resources for Art and Antiques* was published, nearly one thousand copies have been sold, and it is now being carried in local museum shops and national archival catalog companies. We are pleased to present this second edition, which includes new and revised chapters as well as updated conservator listings. The primary goal of this book remains to provide those in need of conservation services with information that describes conservation practices, gives guidance on finding reputable help, and lists local conservators with descriptions of their backgrounds and specialties.

The essays in this reference guide, written by conservators, provide valuable information on preservation principles for various materials (including paintings, metals, stone, textiles, photographs, books, ceramics, furniture, graphics, and more). They also present practical information on why, when, and how to seek help from a conservator. The goal is to enhance the reader's understanding of various treatment options available and the risks involved in any course of treatment.

The Washington Conservation Guild, founded in 1967, is a local non-profit organization dedicated to the conservation and preservation of cultural property. Our members include conservators, curators, framers, students, and others interested in our goals. The all-volunteer board organizes eight meetings a year, with lectures presented on various conservation topics. Many of our members and board members also contributed time and expertise to this publication project, and we are grateful to all who made this resource guide possible. The Washington Conservation Guild sincerely hopes it will continue to be a standard reference for all those in the Washington area in need of conservation services.

We would like to dedicate this second edition to the memory of local conservators who have passed away during the last several years. Many of them have contributed to the success of the Washington Conservation Guild, several in leadership positions, and all have inspired fellow conservators with their skill and professionalism. This publication is in their memory:

Bethune Gibson

Bettina Jessell

Kendra Lovette

Eleanor Quandt

Stanley Robertson

Carolyn Rose

Peter Waters

Sidney Williston

Introduction

CONSERVATION RESOURCES FOR ART AND ANTIQUES, PUBLISHED BY THE Washington Conservation Guild (WCG), provides information relevant to the preservation and treatment of valued and cherished objects. It is a collaborative effort of many WCG conservators over a three-year period. One of the primary objectives of this resource is to link those in need of conservation services with those who provide such services in the greater Washington-Baltimore area. Other useful features of this book include introductory essays about objects and materials, a statement of professional standards for conservators, a glossary of conservation-related terms, and advertisements for sources of conservation materials and equipment. Combining collections care information and referrals in a single source, this is the first publication of its kind by a regional conservation guild in the United States.

Why Some Things Last and Others Don't

Preservation deals with time, matter, and energy; ours, after all, is a material world. Objects, artwork, and natural history specimens are made from matter. Materials are composed of atomic elements and combinations of those elements (compounds). The properties of materials are determined by their atomic structure. Craftspeople and artists have long undertood those properties intuitively, through experience and observation, and the skill of the artisan working with the material is one reason exceptional art and artifacts are appreciated so highly. Discoveries were made by trial and error and even by accident. Trade secrets were carefully protected by guilds and passed on through an apprenticeship system. It does not matter that Michelangelo did not know the chemical composition of marble or da Vinci the chemistry of paper or fresco.

But for collectors and custodians of art and artifacts and for conservators, it is important to know what a thing is made of in order to preserve it. Development of the periodic table and the scientific understanding of materials began in the eighteenth century and continues today. In contrast to past practices, material scientists now first determine what the desired properties are and then either manipulate traditional materials or invent new ones to answer those needs. Many new materials are an outgrowth of the space program. Consider, for example, the many ways that plastics have replaced wood, glass, and metal.

The other consideration in preserving artifacts is energy. Most of us are familiar with energy in the forms of heat, light, chemical reaction, and electricity. The interaction of matter and energy is dynamic. Frequently energy is used in the creation of an artifact, such as the firing of clay to produce ceramics or the hardening of soft steel through tempering. Likewise energy is also involved in the deterioration of an artifact, such as the tendency for metals to corrode or for textiles and paper to fade in sunlight.

Once created, most material objects begin to deteriorate either because of the inherent nature of the material or because of exposure to environments that promote their deterioration. In extreme cases they are damaged or destroyed by accident. The condition of art and artifacts can be maintained, however, and their life extended by proper care and treatment. To provide that care, one must understand the scientific nature of the materials and the agents that influence both deterioration and preservation. This is what conservation is all about.

About Conservation

It is important to know the meaning of the terms **conservation, preservation**, and **restoration** (see the glossary for concise definitions) and to understand how they relate to what we as conservators do with artifacts.

Conservation is a relatively young profession; the term has been applied to the preservation of art only since the 1930s, when knowledge of modern chemistry began to inform the practice of restoration. Similarly modern chemistry had its origins in alchemy and applied material science in the craft tradition. Like the craftspeople and the artists of the past, restorers had a working knowledge of materials but not, in most instances, a scientific understanding of them. In fact, many early restorations were accomplished by artists and craftspeople using traditional materials and techniques. Frequently the intent of restoration was, and is, to repair damage and to return the appearance of an artifact to an earlier time. Risks in such an approach include the loss of historic information, alteration of the artifact from its true character, and methods and materials that can induce further deterioration later on. The risks increase if the restorer knows little about the material composition of the artifact and the nature of the materials used in treatment. The approach of conservation science minimizes these risks. An additional benefit of conservation for museums and collectors is the recovery of information about the techniques of an artist or artisan and about the authenticity of a piece.

The primary distinction between conservation and restoration is that **conservation treatment** requires a scientific understanding of the material. Ideally the conservator has both the understanding as well as the skill of the artist or craftsperson. There are many other differences as well. Conservation is a profession in the true sense of the word, as it requires specialized training and is guided by ethics and standards.

The Conservation Professional

The first graduate-level conservation programs in the United States dealt with the preservation and treatment of works of art. Soon the need for such expertise in related areas, such as the decorative arts, became apparent. Conservators now specialize in a wide range of subject areas, including paintings, sculpture, archival material and paper, three-dimensional objects, photographs, furniture, glass and ceramics, archaeology and ethnographic materials, and textiles.

Previously an aspiring conservator could apprentice himself or herself to a conservator or restorer practicing in a given specialty. There are still very competent conservators who have gone through apprenticeship programs or are self-taught. There are also some very good craftspeople who specialize in materials and objects, such as watches and clocks, that fall outside the normal realm of conservation practice.

But today entry into the conservation profession is defined and focused. The aspiring conservator takes chemistry (usually introductory chemistry, physical chemistry, and organic chemistry), physics, art history, history, and studio art courses during undergraduate studies. Most of the graduate programs offer an M.A. or a Ph.D. in conservation. Following graduate work the new conservator usually serves an internship with a conservator in private practice or with a museum conservation laboratory. A separate area of study is conservation science, which focuses on the analysis of materials rather than the treatment of objects.

Most people are initially surprised by the cost of conservation services. It must be remembered that the conservator in private practice is a trained professional who among other things must maintain a conservation laboratory fully outfitted with materials and supplies, provide security, fire protection, and insurance for artifacts in his or her care, and manage a business with its related expenses.

Most practicing conservators in the United States are members of the American Institute for Conservation of Historic and Artistic Works (AIC), the nationwide professional association of conservators. There are three categories of membership within the AIC: associate, professional associate, and fellow. Admittance to the latter two categories requires specialized training and peer review of a conservator's past treatments. Conservators who have been trained as apprentices or who are self-taught must have a B.A. or B.S. degree. Additionally, professional associates and fellows agree to abide by the AIC *Code of Ethics* and *Standards of Practice* (see the appendix).

Selecting a Conservator

Prior to selecting a conservator, owners of valued objects should take the time to learn more about their objects as well as the qualifications of potential conservators. This is one of the intents of this directory. In essays discussing treatment for objects, more than one opinion is described. Often there are several treatment options, depending upon the desired outcome and related costs. At minimum, basic stabilization may suffice; alternatively, extensive intervention may be necessary.

The AIC suggests the following steps in selecting a conservator:

- Learn about the field of conservation.
- Learn about your object—its history, composition, and care.
- Contact previous clients of the prospective conservator.
- Request information regarding the conservator's training and experience.
- Inquire into his or her facilities (storage space, treatment area, and fire detection and suppression and security systems).
- Inquire about insurance.
- Find out who will actually conduct the treatment—the conservator, an associate, or an intern.

Remember that the conservator cannot provide a reasonable treatment proposal and cost estimate without seeing and/or examining the object. Frequently, a limited treatment may be advised in the interest of preserving the artist's intent and the value of the object. Conservators are bound by a code of ethics and may decline to perform certain treatments that would constitute a violation of the ethical code. A conservator could lose his or her membership standing within the AIC if the violation is serious enough to warrant such action.

In turn, you may expect from the conservator you select:

- a treatment proposal and a cost and time estimate
- photo documentation—before, during, and after treatment
- notification during treatment of necessary changes in the proposed treatment
- a final written report.

Conclusion

It is the intent of the Washington Conservation Guild that this resource will serve as a valuable reference for those seeking conservation services in the Washington-Baltimore area and to the WCG members in private practice.

Further Reading

AIC. *Guidelines for Selecting a Conservator.* Washington, D.C.: American Institute for Conservation of Historic and Artistic Works, 1991.
Ward, Phillip. *The Nature of Conservation: A Race against Time.* Marina del Rey, Calif.: Getty Conservation Institute, 1986.

CHAPTER I

The Environment and Conservation

IN VARYING DEGREES ALL MATERIALS CONSTITUTING ARTIFACTS AND WORKS of art are affected by the natural processes of decay. Research has been conducted in recent years into the harmful effects of the environment—for example, excessive light and heat, humidity fluctuations, and the presence of atmospheric pollutants. This chapter summarizes the damaging effects of various environmental agents and provides advice on how to control them in domestic surroundings. Although today we have a better understanding of the mechanisms of environmental deterioration, many of the commonsense preventive measures discussed below derive from housekeeping practices developed generations ago by those responsible for the maintenance of houses and their contents.

Light

All of us have observed the destructive action of light. For example, sunlight turns the morning newspaper yellow and brittle. The range of materials that are sensitive to light and the extent of discoloration and deterioration light can produce should be of concern to all owners of works of art. Regardless of the rate at which it occurs, the damage caused by light is both cumulative and irreversible. Neither **conservation treatment** nor placement of the object in darkness can return the object to its original condition.

Objects made from **organic materials** are light sensitive. This group includes **textiles** (costumes, furnishing fabrics, embroidery), works on paper, portrait miniatures on ivory, dyed leather, taxidermy, and **ethnographic objects** that are made wholly or in part from fur or feathers. **Inorganic materials** such as **metals** and **stone** are insensitive to light. **Glass** and **ceramics** are also generally insensitive to light (see Chapter 11).

A noticeable sign of damage by light is fading or color change. Less easily observed is the process known as **photodegradation,** the breakdown of the chemical structure of light-sensitive material that results in embrittlement and loss of strength. In general, the extent of damage caused by light depends on three factors: the strength or intensity of the lighting, referred to as **illuminance;** the length of time an object is exposed to light; and the spectral distribution, or wavelength, of the light source. The wavelength indicates the energy of light sources in the different regions of the **electromagnetic spectrum.** The electromagnetic spectrum includes all energy sources, both visible and invisible.

Beyond the violet end of the **visible light** spectrum lies **ultraviolet radiation,** which has shorter, more energetic wavelengths than visible light. UV is particularly destructive. Since we cannot see it, UV radiation does not contribute to our appreciation of objects, and we can eliminate it. Daylight, the strongest emitter of UV, can be filtered by thin plastic films, adhered to the interior surface of windows, or rigid acrylic sheets fabricated as interior storm windows. Each product has advantages and disadvantages. Individual collectors may wish to contact a conservator to discuss the most effective method for their own circumstances. Although the UV content of **fluorescent tubes** varies, most tubes require filtration. Transparent plastic films or rigid acrylic sleeves can be applied over the length of the tube. UV protection is not necessary for tungsten **incandescent lamps**—standard light bulbs—since they emit a weak amount of UV. Newly developed **dichroic glass filters** are available to reduce the UV emission from high-intensity **tungsten-halogen lamps,** which have lately come into more popular use. The filters act both to lower the UV emission to acceptable levels and to reduce the heat generated by the lamps. Although the above measures will reduce the amount of UV striking sensitive material, it is important to emphasize that UV filtration does not preclude the need for other measures of light control.

Visible light is controlled by reducing the intensity of the illumination striking sensitive objects and/or restricting the length of exposure time. For example, the intensity of light can be reduced by extending the distance between strong artificial light sources and vulnerable items, lowering the wattage of spotlights, or redirecting their beam of light, as well as by moving objects away from windows. When a room is unoccupied, blinds or curtains should be drawn. Light-sensitive objects should not be exhibited permanently. To decrease cumulative exposure, it is wise to rotate, systematically, the objects in and out of storage areas, limiting the annual exposure time to six months or less. For the remainder of the year, the objects can be placed in a darkened storage room or suitable container.

Some strong artificial light sources generate sufficient heat to raise the temperature of an object above that of its surroundings. To minimize the possibility of damage, such as cracking or warping, care should be used when directing strong light on objects. Preventive measures include decreasing the strength of the light and/or increasing the distance between the object and the light source.

Temperature and Relative Humidity

Although heat speeds up the chemical decay of objects and promotes biological activity such as **mold** growth, in general it is the effect temperature has on **relative humidity** that is the cause for concern. All organic objects have a **moisture content** that is directly affected by the humidity level in the surrounding air. To maintain an equilibrium with their changing surroundings, these objects will absorb or release moisture. At low RH levels, when moisture is released, shrinking, cracking, and embrittlement of materials constituting these objects can occur. The resulting damage may be irreparable. At high RH levels, swelling can take place, sometimes leading to permanent distortion of the material. Fluctuating relative humidity may culminate in major structural damage due to repeated dimensional changes arising from cycles of expansion and contraction. Although organic objects are generally considered to be more vulnerable to their surrounding environment, inorganic items also can be at risk. For example, high levels of temperature and relative humidity may accelerate **corrosion** of metal antiquities.

Fine art and decorative objects benefit from moderate, relatively constant levels of temperature and humidity. For specific recommendations on temperature and humidity control for a particular category of material, refer to the other chapters in the directory. For collections containing a diverse range of materials, the levels commonly recommended are 70°F and 50 percent RH. Ideally, these levels should be maintained continuously, without intermittent, rapid fluctuations or repeated cycles of change. For example, cycles of fluctuating environmental conditions are created when heating or air-conditioning systems are switched on in the morning and off at night. For humidity-sensitive material, the extent to which environmental damage may occur due to fluctuations or constant conditions above or below 50 percent will largely depend on the nature, history, and condition of the item concerned. Most, but not all, organic objects tolerate variations of ± 20 percent RH with low risk of damage. Vulnerable objects such as ivory carvings or inlaid furniture may require more stringent humidity control.

During the winter, central heating significantly lowers the relative humidity to levels that may cause damage to objects made of organic materials. Vulnerable objects are likely to incur further risk when unsuitable, localized conditions are inadvertently created, for example, by placing furniture too close to radiators or over floor registers. A straightforward method of compensating for the lowering of RH levels is to reduce the thermostat's temperature setting as well as to maintain relatively constant, moderate temperatures throughout the day and night. In practice, human comfort needs will principally dictate the extent to which temperatures can be acceptably lowered. It will probably be necessary to add humidity to the air by installing a humidifier in order to provide adequate RH levels for especially sensitive objects. In homes with forced-air central heating, a humidification system can be added, near the furnace or air-handling unit, with a **humidistat** for control being located within the humidified areas.

For dwellings without central ductwork, portable or room-based humidifiers are available. The different principles of operation include unheated evaporative drum, ultrasonic, and vaporized steam. Varied capacities correspond to different-sized rooms. There are advantages and disadvantages to each type of humidifier. To provide a continual supply of humidified air, the humidifier's water reservoir will need to be refilled frequently by hand. Ultrasonic and evaporative humidifiers require regular cleaning (once a month if tap water is used) to prevent microbiological contamination of the water, and demineralized or **distilled water** needs to be used with the former to avoid the distribution of mineral particles into the air. Units equipped with a built-in humidistat, which enable automatic on/off switching based on a predetermined level of humidity control, provide conditions that are generally more constant.

It is important to note that when humidity is added in the winter, the likelihood of condensation increases, with a consequent risk of damage to surface and structural elements of the house. A balance may need to be struck between the competing preservation needs of the objects and those of the building. Because of the complexity of the issues involved, advice should be sought from a mechanical engineer and conservator.

During the summer months there is usually a need to remove excess humidity from the environment. Standard window air conditioners and central air-conditioning systems are designed to control room temperatures for human comfort; therefore they cannot be considered an effective means of maintaining relative humidity at a specified level. Nevertheless, they do remove moisture from the air, with the added benefit of reducing the entry of pollutants, since windows and exterior doors will be closed. In most domestic rooms a portable dehumidifer, when properly sized, can be effective. Unless the container can be manually emptied on a regular basis, however, the dehumidifier should be fitted with a condensate pump that will remove the collected water to a nearby drain or directly to the exterior of the building. If drainage of the water is inadequate, flooding will occur.

It is worth noting that humidity-sensitive objects that have been kept in unfavorable conditions for a long period—whether humid or dry—become adjusted to those conditions. Moving these objects to a different environment, perhaps with the intention of providing optimal conditions, may be placing them at risk unless they are given time to acclimatize to their surroundings gradually.

Dust and Air Pollution

Dust is an abrasive material composed principally of microscopic mineral particles. If allowed to accumulate on objects, it will cause soiling, thus marring the surface appearance. Since dust particles attract moisture and gaseous pollutants in the environment, they can become active sites of chemical deterioration. The removal of dust typically necessitates wiping, washing, or some form of agitation—hastening general wear and tear and increasing the likelihood of loss of surface detail. Gaseous or air pollution is most problematic in urban areas, due to the proximity of industrial activity, motor vehicle emissions, and the release of by-products from heating systems. In coastal regions, pollutants in the atmosphere will mix with chloride salts and other compounds to create a corrosive environment.

Within the home, a variety of contaminating sources are present: wood-burning fires and candles produce soot. Smoke from tobacco products forms a tar-based coating on objects. Other potential sources of pollution include components in certain interior finishing materials, such as carpeting and paint, as well as home cleaning supplies. In confined areas, such as display cases and storage containers, damaging vapors can be emitted by a range of poor-quality materials that include cardboard, chipboard, and plywood made with urea formaldehyde adhesives, among others.

To reduce the effects of pollution, objects should not be located next to open windows or in hallways near screened doors. Small, vulnerable items can be housed in **vitrines** or display cases made from Plexiglas. To improve filtration of dust and other particles, open-weave filters that are commonly used in forced-air heating systems need to be replaced with a filter of higher efficiency. High-efficiency filters can be purchased at a large hardware store. The costs and maintenance involved in removing air pollution as part of an **HVAC system** are usually not justified in a private home.

Pest Control

A wide range of objects, especially those of organic origin, are at risk from biological activity. Insects bore tunnels in wood and consume the glue in bindings, the **sizing** on paper, or indeed the paper itself. They also eat textiles, fur, hair, and feathers. Common insect pests, which may be present as larvae or adults, include dermestid beetles, carpet beetles, furniture beetles, clothes moths, silverfish, booklice, and cockroaches. Sources of an insect infestation in the home include flowers and plants, firewood, and garbage areas. In addition, termites can move from structural timbers to furniture. Mice, rats, and other small rodents that infest buildings may damage objects during nest building or food gathering. Extensive damage or complete destruction of the object may occur in a very short time as a result of biological activity, which include molds and mildews. In warm, still, humid environments, mold that appears on objects can sometimes cause more than superficial damage.

Objects infested by insects should be isolated and wrapped in a sheet of plastic to prevent dispersal of any eggs, larvae, or adults that may widen the area of infestation. Pesticides have traditionally been employed to control pests, but recent research has indicated that a number of chemicals, especially when not used in a controlled manner, may damage the materials of which many objects are made. In addition, certain pesticides are known to be toxic to humans. Before proceeding to eradicate an infestation among a collection of antiques or works of art, it is recommended that the advice of a conservator be sought.

Much can be done in the home to prevent infestations. Good housekeeping and regular inspection of vulnerable objects and their immediate surroundings will deter most pest activity. Items such as textiles, books, photograph albums, frames, and small wooden historic artifacts or pieces of furniture should not be stored in areas that are dark, humid, and seldom disturbed. Therefore, an attic or basement is generally not a suitable location for objects unless an adequate environment has been established with storage in mind. To minimize the potential for biological attack, relative humidity levels should be kept below 70 percent. Adequate air circulation should be provided to avoid stagnant conditions.

Questions To Ask A Conservator

- How many years have you been working as a conservator?
- What is your experience in dealing with environmental issues, and what percentage of your practice is devoted to this area?
- Can you provide a short list of references?
- Do you have equipment to measure the environmental conditions in my home or museum?
- What remedial measures can I take now to deal with my environmental problem?

Questions To Be Prepared To Answer

General

- Have you identified the source of the environmental problem?
- How long have you had the problem? Is it a recurring problem?
- How has the problem affected your work of art or collection?

Light

- What kinds of light-sensitive material do you have?
- How is your light-sensitive material illuminated?
- How long has the material been illuminated?
- What measures are you taking to protect your light-sensitive material?
- Have you measured the lighting conditions?

Temperature and Relative Humidity

- What kind of heating and air-conditioning system do you have?
- Do you use a humidifier or dehumidifier to control relative humidity? If yes, please describe.
- Have you measured the temperature and/or relative humidity levels? If yes, please summarize.

- What measures are you taking to adjust temperature and/or relative humidity levels?
- Have you consulted an HVAC contractor or mechanical engineer about the problem?

Dust and Air Pollution

- What problem do you have controlling dust and/or air pollution? How is it affecting your work of art or collection?
- Is it a recurring problem during a certain season or time of year?
- What measures are you taking to protect your work of art or collection from dust and air pollution?
- Have you consulted an HVAC contractor or mechanical engineer about the problem?

Pest Control

- What pest problem do you have (insects, rodents, mold, bats, birds)?
- Where is the pest problem, and where does the pest come from?
- Is it a recurring problem during a certain season or time of year?
- Are you currently using a chemical or nonchemical treatment to deal with the problem?
- Does the problem continue to persist?

Further Reading

Appelbaum, Barbara. *Guide to Environmental Protection of Collections.* Madison, Conn.: Sound View Press, 1991.

Craddock, Anne Brooke. "Control of Temperature and Humidity in Small Collections." In *Conservation Concerns: A Guide for Collectors and Curators,* ed. by Konstanze Bachmann, 15–22. Washington, D.C.: Smithsonian Institution Press, 1992.

Harmon, James D. *Integrated Pest Management in Museum, Library, and Archival Facilities: A Step by Step Approach for the Design, Development, Implementation and Maintenance of an Integrated Pest Management Program.* Indianapolis: Harmon Preservation Pest Management, 1993.

Olkowski, William, Sheila Darr, and Helga Olkowski. *Common-Sense Pest Control.* Newtown, Conn.: Taunton Press, 1991.

Rose, William B. "Heating, Cooling, and Ventilating Systems." In *Caring for Your Historic House,* ed. Harriet Whelchel, 165–77. Heritage Preservation and National Park Service. New York: Harry N. Abrams, 1998.

Story, Keith. *Approaches to Pest Management in Museums.* Washington, D.C.: Conservation Analytical Laboratory, Smithsonian Institution, 1985. Free copies are available to the public upon request. Contact: Ann N'Gadi, SCMRE MRC 0534, Smithsonian Institution, Washington, D.C. 20560-0534 Tel. 301/238-3700, ext. 134; e-mail: **abn@scmre.si.edu.**

Thomson, Garry. *The Museum Environment.* 2nd ed. Woburn, Mass.: Butterworth-Heinemann, 1994.

Weintraub, Steven. "Creating and Maintaining the Right Environment." In *Caring for Your Collections: Preserving and Protecting Your Art and Other Collectibles,* 18–29. National Committee to Save America's Cultural Collections, Arthur W. Schultz, chairman. New York: Harry N. Abrams, 1992.

Conservators

Brian Ramer, Aiken & Ramer 126

CHAPTER 2

Western Paintings

WESTERN EASEL PAINTINGS NEED NO INTRODUCTION TO THE ART
enthusiast, as they are nearly synonymous with "fine art" in our
culture. To a greater extent than at any other period, Western
culture in the twentieth century viewed easel painting as the definitive artistic expression. Although the history of painting begins with prehistoric cave
paintings, the large majority of paintings in private collections today fall into
the general description of easel painting: images on lightweight, portable **supports** (the material on which the paint is applied together with any auxiliary
elements). Caretakers of public spaces may be responsible for some other categories of painting, such as murals, altarpieces, or large contemporary as-
semblages with painted elements. Whatever the purpose or format, all paintings share a common characteristic: unlike the three-dimensional arts, which
may retain artistic value even with portions missing (such as an arm or a nose
of a sculpture), the essential artistic value of a painting depends upon original paint on the intact support, and the more original paint that is missing
or concealed by later interventions, the less distinctive the painting.

Paintings may be on a wide variety of supports: usually linen in traditional paintings, and often cotton duck in modern works. Wood, Masonite,
paper and manufactured paperboards, other **textiles, metal, glass,** and **stone**
are also found. Traditional paintings are usually executed in oil paint, with
the **media** composed of nut or seed oils. Modern works are often painted in
acrylics, with the paint media polymer products of the chemical industry.
The coloring agents in paint, called **pigments,** are particles of refined earth,
chemically manufactured powders, and **dyes.** Paintings executed on fabric
are usually mounted on **stretchers,** which are lengths of wood joined together
so that the corners can be expanded to maintain tension in the cloth. Paintings on fabric are also sometimes mounted on **strainers,** which are similar to

stretchers except that they have fixed, nonexpandable corners. Mural paintings are permanently mounted to walls with no intention of portability.

Most paintings were intended to be placed in a frame of separate manufacture; today we acknowledge that frames are often works of art in themselves. (Moreover, frame conservation is a separate specialty, and skilled frame conservators are best consulted when questions arise about frames; see Chapter 15.) Historically, paintings were designed with an integral frame attached, while modern paintings are sometimes created with no frame intended at all.

Context

The services of a professional painting conservator usually are sought because the institution or private owner observes deterioration of the image or structural damage that detracts from the appearance of the picture. In general, it is the desire of the client that the painting be made stable and suitable for display. Recommendations for treatment will depend on a number of factors—historic or market value and sentimental and/or decorative considerations. Family portraits, for example, often have limited market value, but their high sentimental value may more than satisfy the criteria for treatment. By the same token, portraits of minimal aesthetic merit owned by historic houses often possess great cultural significance and easily meet the criteria for **conservation treatment**. On the other hand, the same historic home may possess badly torn, mildewed, unidentified portrait fragments for which managed storage without restoration is selected. The preservation and restoration of fragmentary evidence of painted wall decoration may also be a priority in that fictional historic home. It is important to discuss the value of a painting in personal as well as financial terms and to be aware that there are many intermediate choices between simple **preservation** and complete **restoration.** It is equally important to distinguish between necessary and excessive measures.

Painting preservation seeks to ensure that the original materials, including the design layer(s) or paint, the support, and the frame (if it is original to the painting) are sound and protected from damage in the best possible manner. Painting restoration seeks to restore the aesthetic qualities the artist intended, including those inherent to the support, the ground layer, the paint, the surface finish—and, in some instances, even the display setting. A high value is conferred on original materials in good condition, from the unseen (stretchers, panels) to the surface coating or lack of a surface coating. With that in mind, it may be desirable to preserve rather than replace when possible. Likewise, it is prudent to anticipate that the repairs or restoration materials will eventually deteriorate. Selecting conservation methods that can be undone or removed, returning the treated portions of the painting to nearly the original condition, will give future generations wider options when the time comes to repeat the restorations with fresh materials.

Common Problems

The primary causes of problems with paintings are an unsuitable **environment**, instability of the artist's methods and materials, accidental and deliberate alterations by the owners, and discoloration caused by degraded coatings and accumulated dirt. In terms of the environment, the seasonal cycling of humidity levels can initiate cycles of shrinkage and swelling that eventually cause damage. The effects of sudden shifts in humidity (flooding or water from burst pipes) are sometimes immediately evident in the form of cracking and flaking paint, bulging canvas, corner puckers, and, in extreme cases, **mold**. If the support that is being subjected to distortions by seasonal cycling is more flexible than the dried paint film, the paint will crack and may eventually flake off. Maintaining a constant humidity is the most important and the most difficult thing that one can do to safeguard works of art.

Probably the most famous example of faulty artist's technique is Leonardo da Vinci's fresco, *The Last Supper,* which was painted over a dry, rather than a wet, wall. The paint never permeated the wall properly and began to flake off during Leonardo's lifetime. Recently the decision has been made to remove the centuries-old repainting applied by many later hands, leaving the fragments of Leonardo's paint in a wall lightly toned with **watercolor.** This is an unusual, rather than a common problem, but it serves to illustrate the difficulty of preserving inherently unstable original materials. Unstable pigments are a more typical problem, with results ranging from fading to color change to development of large cracks. Such pigment alterations revise the intended spatial and atmospheric relationships as well as the palette. Unfortunately, deterioration of the materials chosen by the artist cannot be reversed, and disguising the result (for example, painting over the affected area) is often less desirable than accepting the changed appearance.

Accidental damage is one of the most frequently encountered problems that impels a client to seek out a conservator. These damages can include tears and punctures, burns and smoke accumulation, scrapes and scratches, and all the other problems that result from inexpert handling. In addition, deliberate alterations often take place, such as the repainting of facial features and backgrounds in portraits, vandalism by disgruntled family members, and the cutting down of canvases to fit smaller frames. Past restorations by poorly trained practitioners can also be the cause of damage in a painting. These damages most often take the form of inadvertent overcleaning and abrasion of original paint, along with deleterious and misguided structural treatments. Sometimes the retouching completed in the most recent treatment ages poorly, changes color, and becomes a disfiguring element in itself.

Often the first indication the owner has that a picture needs attention is the gloomy image caused by darkened surface coatings and accumulated surface dirt. In spite of the fact that these surface effects usually produce no long-term damage, they interfere dramatically with enjoyment of the picture.

Assessing Condition

The assessment of condition requires a thorough knowledge of the particular type of painting in question. From the foregoing paragraphs it should be evident that the scope of materials and techniques grouped together under the category of paintings is large and that painting conservator might well build a career on an expertise in a subcategory—say, mural paintings or modern paintings. An expert opinion is most reliable when the background of the expert is in the field of the painting at hand (the best surgeon might not provide the best advice on an endocrine disorder). The conservator will require good light and access to the front, rear, and edges of the painting in order to give an initial assessment of physical condition. If the assessment is purely aesthetic, it may be less exhaustive, whereas questions involving authenticity and authorship may require more sophisticated techniques, such as **x-radiography**, pigment identification, and sampling. In most cases these services will be priced separately from **conservation** and/or **restoration.**

Treatment Options

When clients bring a painting to a conservator, they are hopeful that cleaning will make the image clearer and closer to the artist's intent. Layers of atmospheric grime, old darkened **varnishes**, and discolored repaints from previous restorations can all obscure original paint. A competent painting conservator will determine which elements of distortion can be safely removed, together with options for doing so. This type of treatment is probably the most commonly performed and provides the most pleasure to the owner.

Regarding the structural needs of the artwork, the modern approach is to intervene as little as possible: if the support can safely be left alone, nothing is done to it. However, if the support is not sound, a structural remedy must be applied. The remedy may need to include removal of past treatment if there is evidence that it is preventing effective treatment or creating new damage.

A number of treatment options are available to repair structural problems in paintings on canvas. Small tears can be mended on the reverse, and weak tacking margins can be reinforced for increased strength. When the picture has longer tears or holes in the fabric, or is missing tacking margins, **lining** is often recommended. This involves attachment of a layer of fabric to the reverse of the painting with an adhesive, usually with vacuum pressure and heat. Loose linings, which add a layer of fabric directly behind the original support without the use of an adhesive, can also be executed.

Oil paintings on wood panels frequently develop cracks and splits of the wood. Split panels are glued and clamped together until set. In general, warped, twisted, or curved panels are not flattened, since such an operation will introduce interior stresses in the structure of the wood. In some rare instances it is necessary to reshape the wood to allow a crack to be realigned and glued.

In addition to seasonal humidity fluctuations, structural deteriorations such as those listed above will produce instability and flaking in the paint layer. Unstable, flaking paint is meticulously readhered to the picture surface with appropriate adhesives, taking care to respect and preserve the original surface texture and sheen. Pablo Picasso's cubist pictures, for example, were created using matte and glossy paint in specific areas as a design component. Consolidation of pictures with matte, unsaturated paints (some of Claude Monet's paintings have retained the original unvarnished surface) is best performed using materials and methods that do not darken the paint film or leave a glossy surface.

Finally, it is important that the **inpainting** materials used to compensate for losses of flaked or abraded original paint be removable without risk to the original paint. Any varnish should be chosen to provide a surface finish that is compatible with the preferences of the artist and the aesthetic of the period and can be applied with the certainty that it can be removed without damage to the artist's materials. It should be mentioned, however, that certain paintings were created with no intent of a varnish finish, and it is the conservator's responsibility to respect the artist's intent in this matter. There can be no doubt that the inpainting and varnish will require replacement at some future time, and selecting materials that will be readily removable without endangering the genuine artist's materials will help to guarantee that no less of the painting will survive for future generations. In the same vein, selecting a conservator whose résumé reveals a history of practice and study of paintings of a similar quality and category as the picture at hand will help to guarantee a comfortable familiarity with and knowledge of the special properties and intricacies of your painting.

Questions To Ask A Painting Conservator

- How long have you been working in painting conservation?
- With whom or where did you acquire your knowledge of the field?
- Is my picture typical of the pictures in your practice?
- Do you have assistants, what are their responsibilities, and to what degree do they require supervision?
- Does the price of conservation include copies of the documentation for my files?
- What will the picture look like after treatment?

Further Reading

Bachmann, Konstanze, ed. *Conservation Concerns: A Guide for Collectors and Curators.* Washington, D.C.: Smithsonian Institution Press, 1992.

Bomford, David. *Conservation of Paintings.* Pocket Guides series. London: National Gallery Publications, 1997. *[This is a title of a series]*

Carr, Dawson W., and Mark Leonard. *Looking at Paintings: A Guide to Technical Terms.* Malibu, Calif.: J. Paul Getty Museum, in association with the British Museum Press, 1992.

Kirsh, Andrea, and Rustin S. Levenson. *Seeing Through Paintings: Physical Examination in Art Historical Studies.* New Haven, Conn.: Yale University Press, 2000.

Stout, George. *The Care of Pictures.* 1948. Reprint, New York: Dover Publications, 1975.

Conservators

CHAPTER 3

Portrait Miniatures

THE PORTRAIT MINIATURE IS DEFINED BY PAINTING TECHNIQUES AND materials, not by size, despite the fact that miniatures are rarely larger than several inches in either dimension. The earliest known miniature portraits, identified with the French and English courts of the 1520s, were painted in opaque **watercolors** on **vellum** and **paper.** By the mid-1500s some miniatures were painted in **oil** colors on thin sheets of various **metals.** At the beginning of the eighteenth century, miniature painters began to experiment with watercolors applied to supports of ivory, the combination of materials that eventually dominated the other **media.** Today portrait miniatures are routinely defined as small portrait images painted on ivory, a definition that reasonably reflects the heyday of miniature painting from approximately 1750 to 1850 in the United States and in Europe. The use of specialized techniques of paint application—**stippling, hatching,** and **washing**—further define traditional miniature painting, whether the image is a portrait or a scene. The varied styles and techniques of painting can assist in identifying the period and country in which a miniature painting was produced.

Importance of the Case

The type of frame or case that contains the miniature painting also contributes to the identification of a painting's origins. At the same time, the **housing** plays a vital role in protecting the miniature by isolating it from the surrounding environment. Exposure to light and the fading light causes are prevented by cases having lids that, when closed, provide additional protection not offered by the cover glass alone. Cases and frames help buffer moisture-sensitive supports of vellum, ivory, and paper from changes in the ambient **relative hu-**

midity and protect fragile painted surfaces from misapplied cleaning solutions and perspiring hands.

Assessing a Portrait Miniature

The **conservation treatment** of a portrait miniature is based on a careful assessment of condition weighed against the appropriateness of remedial action. An assessment for the purpose of treatment begins with the identification of the materials that were used to create the miniature.

Each material found in a portrait miniature has distinguishing physical characteristics, though magnification is sometimes required to confirm an identification. Under magnification, vellum appears as densely packed fiber bundles having a waxy sheen. Paper surfaces exhibit matted fibers of varied hue. Some papers may be marked by the regular lines of the screen used in making the paper. Ivory is a hard, compact material that sometimes has a discernible grain. Fine scratches may be visible on an ivory surface, underneath the paint layer, evidence of the preparatory process.

The paints used on these supports were made of **pigments** bound in water-soluble **gums**, with the occasional addition of sugars and emulsifying waxes. Although the basic paint mixtures remained remarkably consistent over several centuries, differing techniques of application led to considerable variety in the visual characteristics of the painted surfaces. They range in appearance from flat and opaque to dense and velvety to transparent. At one extreme are rich, saturated, glossy paint films that are sometimes mistaken for oil paints but which can be identified as **watercolors** by their stippled or hatched brushwork. Bright, rich colors are also characteristic of **enamel** miniatures, made by painting metal oxides over an opaque white ground on metal or **porcelain** before firing in a kiln. The resulting glasslike surface is smooth and relatively permanent.

Common Problems and Accepted Treatments

Some of the problems commonly associated with miniature paintings stem from certain artists' failure to use stable materials or sound techniques, problems known collectively as **inherent vice**. To avoid such problems for the future, other miniature painters tried to avoid pigments with a reputation for discoloring, disappearing, or having a detrimental effect on adjacent colors. These artists mixed binding media with care to ensure that the paints they made would be stable and not tend to flake or peel. They also prepared the supports carefully, removing residues that might cause poor adhesion of paint films. But use of good materials and techniques offers no protection from aging, wear, the cumulative effects of the **environment**, or the results of accidental damage. Fortunately, it is often possible to improve a diminished condition through combinations of basic maintenance and more extensive treatments.

Dirt and Mold

Fine dust and dirt inevitably collect on the surface of a miniature image and the interior of its cover glass when a case or frame is not sealed properly. Dirt on the surface of a miniature portrait is often found in conjunction with **mold**. Mold spores, ubiquitous in the environment, will flourish when nutrients (provided by the gums and sugars used in the **binders** for miniature painting), humidity levels, and temperature provide optimum conditions. Care must be taken to protect miniature portraits from the conditions that support mold growth, which as a general rule are humidity and temperature levels concurrently above 70 percent and 70°F, respectively. The presence of mold on the surface of a miniature can lead to deterioration in a paint layer, occasionally accompanied by staining. Mold that develops on the surface of a miniature can usually be removed by conservation treatment, though damage caused by pigment alteration may be permanent.

Damaged Supports

Miniatures on ivory may develop distortions such as warping, cracking, or splitting, especially when an ivory support is backed with an attached card or paper. Such backings were routinely applied by miniature painters as they prepared an ivory for painting and were left in place when the ivory was framed. However, an ivory and its backing respond differently to changes in ambient humidity. As a result, tensions may develop that can lead to damages in the ivory support. During conservation treatment, the removal of a backing from a warped or split ivory support is one means of encouraging the ivory to relax and flatten. Miniatures were also painted on vellum mounted on cards. Vellum supports are not as susceptible as ivory to warping, but **cockling** (wrinkling) is occasionally noted. Miniatures on paper supports are susceptible to problems that generally affect works of art on paper, including staining and tears. These damages are treated by methods used by paper conservators.

Damaged Paint Layers

Dimensional changes in supports made of ivory, vellum, or paper may lead to flaking in paint layers, with subsequent losses. Damage caused by exposure to moisture may also lead to paint loss, chemical reactions, or alteration of hues. Minor losses can usually be successfully toned to match surrounding colors, but major damage and loss in a painted surface are sometimes irreparable in the context of a miniature. Pigments in the water-based paints used in miniature paintings are vulnerable to fading caused by light. Although faded colors are irreversible—lost colors cannot ethically be renewed or enhanced—extensive fading can be prevented by limiting exposure to light.

Framing Problems

Intricate metal cases were provided for miniatures originally worn as lockets, brooches, and bracelets. These cases may contain decorative elements that include monograms, seed pearls, and hair motifs to personalize an image. Miniatures also were painted to be displayed in flat frames of wood or **papier-mâché** as well as in oval or rectangular cases covered in leather. The discoloration of metal cases and metal frame mounts occurs with time. Improperly attempting to clean metal cases or frame mounts can lead to irreparable damage of the materials within. Unless all contents are removed before the cleaning of cases and cover glasses commences, cleaning solutions can damage paint and promote mold growth. With correct methods of cleaning, worn and dirty cases and frames of every type can be improved by maintenance or more comprehensive treatments.

The appearance and condition of its housing are important elements in the presentation of a miniature portrait. The original housing is an integral part of the history of a miniature portrait, and it should be preserved, together with all materials found within. Ideally, a miniature will be reframed with all materials found with it, unless the presence of some or all of the material is considered detrimental for the long-term preservation of the miniature. When such materials are identified, they should be retained with treatment documentation, not reframed.

Cover Glasses

A significant threat to the safety of a miniature is the deterioration of its cover glass. Glass is susceptible to deterioration as the result of a chemical imbalance in its original composition that can lead to conditions called **weeping** or "sick" glass. Small droplets of moisture and hazy films develop on the surface of the affected glass. Contact with deteriorated glass can damage painted surfaces and corrode metal frame components. Deteriorated or broken cover glasses should be replaced, but stable glasses that are scratched or abraded can be polished and then returned to their settings. All glass is liable to "sweat" if the temperature of a miniature drops quickly; abrupt climate changes must be avoided.

The comprehensive treatment of miniature paintings and their housings is generally outside the scope of other conservation specialities. Miniature paintings were created using a wide variety of materials. They are presented in complex housings that can be difficult to enter. Treatment of portrait miniatures requires a sound knowledge of the painting styles and techniques used during various historical periods in many different countries. While individual conservators may not propose exactly the same treatment for a given object, each conservator should be able and willing to justify recommendations to your satisfaction. The successful treatment of miniature paintings must blend historical knowledge with a mastery of technical skills developed in response to the unique needs of miniature portraits.

Further Reading

Aiken, Carol. "Techniques and Methods of the American Portrait Miniaturist," In Dale Johnson, *American Portrait Miniatures in the Manney Collection,* 27-37. New York: Metropolitan Museum of Art, 1990.

Eirk, Katherine. "The Care and Conservation of Miniature Portraits." In *Charles Fraser of Charleston,* ed. Martha Severens and Charles Wyrick, 147-50. Charleston, S.C.: Carolina Art Association, 1983.

Murrell, Jim. "Miniatures." In *Sotheby's Caring for Antiques,* 110-13. New York: Simon and Schuster, 1992.

Murrell, Jim. "The Restoration of Portrait Miniatures." In *Conservation and Restoration of Pictorial Art,* ed. Norman Bromelle and Perry Smith, 129-33. London: Butterworths, 1976.

Ridley, Jo Ann. "Ivory and the Art of Miniature Painting." In Ridley, *Looking for Eulabee Dix,* 285-92. Washington, D.C.: National Museum of Women in the Arts, 1997.

Conservators

CHAPTER 4

Works of Art and Manuscripts on Paper

ORKS OF ART ON PAPER EXHIBIT AN IMMEDIACY OF EXPRESSION THAT draws the viewer into the creative process. Little separates us from the paper surface, and the artist's hands and thoughts are revealed more spontaneously than in art forms made by more complex processes, such as sculpture or furniture. Just as a historic letter reveals the character of its author not only by its content but in the style of writing and the selection of paper, so a drawing or print displays the focus of the artist in the choice of subject, nuance of line, palette of color, and texture of paper. These features begin to explain why works on paper have been treasured by collectors the world over.

The Care of Works on Paper

Paper is generally thought of as a delicate and fragile material, vulnerable to damage. It is easily torn, abraded, and stained. Yet some ancient paper artifacts, such as Chinese scrolls made more than a thousand years ago, have survived in excellent condition. Why is this? One essential reason is the protective manner in which they have been cared for. Traditionally in East Asia, important scrolls were kept carefully rolled in cedar boxes under controlled environmental conditions and exposed to light only occasionally, for viewing. In a similar fashion, European print collectors from the Renaissance onward often stored prints and drawings in beautifully handcrafted albums of fine-quality paper and kept them in cabinets out of the light and protected from dust and moisture, thus ensuring their survival for centuries. Today museums regulate temperature and humidity in their galleries and storage areas, limit the exposure of objects to light, filter out air **pollutants**, and restrict the handling of collections in order to protect objects from dirt and abrasion, chemical degradation, and insect damage.

Although individual owners may not be able to replicate museum conditions, simple **preservation** measures, such as storing objects in **housing** materials of good quality and limiting their display, can help prevent common forms of damage. Learning about an object's needs and vulnerabilities, and caring for it accordingly, will promote its longevity and protect the owner's investment.

The Importance of Environment

Let us first look more specifically at the effects that uncontrolled climate can have on paper artifacts. Wide variations of temperature and humidity over time cause deterioration ranging from **planar distortions**, discoloration, and embrittlement to **mold**. A picture hung in a bathroom, for example, may be exposed to excessive moisture that shows up as staining over the long term or as actual water damage. Works on paper should not be stored in attics or basements where extreme heat, dryness, and dampness can occur, though humidifiers and dehumidifiers can help moderate severe conditions. Nor should these works be displayed above a fireplace, over radiators, above heat vents, or near sunny windows. Without protection against dust and air pollutants, a paper surface becomes soiled, and once the dirt and pollutants have settled down into the exposed fibers, they are difficult to remove. Even with the best-quality framing and light control, works on paper cannot withstand permanent exhibition without eventual deterioration, usually in the form of discoloration or fading. The seasonal rotation of objects on display, a standard practice in institutions, is advisable even for the private owner.

Paper Conservation Services

Suppose a paper artifact or collection has suffered damage that you wish to address. A conservator can help you understand the cause of the object's problems and suggest options for improving its condition. In addition to providing treatment for individual items, a conservator can offer broader assistance: advice about how to house and store objects, how to improve display and storage environments, or how to formulate a **disaster plan** to minimize damage in the case of fire, flood, or other emergency.

During your initial visit with the conservator, it may be appropriate to ask for assistance in precise identification of the object you own. The conservator's trained eye together with specialized equipment can distinguish different types of prints, drawings, and reproductions; and knowing what you have is likely to influence the extent of treatment you select.

Once the type of object has been identified, the cause of damage is determined. Sometimes this analysis will require further investigation beyond what can be immediately observed during the initial visit, and you may decide to leave the object with the conservator for a more extensive evaluation. Following this examination, the conservator will suggest several options for treatment, from **stabilization** of an object physically and chemically so that it can be stored without expectation of continuing degradation, to improvement of the appearance to prepare the object for display or sale.

Some Common Problems and Conservation Solutions

Poor-Quality Housing and Framing

Sometimes the immediate materials used for housing an object may be the cause of visible damage to a paper artifact. Unfortunately, much unintentional damage has been done to works on paper from use of unsuitable materials and techniques for housing and framing. Poor-quality materials, such as mats made of wood-pulp board, and **backings** of wood or **acidic** cardboard, have often been used in framing, resulting over time in discoloration and staining of the original. Pressure-sensitive, gummed linen, or paper tapes may have been used to attach the artwork into the mat and can be difficult to remove and may cause staining. Improper sealing of the frame may have allowed dust or insects to enter the package and do damage as well. Perhaps the glass of the frame has broken and sliced the surface of the picture.

The conservator can evaluate the type of matting and framing material used for an artifact and advise you as to its appropriateness. Removal of damaging materials can be complicated when the artwork is fragile, but it can usually be accomplished by a conservator. Removing hinges, tapes, and adhesives safely requires knowledgeable choices among the solvents and techniques available.

Conservation matting, hinging, and framing are basic for preserving works on paper. Mats function as presentation formats as well as protective ones; a four-ply window mat serves as a spacer, keeping artwork from touching or adhering to the **glazing**. Museum-quality mats are usually constructed of a window and a back mat of four-ply matboard hinged together with gummed linen tape on the long side. If a drawing is executed on paperboard, or a print is mounted to an illustration board of some depth, the back mat is built up to accommodate the dimension of the board, resulting in a thicker mat package. The fiber content of the matboard for most prints and drawings should be 100 percent ragboard with an alkaline buffer of calcium carbonate to help neutralize acidic materials. Hinging of the artwork is normally done with long-fibered **Japanese paper** (kozo) and **wheat starch paste** freshly made by cooking a highly purified wheat starch. Most prints and watercolors can be framed with **ultraviolet**-filtering acrylic glazing. An **acid-free** paper is recommended for the cover on the back of the frame, where it reduces the potential for damage by dust, dirt, and insects.

Some **media**, such as soft graphite pencil, charcoal, chalk, and **pastel**, require mats approximately one-quarter inch deep. These types of media have similar properties and are **friable**; that is, the particles are not firmly attached to the drawing surface and can be easily dislodged by careless handling and improper framing and storage. The static charge of an acrylic glazing can attract particles to its surface, which is why drawings with friable media are framed with ultraviolet-filtering glass, a deep mat, and one-quarter inch spacers in the frame. The mat and spacer keep the media an appropriate distance from the glass. For travel, a special shatter-resistant, thicker, ultraviolet filtering glass is recommended; regular glass should be taped to prevent damage to the art if the glass is broken. However, some friable drawings are not recommended for travel at all due to the risk of losses to the medium. Nor are **fixatives** for friable media recommended, because they tend to pool, compact the media, and can stain the paper over time.

Fortunately, higher standards for framing have been established in recent years, and a wide variety of high-quality framing materials, folders, mats, and storage boxes are available. The conservator can recommend reputable supply sources and experienced framers to the prospective client.

Poor-Quality Secondary Supports

Sometimes a work on paper has been glued in areas or overall to a rigid **support** board that is not composed of good-quality material. In fact, wood or acidic cardboard may cause discoloration or contribute to the acidity of the original. After aging, the embrittlement of this secondary support may create serious risk of breaking in two, and so in many cases the support should be removed. In some circumstances the attachment to the board may be causing planar distortions or even splitting of the original paper. The artwork may have become adhered to the glass in its framing, presenting yet another problem. In most cases the object can be safely removed from its glass or poor-quality backing by a skilled conservator. Sometimes, however, the surface of the original may be too delicate for manipulation or the mount may have historical importance and the conservator may recommend a different treatment, such as adding a reinforcing backing board or supportive mat.

Surface Dirt and Dry-Cleaning

Because paper artifacts are not usually **varnished** like paintings, the exposed fiber surface is especially vulnerable to dust and dirt. Once dirt becomes embedded in the paper, it is sometimes impossible to remove completely. A conservator might use various methods such as **dry-cleaning** crumbs, assorted soft brushes, and mechanical tools like scalpels to dislodge surface dirt or insect droppings. If the soil is mixed with mold damage, additional treatment is often necessary to halt further deterioration.

Mold Damage

An object with actively growing mold is at great risk and should be taken to a conservator for immediate assessment. Because mold spores are a health hazard and can drift through the air to contaminate objects nearby, place the affected object in a bag or box before moving it. You may want to wear a mask and gloves when packing the object, and you should wash your face and hands after handling it.

The conservator will establish through examination whether the mold is still moist and active. If it is, the entire object must be completely dried out before thorough mold removal can take place. Once it is dry, removing the mold quickly will prevent severe stains that are difficult to remove. The conservator may vacuum or aspirate the dried mold using protective equipment. After treatment the object must be returned to an environment of controlled temperature and humidity to prevent reactivation of the mold. **Fumigant** chemicals have been used in the past to kill mold, but recent research has shown that many of them are toxic to humans and that the best way of controlling mold growth in the long term is to control the climate in which an object or collection is stored.

Closely related to mold damage are the amorphously circular, rust-colored stains called **foxing**. Although the precise cause of their growth remains uncertain, high **relative humidity** levels are known to be involved, so, as with mold, preventing their appearance depends on maintaining a controlled environment.

Water Damage and Staining

Water damage can ruin a paper artifact. If the situation is dealt with quickly, however, the damage can be minimized. As soon as a paper object is discovered to be wet, consult a conservator. Immediate treatment may be advised to halt staining or mold growth. If, on the other hand, the water damage is old and the paper is now dried out, the stains or **tide lines** can be addressed with controlled bathing and use of ammoniated water, **alkaline** solutions, and/or possibly **bleaching**. An artwork that is hand-colored or pastel may require a modified local treatment, employing a suction table or ultrasonic mist, for example, to limit the use of water.

Stains in the paper may be caused by something other than water, in which case the conservator can determine the cause through a thorough examination. Illumination with different types of light and use of chemical spot testing may be employed. Sometimes removing a disfiguring stain will require bleaching, a treatment that must be done with great care to avoid damage to the paper or media. Selection of the appropriate bleaching treatment for the stain requires expertise in both art and science on the part of the conservator, who must be familiar with the materials used in making up the object as well as their chemical behavior.

Oversize or Weak Paper

For large items such as posters or maps, large drawings, or contemporary art, the conservator may recommend and prepare a mount of archival-quality materials that will protect the artwork during handling, display, or storage, providing a rigid support rather than a conventional mat, which would be too flimsy for the object's size and weight. Experienced framers also may be able to provide this service. Items suffering physical damage, such as large tears or weakness due to very thin paper, mold damage, or pigment deterioration of the paper, may also require treatment. Selection of the proper weight of paper and execution of the appropriate **lining** method require practice and finesse. The conservator is aware of the importance of designing, in some cases, a **reversible** treatment that can, if necessary, be undone in the future without harm to the original.

Unstable Media

Cohesive failure within a medium (e.g., paint, ink, and pastel) or among materials in an object may be due to an individual, poorly made material, its interaction with other materials, or fabrication methods. All media must be compatible with the paper and with each other in order for all layers of the object to remain intact. For example, a flexible paper cannot support thick, brittle paint: stiff paint requires a rigid support. Similar symptoms appear when a very dry environment has caused media to become desiccated. Cracked, powdering, or flaking media are a serious problem and should be addressed as quickly as possible to ensure that the image is not lost.

It is essential, and often challenging, for a conservator to find the material and technique that will secure unstable media without altering surface colors or causing eventual discoloration. Occasionally an artifact that requires consolidation is mounted to a rigid support by the conservator to prevent the sheet from continuing to move beneath the vulnerable media. These situations are exceptions to the general rule that paper artifacts should be free to contract and expand in response to environmental changes.

Planar Distortions

Undulations or distortions in the paper of an artwork can interfere with the aesthetic reading of the piece. These distortions are often caused by poor-quality matting and framing practices combined with exposure of the paper to fluctuating temperature and humidity levels. Using gentle, gradual procedures, a conservator usually can reflatten a sheet while preserving the texture of the paper, as well as the design media.

Tears and Losses

Tears and holes in the paper can be repaired using compatible but unobtrusive mending papers and nonstaining reversible adhesive. Japanese papers have traditionally been used by conservators to strengthen weak areas and fill in losses, and they can be very successful in returning a sense of full sheet to a damaged original. The ability of the conservator is, of course, a major factor in how well these repairs are integrated into the original. The manner in which missing media is compensated for in a repaired loss depends largely on the type of artwork and the intention of use by the owner. Missing manuscript ink in a document, for example, is never filled in, but a missing area of a print could be. There are two reasons for this difference in approach: documents are valued for their connection to history, while art objects are valued for the image they convey. In the case of a print issued in an edition of the same image, the conservator can sometimes make a correct reproduction of a lost print area. Otherwise, unless a document or drawing was photographed the before loss occurred, there is no way to know exactly what the lost passage looked like. Most conservators aim for reversibility of treatments in these instances and use high-quality materials that age well.

Conclusion

Some paper conservators are generalists akin to general practitioners in medicine, while others have expertise in specific areas. Some specialize in sophisticated **conservation treatments** for individual objects, developing their craftsmanship and perhaps even narrowing their attention to one particular period of art, while others engage in treating masses of material efficiently, managing statistics, making projections through surveys, and designing housings and storage. Working in emergency situations requires knowledge about dangerous environments and stabilization procedures. Contemporary objects are made with new materials used in unconventional ways, requiring a conservator to keep abreast of commercial developments that someone working with traditional artifacts need not consider. Similarly, a conservator who works with older objects needs to be able to detect traces of materials that have altered over time. Very large objects such as wallpaper and globes may require particular equipment as well as experience. Asian or Middle Eastern paintings also demand specialized knowledge. It is important to find someone with the experience appropriate for your object or problem.

In addition to these specializations, some objects require the expertise of two different kinds of conservators. Among the most common are **oil paintings** executed on paper or cardboard and works on **parchment**, which is not paper but treated animal skin. Because parchment predated paper as a surface for writing and painting in the West, parchment objects may seem to require the expertise of a paper or book conservator rather than an ethnographic objects conservator (see Chapters 6 and 9). However, the chemistry, character, and needs of parchment objects are quite different from those of paper artifacts. Other objects not made from paper but sometimes treated by paper conservators include works on papyrus, **tapa cloth**, and **pith paper**. Depending on the particular problem, a paper conservator may refer you to a colleague or propose a collaboration.

Whatever treatment course is chosen, its success depends on a combination of factors. The currency of a conservator's knowledge is critical because significant advances in the profession are continuously being made. Techniques and materials that were accepted twenty years ago may not be the best options today. At the same time, there is no substitute for years of experience and observation. The quality of materials, tools, and equipment used also affect the treatment outcome. Finally, and most important, a fine conservator needs skillful hands, thoughtfulness, concentration, and a sense of professional ethics to make a treatment a success.

Further Reading

Gascoigne, Bamber. *How to Identify Prints*. New York: Thames and Hudson, 1986.

Goldman, Paul. *Looking at Prints, Drawings, and Watercolors: A Guide to Technical Terms*. Malibu, Calif.: British Museum and J. Paul Getty Museum, 1988.

Hunter, Dard. *Papermaking: The History and Techniques of an Ancient Craft*. New York: Dover Publications, 1978.

Lawrence, Patricia O. R. *Before Disaster Strikes: Prevention, Planning, and Recovery*. New Orleans: Historic New Orleans Collection, 1992.

Perkinson, Roy, and Francis Dolloff. *How to Care for Works of Art on Paper*. 4th ed. Boston: Museum of Fine Arts, 1985.

Smith, Merrily. *Matting and Hinging of Works of Art on Paper*. New York: Consultant Press, 1986.

Weintraub, Steven, and Gordon O. Anson. "Natural Light in Museums: An Asset or a Threat?" *Progressive Architecture*, May 1990, pp. 49–54.

Subspecialties

Analytical services, archival collections, collages, contemporary art, drawings, globes, manuscripts, maps, parchment, posters, prints.

Conservators

CHAPTER 5

Photographs

THE MANY DIFFERENT KINDS OF PHOTOGRAPHS AND THE LARGE NUMBER of them in most collections can make caring for photographs a daunting task. Since most photographs are sensitive to physical and chemical damage, **preservation** must begin with an understanding of the structure of a photograph and the needs of the materials that make up the photograph. A photograph conservator can provide advice concerning the avoidance of damage as well as the treatment of damaged photographs. Because many types of damage are permanent and cannot be reversed, the value of preventing damage cannot be overstated.

Structure of Photographs

Photographs are comprised of a variety of materials that can be categorized by their function. The most common structural parts are the image material, the **binder**, and the **support**. The binder adheres the image to the support. The most common image materials are silver (in various forms) and chromogenic **dyes** (used in most color photographs). The most common binders are gelatin, **albumen**, and **collodion**. **Paper**, plastic, **glass**, and **metal** have all been used as photographic supports. Additional materials, such as retouching and other applied color, coatings, cases, mats, and mount boards may also be part of a photograph.

The variety of materials that may be found in a photograph pose a challenge to the photograph conservator. All photographs do not have the same components. For example, a typical color photograph made today has an image made of dyes in a gelatin binder on a support made of paper and plastic.

On the other hand, albumen photographs are a common type of photograph from the nineteenth century. They have a silver image in an albumen binder on a thin paper support. The photograph is typically adhered overall to a thicker card support. What is an appropriate treatment for one type of photograph may be disastrous for another. For example, a photograph with a binder of collodion (another common nineteenth-century photographic process) may be badly damaged in treatment by solvents that would not harm a photograph with an albumen binder.

Damage to Photographs

Poor handling and chemical deterioration caused by poor storage environments are the primary causes of damage to photographs. Poor handling results in damage such as tears, breakage, cracking, and losses. Chemical reactions cause deterioration such as fading of image materials, discoloration of binders, and embrittlement of supports. These types of problems are typically not treatable, and maintenance of a good **environment** is crucial to preventing chemical deterioration.

A primary concern with photographs is chemical deterioration of the image material. Image deterioration is mostly the consequence of poor storage conditions such as high levels of temperature, **relative humidity**, light, and pollutants. While poor processing can be a factor in the deterioration in some photographs, it is usually not the cause for deterioration. When most image materials deteriorate, they become less visible; eventually their deterioration will be noticeable as fading. Fading is usually first seen in the lightest areas of a photograph. If fading is extensive enough however, it will become noticeable even in darkest shadow areas.

A related deterioration phenomenon is a shift in image tonality. For example, photographs with a silver image, such as an albumen photograph, can shift in tone from deep purple to reddish brown, due to chemical deterioration. A similar shift in tonality can be seen with more recent black-and-white photographs fading from a black tone to a brown one.

Another concern is staining. Rather than fading upon deterioration, some materials darken in appearance, causing staining. Because of the vulnerability of photographs to chemical deterioration, it is critical to store photographs in a good environment and to limit exhibition of photographs to fairly short periods of time. Changing the photographs you display twice a year is a good idea.

Treatment of Damaged Photographs

While chemical deterioration such as fading is largely irreversible and cannot be treated in most cases, a photograph conservator can treat physical damage. Treatment procedures exist for a variety of kinds of damage: surface grime; structural damage, such as tears and cracks; flaking binders; mold damage; and removal of tapes and adhesives.

Treatments for photographs can be divided into two broad categories: structural treatments that stabilize the condition of a photograph, and **cosmetic treatments** that improve the appearance of the photograph. Some treatments, such as the reduction of adhesive, are both a **stabilization** and a cosmetic treatment. Photograph conservators may differ in approach concerning the amount of cosmetic treatment they feel is necessary. They may also differ concerning the importance of retaining original mounts, housings, and other materials.

While many photograph **conservation treatments** are similar to paper conservation treatments, they should be done by a conservator trained in applying these methods to photographs. Photographic materials can be unpredictable in treatment. Of particular concern are treatments such as adhesive removal and surface cleaning that involve the use of water or solvents either in localized areas or by immersion. Binders are especially vulnerable to water or solvents. The **treatment proposal** should describe the rationale behind the treatment, the benefits and risks of the plan, and the expected outcome.

Enclosures for Photographs

A photograph conservator will be able to make recommendations for proper storage enclosures. Any storage enclosure should do two things: it should provide physical protection, and it should not harm the photograph. Since enclosures are either in direct contact or in close proximity to photographs, it is vitally important that the materials used to make enclosures do not harm the photograph. Poor-quality materials, such as groundwood paper, can cause extensive chemical degradation and often do not provide sufficient physical protection. Poor-quality storage enclosures may also contain a variety of harmful components, including oxidants, acids, and sulfur. In addition to causing chemical degradation, enclosures with these components tend themselves to degrade. Consequently, they provide the photograph with less and less physical protection. Using good storage enclosures can substantially reduce damage caused by handling.

Fortunately, a test exists for evaluating the materials used to make enclosures. The **Photographic Activity Test (PAT)** is described in a standard written by the American National Standards Institute (ANSI). This standard provides a way for buyers of enclosure materials to know that what they buy will not harm their photographs. Many manufacturers and suppliers of housing materials now conduct this test on their products. Owners of photograph collections are urged to purchase only products that have passed the PAT or to specify that any enclosure must pass the PAT. If you have photographs framed, by sure to ask for materials that "pass the PAT."

If a plastic enclosure is preferred, and there is no indication that it has passed the PAT, be sure the plastic is one described as acceptable by ANSI. Acceptable plastics include polyethylene, polypropylene, and polyester. They may be purchased through reputable preservation supply companies and some photo finishers. Avoid polyvinyl chloride (PVC) sleeves and self-adhering magnetic photo albums.

Copying Photographs

Making copies of exhibition photographs is a beneficial preservation technique. Copies of photographic prints can reduce handling of valuable or fragile originals. Using copies for long-term display can also prevent damage to originals during exhibition.

In general, the greatest concern when making copies of photographs is physical damage caused by handling. Special care must be taken if photographs are turned over during copying or scanning. Overhead copystands require less handling and are safer for making copies than photocopiers or flatbed scanners. Photographs on brittle mounts are especially vulnerable. Heat from light sources can be damaging and should be minimized. Even so, the light exposure from a typical copy, photograph, or scan is very small when compared to the daily light exposure in a typical home.

While conservators do not usually copy photographs, they can help you find someone who can do the work well. Most important is to use a photographer or lab that is familiar with handling the type of photograph you desire to have copied. While many photographs have only one image tone, often this tone is not completely neutral and will be lost if the copy is in black-and-white only.

Further Reading

ANSI. *American National Standard for Imaging Materials: Reflection Prints—Storage Practices.* ANSI IT9.20-1996. New York: American National Standards Institute, 1996.

ANSI. *American National Standard for Imaging Media: Photographic Activity Test.* ANSI IT9.16-1993. New York: American National Standards Institute, 1993.

ANSI. *American National Standard for Imaging Media: Photographic Processed Films, Plates, and Papers—Filing Enclosures and Storage Containers.* ANSI IT9.2-1998. New York: American National Standards Institute, 1998.

ANSI. *American National Standard for Imaging Media: Processed Safety Photographic Films—Storage.* ANSI IT9.11-1998. New York: American National Standards Institute, 1998.

McCormick-Goodhart, Mark H. "Conservation Forum: The Allowable Temperature and Relative Humidity Range for the Safe Use and Storage of Photograhic Materials." *Journal of the Society of Archivists* 17, no.1 (1996): 7-21.

Norris, Debbie H. "Photographs." In *Caring for Your Collections: Preserving and Protecting Your Art and Other Collections,* 64-75. National Committee to Save America's Cultural Collections, Arthur W. Schultz, chairman. New York: Harry N. Abrams, 1992.

Reilly, James. *Care and Preservation of 19th Century Photographic Prints.* Rochester, N.Y.: Eastman Kodak Co., 1986.

Wilhelm, Henry, and Carol Brower. *The Permanence and Care of Color Photographs: Traditional and Digital Color Prints, Color Negatives, Slides, and Motion Pictures.* Grinnell, Iowa: Preservation Publishing Co., 1993.

Sub-specialties

Nineteenth century, twentieth century, contemporary, art, family, negatives and film, copying

Conservators

Dianne van der Reyden 195–196
Sarah S. Wagner 200

CHAPTER 6

Books

A S ONE MIGHT EXPECT, BOOKS AND "FLAT" **PAPER** ARTIFACTS HAVE SOME fundamental similarities in the way their **conservation** is approached. However, there are some important differences: books are not made of paper alone; they are **composites** of paper (or sometimes an animal skin called **vellum**), cloth, leather, thread, adhesives, paperboard and occasionally wooden boards, **metal** clasps, and even ornate **textiles**, precious metals, and jewels. Furthermore, many books hold still more materials, such as photographs, botanical specimens, or newsclippings. Book conservators determine appropriate treatment options after considering all the materials involved, not just the paper pages.

In addition, the paper in books may be treated differently from paper in a work of art. Unlike art, which is usually framed and not handled, books are meant to be held and used. They are functional objects, and their paper must be able to move.

Before deciding on a treatment protocol, a book conservator will consider not only how the treatment will improve the appearance and chemical stability of the paper but also how its strength and flexibility will be affected. While some treatment options, such as alkalization and page repair, are identical to those used by conservators of flat paper objects, others must efficiently address the large number of pages in books. Therefore, except for extremely valuable books, book conservators often resist extremely labor-intensive treatment options, such as bleaching brown spots from pages. Ideally, the cost of a **conservation treatment** is kept proportionate to the value of the artifact.

Value

Value is, however, a difficult concept to define, and client and conservator must come to an understanding of a book's value before treatment begins. Some books and documents are valuable for historical reasons; others may be rare imprints. Some are valuable for their information, while others may be valued for their association with a famous person or book collection. Sometimes a book is valued for an autograph it contains or simply for its beauty or fine craftsmanship.

Once the conservator and client have established why and how the book is valuable, they can discuss the client's expectations for its conservation, whether those expectations can be met, and what treatment approach is or is not appropriate. For example, a book in its original binding and with historic significance probably should be kept as close as possible to its original condition: replacing a historical binding structure with a new cover would adversely affect the historical value. However, for another book with informational or sentimental value only, recasing in a new cover may be a reasonable option.

Use

The conservator and client must also discuss how the book is to be used. Is it in high demand, or will it sit on a bookshelf more often than not? Books that are used heavily may require more interventive treatment to ensure sufficient physical stability, while books used infrequently often can survive with more conservative treatment, such as providing a protective enclosure.

Common Problems

Brittle Paper

Brittle paper is one of the most common and devastating problems suffered by books. When poor-quality materials are used to make paper, book pages often become brown and so brittle over time that they can virtually shatter. Even ordinary use causes the paper to break out of the book. Unfortunately, there still is no cure for brittle paper. Even conservation methods that stabilize **acidic**, brittle paper chemically do not strengthen the sheets. Interim solutions are few.

Encapsulation is a technique whereby a brittle sheet is placed between two sheets of clear **polyester film** (Mylar) and sealed along the edges. The advantage of this treatment is that the paper is fully supported and can be used freely without danger of breaking further. The disadvantages are that the paper must be stabilized chemically before encapsulation and then "post bound" rather than sewn back into a book format. A post binding looks fundamentally different from a sewn binding—somewhat like a refined loose-leaf binder with posts rather than rings.

An alternate way to support brittle paper is called **paper splitting**. Rather than supporting the outside of the brittle leaf, as with encapsulation, support is placed inside the leaf. Each page is literally split apart through its cross-section, and a thin support paper is sandwiched between the two halves before they are readhered. This technique is extremely labor intensive, however, and not often done in the United States. (A German factory is marketing a massive, mechanized paper-splitting service, and it may be possible to send brittle paper there if this treatment would be appropriate.)

Acidic Paper

Whether the materials used to make the paper were inherently acidic or have become so due to an acidic environment, paper that is acidic ages poorly. The acid will "eat" at the cellulose fibers unless a base is introduced to counteract it and **buffer** the paper from **inherent vice** and air pollutants—sulfur dioxide, for example, which becomes sulfuric acid in the presence of atmospheric moisture. This deacidification or alkalization process is accomplished using calcium or magnesium salts to raise the **pH** of the paper to neutrality or alkalinity. The salts can be applied by a variety of aqueous and solvent-based techniques.

Stained, Dirty, or Yellowing Paper

Dirt comes in many forms and is removed by different methods. Dirt sitting on the paper surface can be **dry-cleaned**, a process that lifts it off the surface of the leaf. Staining and yellowing are not, however, surface problems. To clean them from deep within the fibers of the paper, a conservator must use water to treat the sheet. Before **washing**, a conservator must carefully test the inks or other **media** on the pages for solubility. If the inks are not stable in water, it may be possible to wash the pages in a water and ethyl alcohol combination or it may not be possible to wash the pages at all. If washing is possible discoloration can often be reduced significantly. Often washing is followed by a second bath of alkalizing magnesium or calcium salts and resizing with gelatin or methyl cellulose to restore a crisp feel to the sheet and reduce its surface absorbency.

Torn Paper

Usually paper tears are repaired using techniques and materials derived from age-old Japanese craft traditions. Repair papers made of kozo fiber (a **Japanese paper** from the species of mulberry) and **wheat starch paste** (traditionally used to mount scroll paintings) have withstood the test of time. Rather than reinvent the wheel, modern book and paper conservators often use these materials to make mends, which are extremely stable, nearly invisible, flexible, and **reversible**.

Leaf casting is another paper repair technique, appropriate for paper that can withstand immersion in water. Leaf casting cannot be used with water-sensitive ink or paint, but papers with stable inks and many small holes or losses are ideal candidates for this technique. The sheet is submerged in a special sink that has been filled with a mixture of water and new paper fibers. Once the plug is pulled from the bottom of the sink, the water drains following the path of least resistance—through the holes in the paper. The fibers in the bath settle in the holes and fill them. This technique requires disbinding and eventually rebinding a book.

Under no circumstances should pressure-sensitive tapes or adhesives be used for paper repair if they are not reversible in water. Well-intentioned home repairs can have devastating results and cause more damage than what they were meant to redress. Tape and glue residues damage paper and cannot be removed without using organic solvents. Often this treatment requires that the book be disbound into loose sheets, treated, and then rebound—an extremely time-consuming, expensive option.

Loose Covers or Spine

To repair a book with loose covers and a damaged spine, a conservator can consider either reusing or replacing the original materials. Choosing between these options depends on several things. First, the conservator will determine whether the original materials are strong enough to be reused. Then client and conservator need to discuss the value of the book, because reusing old materials often is a more labor intensive and costly option.

Historically valuable materials need special consideration because the solution for their problems may not be as obvious as one imagines. For example, it may seem appropriate to reuse original materials to repair a historic binding, but many curators and researchers do not want a new repair placed on an old book. They may prefer that the artifact simply be protected in a box, untreated and historically intact. Or they may prefer that original materials be removed and saved for study while the book is rebound in new materials in the original manner, with everything housed together in a protective enclosure. Interim solutions may also be possible, such as board tacketing, whereby loose covers are threaded back onto a text block without disrupting the original sewing or covers.

Broken Sewing

Often the pages of a bound book begin to loosen or fall out because the thread used to sew the book together has broken somewhere. If this is the case, most likely the volume needs to be partially or completely disbound and resewn. The steps in this process include adhesive removal, page repair, resewing, relining, and rebinding. The client and conservator should discuss different resewing techniques, as it may be inadvisable to resew the volume in the original manner if doing so could set the stage for repeated structural failure. For example, in "oversewn" books the thread is stabbed through the stack of pages, a method that can cause the paper to weaken and tear at the sewing perforations. Resewing the pages through the centerfold in each gathering of leaves would be a better choice.

Deteriorated Leather

All skin ages, whether it is our own or tanned animal skin on a book, and unfortunately there is nothing we can do to reverse the effects of time. Traditional methods that aim to preserve leather bookbindings by the application of neat's-foot oil and waxes do not increase the longevity of leather or improve its condition. In fact, leather treatments often diminish the clarity of gold tooling on covers, stain the text paper if applied too liberally, and cause dirt and dust to stick to the surface. Like paper, the condition of leather often depends on its manufacturing process, the amount of previous handling, and the storage environment. Some skins do survive better than others, though. Goat, calf, and pigskins tend to survive better than sheep, which is prone to peel due to its high lanolin content.

All leathers are subject to **red rot**, a marring, dry, powdery decay. The fibers of an affected leather rub off the book cover and onto the hands of the user, and may then stain the book paper. Frequently, leather book covers with red rot are too weak to be used without breaking. If the covers are still somewhat intact, an interim solution is the application of a leather consolidant, but the only true fix for covers with red rot is to replace them.

Protective Enclosure

The most common and preferred treatment for treasured books in museums, libraries, and private collections is protection by a custom-fitted enclosure. The advantages are numerous. Such enclosures protect books from light, which causes irreversible damage, and dust, which causes surface abrasion and attracts pests. Enclosures also buffer books against shifts in temperature and relative humidity, both of which accelerate the aging of materials. And enclosures provide protection against atmospheric pollutants. There are many types and styles of boxes available, all very economical when compared to the cost of conservation treatments. Protective enclosure is usually considered the first line of defense and best investment of funds for most books.

Restorer Bookbinders vs. Book Conservators

Without a doubt, at least half the artifacts that book conservators treat have been treated previously by a restorer bookbinder. The fundamental difference between the two specialists is their knowledge of materials: how they age, the mechanisms of structural failure, and what materials and techniques will prevent structural problems while producing repairs sympathetic to the original aesthetic. It is not enough to wield the same level of craftsmanship as the maker of the original book, and one should not reuse techniques that have failed. A book conservator is fully trained in bookbinding history and chemistry as well as craft techniques: all these elements are necessary to produce a conservation solution that will withstand the test of time.

Further Reading

Pickwoad, Nicholas. "Books and Libraries." In *The National Trust Manual of Housekeeping*. Harmondsworth: Penguin, 1993.

Conservators

CHAPTER 7

Textiles

TEXTILES ARE PART OF OUR LIVES FROM THE TIME WE ARE FIRST WRAPPED in a baby blanket. We protect ourselves from the elements with **textiles**, and we adorn our homes with textiles. We celebrate important occasions in special garments such as wedding gowns and Easter hats. The word <u>textile</u> can refer to a great variety of objects: from a lace kerchief to a Navajo blanket, from a machine-made fabric to an archaeological fragment, from an upholstered chair to a teddy bear. Textiles may be collected as decorative art or for their sentimental value.

While you are probably familiar with the care of the furnishings and clothing of your daily life, it is unlikely that you are aware of the chemical and mechanical properties of **dyes** and fibers and of their deterioration. The difficulties of treating a textile are not necessarily obvious. **Washing** and remounting a small sampler seems easy, until you discover that certain dyes bleed or discolor, or that commercial detergents damage the fiber of the embroidery yarns, or that certain treatment and reframing methods can significantly change the intrinsic value of the piece. Larger textiles can present logistical issues when their size and weight are equaled by their fragility. Tears, sagging, and stains can indicate storage and display problems that conservators are trained to recognize and treat. Fading from exposure to light is cumulative and irreversible, but a good conservator can help you minimize this aspect of damage.

Common Problems

Light damage

Light contains **ultraviolet radiation**, **visible light**, and **infrared light**, all of which can cause damage to textiles. Most dyes and fibers absorb light, which weakens the fabric structure by leaving it susceptible to rips or tears and fading the dyes. Because damage caused by light is irreversible and cannot be treated, you should try to protect your important textiles from direct light.

Damage from Handling and Storage

Improper handling and storage can damage textiles over time. Attics and basements tend to have extremes of temperatures and **relative humidity**, which are inappropriate storage conditions for textiles. Conservators can give you recommendations for appropriate storage and handling.

Flood Damage and Mold

Many textiles absorb moisture quickly but desorb moisture much more slowly. This characteristic puts textiles at great risk for **mold**, especially after a flood or water leak. Because conservators are trained to treat both individual textiles and large collections, conservators are adept at helping you respond to emergencies and minimizing damage to your antique textiles.

Pest Infestation

Carpet beetles and clothes moths are the principal insect pests in the Washington, D.C., area. Horsehair stuffing in antique upholstery, woolen fabrics, silk, and feathers are susceptible to damage. The larval stages of clothes moths and carpet beetles do active, serious damage; they prefer higher humidity (about 70% RH) and dark, pleasant (70°F / 21°C), undisturbed surroundings. Textile conservators may give you procedures for handling such infestations in a manner that will minimize damage to your collection. They can also estimate the cost of remedial repairs.

Smoke Damage

Smoke or soot from fires usually has a mixture of oily residue and a carbon deposit. In many cases, textiles act as a filter absorbing this mixture. Conservators can alert you to proper care and handling procedures, assess damage, and provide treatment for textiles or costumes that have been exposed to fire or smoke.

Treatment Options

Methods of Repair and Reweaving

Different categories of textiles have different traditional methods of repair. Carpets, for use on floors, are generally **rewoven** when holes occur in order to keep the weaving adjacent to the damaged area intact. Woven coverlets, **tapestries**, knitted garments, and open-weave flat textiles are most often rewoven if the damage is incidental and the surrounding area is sound. Antique textiles are less often rewoven because the yarns adjacent to the damage usually do not have sufficient strength to tolerate stress and manipulation required for rewarping and rewefting. Consequently, some form of darning, patching, or **backing** may be used to **stabilize** the textile and to provide visual continuity to the design. Finely woven textiles like silk-patterned weaves are not rewoven because the high warp count prevents such work and the expense of reweaving may be prohibitive. The type and amount of appropriate repair are a matter for discussion with a skilled textile conservator specializing in the treatment of the particular category of textile or costume. Other types of **compensation** to minimize the visual effect of a hole or rip may also be possible. These may be discussed in detail with the conservator.

Methods of Cleaning

Washing with water can alter the physical appearance of a textile, especially its surface texture. However, it is also a means to remove discoloring degradation products. Conservators are reluctant to immerse certain types of textiles in water, and textiles with certain dyes, structures, constructions, or finishes are susceptible to damage during cleaning. The conservator will analyze the type of soiling or staining and the type of fiber and fabric to determine the most appropriate cleaning process and the extent of the cleaning required. Since cleaning is an irreversible procedure, the advantages and disadvantages of cleaning are important to consider. Sometimes a local and specific stain removal treatment is sufficient. The conservator will describe the relative merits of a cleaning procedure for your particular textile.

DRY-CLEANING. **Dry-cleaning** refers to the use of nonaqueous solvents to clean textiles. This procedure is carried out with organic solvents. Such solvents dissolve oily soil (grease, fat) that makes dirt stick to textiles, without swelling the fibers of the garment. Once these soils are dissolved, particulate soil adhered to the oil may be dislodged as well.

WET-CLEANING. **Wet-cleaning** refers to washing textiles with water. At home, most contemporary cotton clothes can be washed in washing machines because water swells, and actually strengthens, the cotton fibers. This swelling allows water to dissolve water-soluble dirt and lets detergents emulsify soils that can be suspended in water. Rinsing removes the dirt and soil; spinning helps to remove the excess water. Washing machines utilize more heat and more agitation than are prudent for antique textiles, however, and for many types of fine fabrics and embroideries; therefore washing machines are *never* appropriate for antique textiles.

Textile conservators utilize custom-made baths, trays, and other specialized equipment to wash textiles without excess heat or agitation. Water used for bathing is either **deionized** or **distilled**. **Surfactant** solutions are selected to match the properties of the fibers, dyes, and structures of the textiles and the type of soiling.

Bleaching

Oxidation or reductive **bleaching** is sometimes carried out, after careful consideration, on certain types of textiles in response to certain problems. Some conservators are reluctant to bleach because bleach can, in some instances, lower the strength of textile fibers and also affect other aspects of the textile, like the dyes or the finish.

Adhesives

The use of **adhesives** to consolidate fibers or to provide backing support to antique textiles has been discussed for several decades. There are valid reasons for the use of adhesives in some instances, and there are other treatments in which it is not appropriate. Because of the variety of adhesives and the types of textiles, conservators may differ in their opinion as to whether an adhesive treatment is appropriate for your textile.

What Can You Expect from a Textile Conservator?

Analysis and Examination

A detailed analysis or examination of the fibers, structure, construction, dyes, finishes, and past usage or alterations of the textile should be performed. Textile and costume conservators cannot give appraisals of your objects, but they can provide you with useful, perhaps valuable, information. This initial examination by the conservator may document materials and technologies found in a particular period and culture; it may also detect inappropriate alterations to your piece. Occasionally, this review may find the textile to be inconsistent with its purported date and provenance.

Condition Report

A **condition report** assesses the relative health of the object and whether the problems are inherent to the type of textile or particular to yours alone. While often the condition report is based on visual observation, occasionally specific tests will be necessary to determine chemical or physical conditions, such as testing for fastness to water, solutions, or solvents; testing for **acids** or **alkalis**; testing the type of soiling; and testing the potential for stain removal. These tests may be necessary for individual yarns or portions of fabric, whether or not they are dyed. The conservator will request your explicit permission to test in a small area(s).

Treatment Proposal

Based on the information about the textile or costume developed in the analysis and condition report, the conservator will prepare a **treatment proposal** to address the deficiencies or problems. **Conservation treatment** options may be almost as varied as the types of textiles and costumes there are to treat. In addition, your description of the purpose or goal of the treatment may affect the type of treatment proposed. If the purpose is to prolong the life of the textile, the approach may be primarily structural, while if visual improvement is the goal, the approach may be more **cosmetic**. Some of the treatment steps may be:

- stabilizing, to keep the fabric properly aligned and supported
- wet-cleaning with water-based solutions
- dry-cleaning with organic solvents
- blocking or realignment, if the object has been distorted
- repairing or reweaving, if there are holes or other voids
- attaching a permanent backing with a stronger, new fabric, to support your antique, but fragile, original textile
- **lining** a flat textile, to provide a dust barrier from the back
- mounting a flat textile on a **stretcher** or solid **support** board
- mounting on a specific form or mannequin
- installing the object in a specific case or frame

Treatment Report

The **treatment report** describes in detail all actions taken on the textile or costume. If the treatment has varied from the original proposal, then detailed subsections may be included to document changes in those specific areas. Photographs and, occasionally, sketches of the treatment should be provided.

Maintenance

Conservators can provide guidelines for the care and handling of the object in the future, as well as sources of supplies for maintaining your textile.

Collection surveys

Collection surveys performed by a conservator can help a collector or cultural institution by determining the needs or priorities for treatment, planning displays or exhibitions, developing storage criteria, creating maintenance procedures, assessing future expenses associated with collections, and dealing with emergency situations, especially floods, smoke and fire damage, and/or pest infestation.

Exhibition Mounting and Installation

These services are often carried out by textile and costume conservators who specialize in assisting collectors, museums, or historical societies that lack a permanent staff member who is trained to build and "dress" the custom mannequins necessary for costume display or who is familiar with the criteria for the safe display of fragile laces and embroideries. These conservators work to prepare the individual objects for viewing and to provide procedures for handling, installation, and deinstallation. The conservator may also mount the textiles for the framer to a frame, since the technical criteria for mounting textiles are often quite different from those for mounting paintings or prints.

Questions To Ask a Textile Conservator

- What is your specialty, within the field of conservation? What kinds of textiles do you normally conserve?
- How long have you been practicing textile conservation?
- Are you a member of any professional organizations?

- Do you have examples of projects that you have completed recently? Can you provide a list of clients?
- Will my treatment proposal include detailed explanation of all steps involved in the treatment?
- What if this treatment ends up costing more than your proposal?
- What is the best way to frame or display this textile?
- Can you provide me with practical advice or guidelines for caring for the textile after the object is returned?
- Can you refer me to an appraiser who will tell me the current market value of my textile?
- What is the estimated cost of the treatment?

You may wish to ask the conservator to describe how the process will change your textile structurally and cosmetically. You should ask as many questions as you need to understand why a particular course of action is recommended for your particular object.

Questions To Be Prepared to Answer

- What type of textile do you have?
- What are its dimensions?
- Describe your textile.
- What is the history of the textile, as you know it?
- What is the problem with your textile?
- What would you like done?
- How do you plan to use or display the textile?

Further Reading

Bachmann, Konstanze, ed. *Conservation Concerns: A Guide for Collectors and Curators.* Washington, D.C.: Smithsonian Institution Press and Cooper Hewitt Museum, 1992.

Canadian Conservation Institute. *Textiles and Fibers.* CCI Notes 13/1–13/15. Ottawa: Canadian Conservation Institute, 1990–96.

Fisher, Charles E., and Hugh C. Miller, eds. *Caring for Your Historic House.* Heritage Preservation and National Park Service. New York: Harry N. Abrams, 1998.

Mailand, Harold F., and Dorothy S. Alig. *Preserving Textiles: A Guide for the Nonspecialist.* Indianapolis, Ind.: Indianapolis Museum of Art, 1999.

Story, Keith O. *Approaches to Pest Management in Museums*. Washington, D.C.: Conservation Analytical Laboratory, Smithsonian Institution, 1985.

Wolf, Sara J. "Textiles." In *Caring for Your Collections: Preserving and Protecting Your Art and Other Collectibles*, 86–95. National Committee to Save America's Cultural Collections, Arthur W. Schultz, chairman. New York: Harry N. Abrams, 1992.

Subspecialties

Archaeological textiles, costumes and uniforms, embroidery, ethnographic textiles, fiber art, flags and banners, lace, painted textiles, quilts and coverlets, religious art, rugs and carpets, tapestries, three-dimensional textiles, upholstery and draperies

Conservators

CHAPTER 8

Archaeological Objects

THE CATEGORY **ARCHAEOLOGICAL OBJECTS** INCLUDE ARTIFACTS THAT can be made of any material (ceramics, bone, leather, etc.) in any form, and they may have originated at any time from the recent to ancient past. What distinguishes archaeological objects is that at some point they were buried in the ground, in water, or in some other environment for which they were not originally intended. They were then recovered by controlled excavation, by accidental discovery, or by looting.

What Makes Archaeological Objects Different?

Because of the time these objects spent buried in unusual environments, some artifacts still carry direct evidence of their burial surroundings. For example, they may be waterlogged or covered with dirt. Most archaeological objects display deterioration differently from that found on similar objects that have aged more gradually and without burial. The alterations archaeological objects have undergone may affect not only their appearance but also weaken them significantly and aggravate sensitivity to fluctuations in display and storage environments.

The problems of archaeological objects are complex due to chemical reactions between the objects and the burial environment, and further complications begin when objects are excavated. As the materials adjust to new environmental conditions, objects can deteriorate very quickly. For example, damp objects may develop new cracks as they dry, or their surface decoration may flake. Until they receive a conservator's attention, some objects even need to be kept in a "holding pattern"—stored in conditions resembling the burial environment—to stabilize them. If you are an archaeologist, we recommend that you contact a conservator before an excavation begins so you will be able to include **stabilization** procedures in the excavation process.

Keep in mind that all potentially damaging problems are not obvious. When you consult a conservator for one problem, he or she may find other, less noticeable forms of deterioration. For example, archaeological objects excavated from salty environments, such as desert soil or the ocean, have often absorbed soluble salts that can be extremely damaging. When the objects dry, these salts may become visible as white crystals on the surface, particularly with porous materials like ceramics and some types of **stone**. They may also remain invisible—still hidden in the pores of the object. These continue to react to fluctuations in **relative humidity** and can cause surface flaking and other physical damage over time. Consequently, when you take an object to a conservator for assessment, often he or she will test for the presence of these soluble salts or other hidden forms of potential degradation.

Metal artifacts may also be affected by unstable **corrosion** that may not be readily apparent. For example, a lumpy green corrosion product on the surface might be either a stable **patina** or a symptom of **bronze disease**, a corrosion process that can affect buried copper-based metals. Originating at the core, it may, without stabilization treatment, cause progressive disintegration.

Finally, most archaeological objects reveal their history of use and burial through the cracks, breaks, losses, ancient repairs, residues, corrosion, and burial **encrustations** that may still be on them. An insensitive treatment could alter or destroy this evidence. For example, cleaning up the surface of a ceramic vessel and filling its losses might remove evidence of the drill holes and resinous adhesive left from an ancient repair. Thus, the visual aesthetic for archaeological objects may be very different from that for historic period objects and decorative arts objects.

Why Do You Need a Conservator Who Specializes in Archaeological Material?

Preservation vs. Restoration

Because an archaeological conservator understands the characteristics and complexities that distinguish archaeological artifacts from other objects, his or her approach will emphasize **preservation** of all aspects of the object rather than **restoration**. For conservators, the term *restoration* can be troublesome because it often implies making an object look new. While restoring an object to its original appearance is appropriate in some situations, restoration techniques can change the character of an archaeological object completely. Usually this change is inappropriate. Breaks, losses, and corrosion might be considered flaws on certain kinds of objects (e.g., historic period objects, decorative arts objects), but on archaeological objects they provide evidence of use and burial. Unfortunately in the past, uninformed restorers who treated archaeological artifacts obliterated important archaeological characteristics, decreasing both the financial and scholarly values of these objects.

To repair breaks, fill losses, and remove corrosion and burial encrustation may be appropriate to some degree, but no single approach works for all types of objects and materials. Archaeological conservators are aware of these issues and can discuss them with you to ensure that your object receives the most ethical and sensitive treatment.

Specialized Equipment and Techniques

Archaeological conservators distinguish materials excavated from dry or damp land sites from those from underwater sites because the problems are often very different and treatment may require specialized equipment or conservation techniques. This is particularly true for waterlogged materials that typically are brought from a saturated to a dry state. **Organic materials**, for example, may require **freeze-drying** treatment to prevent severe deformation or shrinkage.

Many treatments for archaeological objects have been adapted from conservation procedures used for nonarchaeological objects made with the same materials. Refer to other chapters in this directory for information about the specific materials found in your objects.

Ethical Issues

What makes archaeological objects precious is their context—that is, the particulars of their "find spots" that enable archaeologists to reconstruct a detailed picture of life at a specific time and place. Treating an object that may have been excavated illicitly raises serious ethical issues for a conservator, so some will not treat objects with questionable origins.

What Can You Expect From an Archaeological Conservator?

Because some problems may be hidden, a conservator will not be able to fully assess an object's need until it has been examined and tested carefully. After that, you will receive a written **treatment proposal**, usually with several options presented and the steps of each option described. These may represent progressive levels of treatment, from basic stabilization to choices about aesthetic compensation.

The first treatment level will be stabilizing the object to prevent or retard further deterioration. This option may be as simple as providing a description of the environmental conditions necessary for safe display and storage, or it may require a complex chemical treatment.

In a level beyond stabilization, the conservator may suggest aesthetic compensation. Generally, archaeological conservators suggest techniques that help to visually integrate lost or damaged portions of an object without hiding or destroying its history. This approach stabilizes artifacts, restores some of the major structural characteristics, but does not hide the history of the object under new restoration materials. For example, after removing soluble salts from a ceramic artifact and rejoining its pieces to restore the object's shape, a conservator might propose filling large losses but leaving small holes and cracks alone.

Finally, the conservator will give you guidelines for display techniques, storage materials, and environmental conditions appropriate for your object. These may be the same as for nonarchaeological artifacts made with the same materials. Once stabilized, most archaeological objects fare well in a stable environment that is comfortable for people. However, iron and other archaeological metals often need to be maintained in a dry environment—for example, below 20 percent relative humidity.

Questions To Ask an Archaeological Conservator

- What is your experience with archaeological objects?
- Have you worked on objects from this culture?
- Have you worked on material from this climate or type of burial site?
- Have you worked on freshly excavated material?
- What are the treatment options for my object, and what are the reasons for each option?
- How will your treatment protect the archaeological character of the artifact?
- How should I display this object?
- How should I store the object?

Questions To Be Prepared To Answer

- What is the object made of (ceramic, glass, metal, textile)? Be ready to describe its material(s) and size.
- What is its geographic or cultural origin?

- What situation or condition prompts you to call a conservator?
- Do you know anything about the excavation history of the object? For example, when was it excavated and by whom?
- Do you know whether the object may have been restored previously and, if so, by whom? Are there any records from that treatment?
- Be prepared to describe surface characteristics. For example, is it covered in dirt? Does it have lumpy corrosion, or is it smooth with an even color?
- What do you plan to do with the object? Where will it be stored and displayed?
- Do you have photographs or slides of the object?

Further Reading

Cronyn, J. M. *The Elements of Archaeological Conservation.* New York: Routledge, 1990.
Robinson, Wendy. *First Aid for Underwater Finds.* London: Archetype Publications; Portsmouth, UK: Nautical Archaeology Society, 1998.
Sease, Catherine. *A Conservation Manual for the Field Archaeologist.* Los Angeles: UCLA Institute of Archaeology, 1992.

Sub-specialties

Damp land site objects, dry land site objects, underwater site objects, field work

Conservators

Alexandria Conservation Services, Ltd. 129–130
Chase Art Services 142
Conservation Anthropologica 145
Conservation Solutions, Inc. 147–150
Catherine E. Magee 169
Maryland Archaeological Conservation Laboratory 171
John Scott Conservator of Art and Architecture 181
Landis Smith 182
Catharine Valentour 194

CHAPTER 9

Ethnographic Objects

THE DESCRIPTION ETHNOGRAPHIC REFERS TO MATERIAL CULTURE THAT
is frequently utilitarian in nature and for which anthropological context is important. The cultural groups producing these objects may
have been historically documented or may still be functioning as a society in
the present. Because the written record on these cultures is often sparse or non-
existent, objects become a primary source of information on the society. Consequently, **ethnographic objects** are collected for the information they may
hold about the people who made them as well as for their aesthetic qualities.

How an artifact is made, used, and perceived indigenously (i.e., within
its own culture) will significantly influence the conservator's approach to treatment. The materials from which ethnographic objects are manufactured can
be either familiar or unusual, and in many instances they may be impossible
to identify. Often these objects are **composites**—made of more than one type
of material. Certain combinations of materials interact detrimentally, a phenomenon referred to as **inherent vice**. For example, oily leather dressing causes
corrosion on brass **metal** hardware. Incompatible combinations of materials
may complicate recommendations for display or storage (metal requires low
humidity whereas wood prefers a more humid environment) or treatment
choice (polishing metal attachments on a leather object could abrade edges of
the leather). The technology of construction also influences the stability of
the artifact (pigments with minimal **binding medium** will flake; **dyes** may be
naturally **acidic**; a poor mix of the ingredients for glass will cause structural
breakdown; feathers are inherently fragile).

Much of the importance of traditional ethnographic material resides in
the context in which it was created: how the objects have been used and valued within the originating society. A conservator will be able to recognize ev-

idence of use and set as a priority the **preservation** of this information. Wear might be the most obvious form of use; areas of the object may be worn down, smoothed, or even rubbed away by indigenous handling. Indigenous repairs are considered part of the history of the piece and contribute to the object's value; these mends should be retained. Patination is the change in the surface appearance through time and use. This buildup of surface characteristics—color, sheen, encrusted applications, oils—indicates that an object has been well used in its cultural setting. Patina is an indication of age and of value to the original society. Further, any treatment an object may have received after being removed from its cultural setting is sometimes considered valuable evidence of its history and **provenance**. However, unsightly **restorations** or poor mounting mechanisms should be removed.

In their cultural context, objects may have been purely functional items, or they may have been more socially important, imparting prestige, providing control, or invoking spiritual responses. In recent years, the cultural perceptions of an artifact have become influential when considering possible **conservation treatments** and the general handling of ethnographic material. For example, material produced by the indigenous people of the Americas is often considered sacred culturally; consequently, these objects may have special requirements for storage, exhibition, and treatment. An ethnographic conservator will provide treatment that is culturally sensitive.

Common Issues Associated with Ethnographic Objects

Infestation

One of the most common problems presented by ethnographic material is insect infestation. It may be recognized by piles of wood "dust" (insect *frass*) beneath, and small circular exit holes in, wooden objects. **Textile** objects may have casings and frass as well as holes. Often insect carcasses will be present; and careful examinations may locate a live specimen in either the larval or adult stage, which should be collected in a small container for identification by a professional. The next action in containing an infestation is to place the affected article in a thick, well-sealed plastic bag; this step isolates the problem and protects other furnishings and objects in the vicinity.

At present, there are three general options for treating infested objects. Selection of the appropriate method depends on a knowledge of the materials to be treated and the insect in question and requires the advice of a conservator. Ideally, the method should kill all stages in the life cycle of the insect with one treatment. Otherwise, a repeated application may be required.

Briefly, the safest treatment for both object and owner is an **anoxic** approach. Placing the piece in an oxygen-free environment for several weeks will kill all stages in the insect life cycle and leaves no residual chemicals in the object. Freezing is another effective treatment that also destroys eggs, larva, and adults, leaving no residues; the process must be carried out in a precise manner using specialized equipment. Third, **fumigation** is available commercially, but a conservator must advise on the specific chemical selected for the materials to be treated. Often fumigation kills only larva and adults, and a second treatment is required after eggs have hatched. Residual fumigant may remain.

Appropriate Mounting and Display

Another problem familiar to the ethnographic conservator is breakage or abrasion caused by the absence or inadequacy of a mount. Although mounting **armatures** must often be custom made and therefore can be expensive, they properly support objects and prevent accidental damage. Never use screws or nails to mount an object; always consult a conservator or an experienced mount maker when an object needs to be secured.

Cleaning and Protection

Apart from gentle dusting and vacuuming, cleaning should be left to a conservator, who will be able to determine how much cleaning is appropriate to preserve evidence of use and protect patinations. The conservator also will be able to make informed decisions regarding appropriate cleaning agents. Commercial products should not be applied to objects; for example, oil or spray dusters have no protective value and may actually damage patinated surfaces and decrease the value of an object. Similarly, certain commercial detergents that are promoted as gentle cleaners for ethnographic textiles may be difficult to rinse away and should be avoided.

Repair and Restoration

Private collectors should never try to repair a valuable object by themselves. Proprietary adhesives, such as **epoxy** and superglues, are difficult to reverse once set. Failed attempts at repair make a conservator's job harder and consequently more costly. A conservator will choose adhesives and materials that should not change chemically through time; in other words, they are and remain **reversible** as they age. The degree of **restoration** or **conservation** can range from a passive, nonintervening approach, such as simple mounting, to structural stabilization and aesthetic retouching. The conservator will also provide photographic and written documentation of the condition of the object before and after treatment.

Technical Analysis

You need to be aware that many of the **organic materials** used in ethnographic objects cannot be definitively identified or dated. Metals and **alloys** can be characterized through instrumental analyses conducted by scientific institutions, universities, or private laboratories. There are, however, some easily accessible techniques that can provide useful information. Long-wave **ultraviolet light** (black lights) can help discern areas of **overpaint** or adhesive in restorations that may be overlooked in daylight. Additionally, x-radiography can be valuable for distinguishing old restorations, such as dowels, pins, and breaks, which may not be apparent with the unaided eye. Structurally weak areas within an object can also be highlighted with this technique. However, ceramic or cast metal objects should not be **x-radiographed** before considering dating possibilities; exposure to radiation can effectively "reset the clock" and render dating results inaccurate.

Methods for dating ethnographic objects remain mostly stylistic as instrumental analysis is not as useful for historical (as opposed to archaeological) pieces. **Radiocarbon dating** is used for organic material (wood, bone, and textile) but provides useful information only for objects more than three hundred years old. **Thermoluminescence** (**TL**) dating is most helpful for distinguishing an older, authentic piece from a modern fake. It is applied to both ceramics and clay casting cores, which might be present in metals.

Finding the Right Conservator

The right conservator for your ethnographic objects should be conversant on factors that affect the condition of ethnographic objects and be able to clarify what the object will look like after treatment. The conservator should have demonstrable experience treating the specific materials and object type presented by your object, should have cultural expertise, and should be abreast of issues that may be sensitive (such as the treatment of sacred objects). Further, the conservator should offer advice on long-term care and be able to recommend relevant forms of analysis and scientists who can provide analytical services.

An ethnographic conservator will have his or her unique combination of the above expertise and experiences, so specific approaches and treatments may vary from one conservator to another. You should be aware that an ethnographic conservator may ethically decline to work on objects that are culturally sensitive, made of materials whose importation is restricted or illegal (such as ivory, pelts, and shark skin) and older objects with questionable provenance.

Further Reading

Rose, Carolyn. "Ethnographic Materials." In *Caring for Your Collections: Preserving and Protecting Your Art and Other Collections,* 138-55. National Committee to Save America's Cultural Collections, Arthur W. Schultz, chairman. New York: Harry N. Abrams, 1992.

Rose, Carolyn. "Preserving Ethnographic Objects." In *Conservation Concerns: A Guide for Collectors and Curators,* ed. Konstanze Bachman, 115-22. Washington, D.C.: Smithsonian Institution Press, 1992.

Conservators

Conservation Anthropologica 145
Catherine E. Magee 169
Landis Smith 182
Catharine Valentour 194

CHAPTER 10

Metals

METALS ARE AMONG THE MOST ABUNDENT ELEMENTS ON THE PLANET Earth, but pure **metals**, as we know them in their utilitarian forms, are an exception in nature. Their scarcity is owing to the atomic structure of pure metals and their tendency to combine readily with other elements such as oxygen, sulfur, nitrogen, and chlorides. When found in abundance these naturally occurring compounds are called ores. Ores must be smelted and refined in order to obtain pure or almost pure metals, which can then be fashioned into utilitarian or decorative objects. The tendency for pure metals to revert to more stable compounds by combining with other elements persists, and metal objects tend to deteriorate with time if not properly maintained. Therefore the **preservation** and treatment of metal artifacts can be thought of as an attempt to achieve stability in an inherently unstable material.

Uses of Metals

The properties of metals include luster, **hardness**, strength, malleability, and electrical and thermal conductivity. Throughout history, dynamic advances in metals' technology have led to new applications in the arts, architecture, and industry. In ancient times metals such as bronze and iron were used for weapons and tools. Precious metals such as gold and silver also were used for vessels, as well as for jewelry and decorative functions. In architecture, metals have been used for both structural and decorative applications. A primary use in the fine arts is for sculpture. Metals also figures prominently in the broad category of functional objects that includes machines, tools, vehicles, armaments, and musical and scientific instruments.

Metallic Elements and Alloys

Each metallic element (zinc, copper, aluminum, iron, lead, tin, nickel, silver, gold, and platinum, for example) has specific properties. Combining one or more of these elements to form an **alloy** produces a metal with different and often more useful properties. Some metals are alloyed to produce **corrosion** resistance; some, to increase strength or workability; some, for color. Typical alloys include the brasses (copper and zinc), **bronzes** (copper and tin), silver alloys (silver and copper), **pewter** (tin, copper, antimony, and/or lead), white brasses (copper, zinc, and nickel), and **steels** (iron and carbon).

Working Techniques and Surface Finishes

How a metal object is formed is often dictated by the properties of the constituent metal. For example, bronze alloys are relatively easy to cast, but difficult to work as sheet metals. Fabrication techniques include casting, stamping, repoussé, raising, hammering, spinning, forging and die-casting, welding, machining, filing, and combinations of these. Knowledge of metallic properties, forming techniques, and finishing processes is requisite to the conservation and maintenance of metal objects and can often be used to date an object or establish its provenance.

A surface finish, or **patina**, can be decorative, functional, or both. A metal surface can be heat-treated or treated with chemicals to produce pleasing colors or corrosion resistance. Examples include blackened silver on Japanese decorative arts, bluing on steel, or niello inlay on hammered copper, silver, or brass objects. Finishes include **plating** and **gilding**, patination, **enameling**, inlay, **polishing**, and coating with colored **lacquers**, waxes, **resins**, oils, and paint. Generally, chemical patination is intentional and corrosion is not, but some metals do achieve pleasing and sometimes stable corrosion films or crusts with time. A patina can refer to either the intentional finish or naturally occurring corrosion.

Another example of beneficial oxidation is the familiar surface film that aluminum quickly forms as it bonds with atmospheric oxygen. This thin aluminum oxide film enables the metal to resist further corrosion and thus gives aluminum its reputation as a corrosion-resistant metal.

Unfortunately, however, most metals and alloys do not form protective films or patinas. Metals will continue to corrode even after an initial corrosion layer has developed, and this corrosion can destroy not only the original surface but, if allowed to continue, cause extensive metal loss. Though rare, and a term often misapplied to other types of copper alloy corrosion, **bronze disease** can occur as the result of the interaction of moisture, air, and chlorides with bronze, resulting in a powdery, light green corrosion product. **Archaeological metal objects**, which have been buried in the soil or submersed in maritime environments, may react with salts and other compounds that consume most of the metal and transform the objects into unrecognizable lumps (see Chapter 8).

Deterioration

Even in normal environments, most metals are quite reactive. High **relative humidity**, moisture, and air **pollutants**, such as **ozone** and compounds of sulfur and nitrogen, are the most common causes of corrosion. Certain storage materials, such as woods, adhesives, **acidic** papers, and rubber emit corrosive gases. Even simply handling a metal object with bare hands can leave behind corrosive ammonia and salts. Ammoniated cleaning and polishing solutions may also cause damage to metals and should be avoided. Metals also are subject to various kinds of physical damage such as cracking, deformation due to heat or bending, joint failure, and surface abrasion.

Care and Treatment

There are two approaches to collections care. **Preventive conservation** involves actions that mitigate the causes of deterioration passively, while **conservation treatment** involves direct intervention. Generally, with good guidance a nonspecialist can provide many forms of preventive conservation. Conservation treatment requires specialized knowledge and training in both materials science and traditional craft techniques.

Sometimes treatment by a metals conservator is absolutely necessary to repair structural damage, to stop active corrosion, or to return an object to its intended appearance. If it has been deemed appropriate to return a deteriorated object to its original appearance, a conservator may need to remove disfiguring corrosion, **repatinate**, or replace missing parts. For any particular object problem there may be several appropriate treatments. The final choice will depend on the objective of the treatment, the training and philosophy of the conservator, and time and cost factors.

You should take the time to weigh the merits of various **treatment proposals**. For example, one conservator might propose welding or **resoldering**, another might recommend using an **epoxy** resin to repair a break, and yet another might recommend a mechanical armature or fastener. Resoldering and welding are traditional types of repair that are strong and suited for objects that will continue to be used. An epoxy repair is less intrusive and adequate for an object that is not going to be used. To weigh the merits of different proposals, you need to become familiar with the properties of your objects and to ask the conservator about the details and implications of proposed treatment procedures. Conservation is a relatively young profession, and treatment options are not static. Different metal objects require different conservation approaches, but all procedures should be designed to preserve the original metallographic structure.

Common cleaning techniques may be **mechanical** (i.e., using hand tools) or chemical in nature. Following cleaning, typical surface treatments could include gilding, plating, repatination, and application of corrosion inhibitors and coatings. Choosing **reversible** coating materials will facilitate their removal and replacement in the future.

Treatment Decisions and Dilemmas

As the scientific understanding of materials advances and new treatment materials and techniques are introduced, gray areas develop. For example, once it was technically and ethically acceptable to clean a sculpture by blasting it with glass beads (peening) and then repatinating the surface. Today many conservators consider the practice too drastic. Some treatment dilemmas you might encounter in your quest for appropriate treatment for your metal object are:

- to strip or not strip patina, paint, or coatings
- to coat or not coat silver
- to wax, lacquer, or both
- to use mechanical techniques versus chemical techniques
- to use traditional metalworking **restoration** techniques or conservation techniques

A common misconception about metals is the assumption that all corrosion is harmful and should be removed. This erroneous assumption often results in unnecessarily drastic actions that produce greater damage than the corrosion itself, often leading to the loss of an original surface finish or the under-lying metal.

Before opting for treatment, monitor the condition of your objects to determine whether they are stable or deteriorating actively. In many cases, monitoring can be done visually. Do you notice a change in color? Does it seem that the corroded area is getting bigger? Do the corrosion products flake off or stain surrounding areas? Is there a noticeable **bloom** of white, orange, or green? To ensure that your object receives appropriate treatment, you should be satisfied that the proposed treatment addresses the cause of the problem and not just the symptom. For example, removal of corrosion products may not address the root cause of the corrosion such as a humid environment. Take a conservative approach to treatment: least is often best. Refer to the following bibliography to learn more about your artifacts and treatment options.

Further Reading

Barkley, Bob, and Charles Hett. *The Cleaning, Polishing and Protective Waxing of Brass and Copper*. CCI Notes 9/3. Ottawa: Canadian Conservation Institute, 1988.

Boyer, Howard E., and Timothy L. Gall, eds. *Metals Handbook*, desk ed. Metals Park, Ohio: American Society for Metals, 1985.

Canadian Conservation Institute. *Recognizing Active Corrosion*. CCI Notes 9/1. Ottawa: Canadian Conservation Institute, 1989.

Hodges, Henry. *Artifacts: An Introduction to Early Materials and Technology*. London: John Baker, 1971.

Drayman-Weisser, Terry. "Metal Objects." In *Caring for Your Collections: Preserving and Protecting Your Art and Other Collectibles*, 108–21. National Committee to Save America's Cultural Collections, Arthur W. Schultz, chairman. New York: Harry N. Abrams, 1992.

"Metalwork." In *The National Trust Manual of Housekeeping*, comp. Hermione Sand-with and Sheila Stainton, 103–15. London: Penguin Books and the National Trust, 1984.

Mulholland, James A. *A History of Metals in Colonial America*. Tuscaloosa, Ala.: University of Alabama Press, 1981.

Untracht, Oppi. *Metal Techniques for Craftsmen*. New York: Doubleday & Company, 1975.

Subspecialities

Archaeological artifacts, architectural components, decorative objects, functional objects, interior sculpture, jewelry, outdoor sculpture

Conservators

CHAPTER II

Ceramic and Glass Objects

CERAMIC AND GLASS ARTIFACTS ENCOMPASS A WIDE VARIETY OF OBJECTS from the decorative arts to archaeology, (see Chapter 8), ethnography, (see Chapter 4), and architecture. They come in a multitude of forms, from glass window sheets and ceramic floor tiles to folk pottery and crystal goblets, from sculpture to lighting fixtures. Almost all cultures have produced ceramics, and those that did not manufacture glass often traded for it. Its use is widespread.

Ceramics and glass often are grouped together because they are made from similar materials; the major component in both is silica. Glass is often described as a very viscous liquid, though generally it is considered to be a solid. Glass is made mainly from silica, sand, or quartz, with other materials, known as modifiers, added to give color and alter its working properties. For example, lead is added to increase clarity and lower the melting point of silica. Different types of glass are named from the type of **alkaline** or metallic additives, for example, soda-lime glass, potash glass, and lead glass.

Ceramics are classified by the description of the clay body, which is determined by the firing temperature of the clay. **Terra-cottas** are generally brown or red, porous, and fired below 900° C. Earthenware is stronger than terra-cottas; it is usually red, tan, or cream colored, porous, usually glazed, and fired between 1000 and 1200° C. Stoneware is usually red, cream, brown, or gray; it is highly vitrified, slightly porous, nontranslucent, and fired about 1250° C. **Porcelain** is white or cream-colored, nonporous, vitrified, translucent when thin, and fired between 1300 and 1450° C.

Some ceramics share similar characteristics with glass. For instance, porcelain is fired at a high temperature, causing the ceramic body to be vitrified (i.e., glasslike). Similarly the glazes on some ceramics are thin layers of glass. At the same time, ceramics and glass are distinct. Glass is actually a nonporous supercooled liquid, while ceramics are made from clay and range in **porosity** from very porous terra-cottas to nonporous porcelain.

Common Problems

Glass

The most common problems with glass artifacts are cracks, chips, and breakage. In functional glass objects these problems result from mishandling or **thermal shock**. Thermal shock occurs when glass is subjected to rapid temperature changes. For example, using a punch bowl for an iced beverage and then plunging it into a hot water wash can cause the object to spontaneously crack or break because the object cannot withstand the stress from the rapid change in temperature.

Less common is what often is referred to as "sick glass." This condition manifests itself in two forms. **Crizzling**, a network of fine cracks, and **weeping glass**, droplets of moisture on the surface, are due to an excess of alkaline materials in the glass formulation. These can cause the glass surfaces to react with atmospheric moisture, causing crizzling in dry environments and weeping in damp environments. Another glass problem is inherent strain in an object due to improper annealing during manufacture. This phenomenon occurs frequently in hand-blown glass and may manifest itself as precipitous or even explosive damage.

A third problem found usually in liquid containers, such as decanters, pitchers, and drinking glasses, is cloudy glass. Sometimes this condition is caused by a superficial coating of some chemical in the container's liquid, which can be removed by washing or chemical means. The more common problem is that the liquid has partially dissolved one the glass components, leaving voids that appear whitish.

Ceramics

The most common problems with ceramics are cracks, chips, and breakage in both the ceramic body and the applied decoration. **Archaeological** ceramics have often been damaged by salts from the burial soil (see Chapter 9).

Not only are different types of ceramics classified by their firing temperatures, but the different firing methods also have treatment implications. And an additional ceramic category, not mentioned above, includes extremely low-fired "ceramics" such as sun-baked mud brick or cuneiform tablets, which will disintegrate in water and require special sensitivity in treatment.

Treatment Considerations

Conservation treatments for glass and ceramic objects, like the **conservation** of other kinds of objects, vary with the owner's intentions and needs. For example, when joining an object that will be displayed, but not used, a conservator relies on the strength of the mending adhesive to hold the object together. If an object is to be used, a stronger adhesive is required, and the conservator may suggest inserting a pin or dowel into the body of the object. This procedure is intrusive to the object but may be necessary if the object is to be used; it is a decision made between the conservator and client. For example, a broken chandelier arm made of either glass or porcelain would most likely need to be doweled.

Adhesives

One difference between conservators and restorers is their choice of materials and techniques to treat objects. Conservators use **reversible** materials sympathetic to the materials being treated. Adhesives have been tested thoroughly to assure their stability, reversibility, and resistance to yellowing over time. These materials range from acrylics to epoxies and cyanoacrylates, and ultraviolet curing adhesive, but rarely include common commercial products due to their variable formulations and uncertain long-term stabilities.

Most types of glass are repaired with stable, reversible acrylic adhesives, **epoxies**, or **UV** curing adhesives. If necessary, **dyes** or **pigments** can be added to adhesives to diminish the visibility of mends. Ceramic objects are treated differently depending on the body type and method of decoration. For all types of ceramics, the choice of adhesives is of utmost importance because each body type calls for a different adhesive strength to adhere it properly. Too strong an adhesive can damage a ceramic body as much as a weak one.

A professional conservator understands the properties of adhesives and chooses them carefully to avoid strain, surface stains, or insufficient bonds. Nevertheless, some ceramic materials are difficult to treat. Low-fired ceramics such as **terra-cottas** are very fragile and often crumble when they break. Frequently, they are difficult to reassemble because they absorb adhesives and consolidants, "starving" the joint of the adhesive or creating adhesive stains on the object's surface. Lower-fired ceramics with a vitreous glaze, such as earthenwares, may be stained by adhesives.

Restoration

After an object has been reassembled, losses may need to be filled and the object returned visually to its predamaged state through toning losses in glass or inpainting losses in ceramics. Inpainting involves painting the filled or repaired area, but not the original artifact, to match surrounding areas and recreate decorative motifs where the design is known. Conservators use reversible materials, often acrylic paints, for inpainting. Restorers routinely overpaint filled areas and often a large area beyond a fill to hide their repairs, whereas professional conservators overpaint the edges of a fill only in exceptional circumstances. Not only does overpaint obscure the original object and thus devalue it, but also the overpaint may change color over time, causing discoloration and possible damage if it cannot be removed or can be removed only with damage to the object's surface.

Conservators do not grind the edges of breaks in ceramics or glass to refit pieces more easily. Grinding is a radical and unnecessary procedure that permanently devalues objects, though it is often employed by restorers. Similarly, conservators do not use chlorine bleach to remove stains on ceramic objects because chlorine can destabilize a vitreous glaze, and it sets the stage for future damage from soluble salts even though the potential damage might not be noticed for several years.

Environment

Problems arising from unstable environments can be mitigated by both storing and displaying glass and ceramic objects in environments that are comfortable to people while avoiding wide fluctuations in temperature and humidity. Humidity adversely affects both ceramics and glass; therefore, precautions should be taken to prevent a **relative humidity** (**RH**) above 60 percent and below 30 percent.

Crowded storage should be avoided, though adequate spacing is often difficult to achieve due to limited storage areas in both museums and homes. A tightly packed shelf sets the stage for damage when objects are removed or replaced and may accidentally hit adjacent artifacts, causing chips, breaks, and large losses.

Another consideration in both storage and display is vibration. From sources as various as **HVAC** equipment, people walking across the floor, or street traffic, vibration can cause objects to "walk" off a shelf and fall or bump into other objects and damage them. To prevent damage from vibration, the shelves in storage areas can be lined with a cushioning sheet of polyethylene foam, available from conservation supply houses. Objects that are being displayed can be stabilized with brackets.

The effects of light also must be considered. Although glass and ceramics are often displayed in home windows, the ultraviolet component in daylight and **fluorescent tubes** can change the color of older glass, and heat buildup inside vessels can cause **thermal shock**.

Questions To Ask A Ceramics And Glass Conservator

- Have you worked on this type of material before?
- What type of treatments have you done to similar objects, and why?
- What types of materials do you use?
- What types of adhesives would you use to repair this object, and why?
- How long have you been a conservator?

Questions To Be Prepared To Answer

- How will the object be used (displayed beyond the reach of visitors, displayed in a place where it may be handled, or returned to use)?
- How do you want the object to look after treatment? Do you want the repair to be as invisible as possible, or do you want a clear distinction between the artifact and repairs?
- Is the purpose of treatment solely to arrest future deterioration, with no effort to fill losses?

Further Reading

Kingery, W., and P. Vandiver. *Ceramic Masterpieces.* New York: Free Press, 1986.

Newton, R., and S. Davidson. *The Conservation of Glass.* Oxford: Butterworth-Heineman, 1989.

Tennent, N., ed. *The Conservation of Glass and Ceramics: Research, Practice and Training.* London: James and James, 1999.

Conservators

CHAPTER 12

Stone Objects and Sculpture

S TONE IS WIDELY ASSOCIATED WITH PERMANENCE; HENCE, ITS USE IN phrases such as "rock of ages." Stone can be more chemically resistant than many artistic materials, and the materials and methods used for cleaning can often be more aggressive than those used for other media. Nevertheless, stone is not immune to damage from human beings, and it can deteriorate dramatically outdoors, especially in polluted atmospheres (see Chapter 13). Stone is heavy and, despite an appearance of solidity, is brittle and can be easily broken when transported improperly. Its weight can also limit the type of adhesive used for repair.

Types of Stone

Different types of stone can present quite different treatment problems, and it is important that the conservator know what type of stone has been used before treatment begins. Rocks are composed of one or more minerals, defined as homogeneous substances of specific chemical composition and characteristic **crystalline structure**. Rocks are divided into three categories based on formation: sedimentary, igneous, and metamorphic. The characteristics of each type of rock can often be correlated with use, deterioration, and appropriate **conservation treatment**.

Sedimentary Rocks

Sedimentary rocks such as **limestone** and **sandstone** are formed by the deposition of sediments in water. As a result, they are relatively porous and have layered structures. One ramification of **porosity** is that dirt can be readily absorbed in the pores: thus, sedimentary rocks can be difficult to clean. Surface layers can scale off if the sedimentary rock is carved with the layers face-bed-ded (i.e., vertical, with the plane facing the viewer). This is a common phe-nomenon for tombstones made of sandstone. The layered structure may have made it easy to make the tombstone in the first place, allowing the sandstone to be split to provide a flat surface for carving. The areas between the layers are vulnerable to weathering, however, and **spalling** off of the surface layer will likely result in loss of the entire inscription.

Because sediments are deposited by so many different natural agents, the chemical and physical properties of sedimentary rock vary considerably, with important consequences for cleaning. For example, the calcite of which lime-stone is made is rapidly attacked by **acids**; thus cleaning limestone with any acid, including mild household acids such as vinegar and lemon juice, will cause damage. Sandstones, on the other hand, are composed of sandy parti-cles (usually quartz) cemented together with one or more of a range of min-erals. If quartz particles are cemented siliceous minerals, they may be cleaned relatively safely with strong solutions, even those containing hydrofluoric acid. If the particles are cemented with calcite, they will be attacked by acid. If there is a substantial component of clay in the cement, the sandstone may be damaged by water alone.

Metamorphic Rocks

Metamorphic rocks are formed by great heat or pressure, resulting in recrys-tallization of minerals and even formation of new minerals. **Marble** is an ex-ample of a metamorphic rock made of the same mineral as limestone, but its recrystallization enables the stone to take a high polish. If highly polished, however, the appearance of marble can be easily altered by cleaning, and mar-ble is attacked by the same acids that damage limestone. It should also be noted that the word marble is often used loosely by nonexperts to mean any stone which takes a polish, and so the conservator will establish what the true composition of a "marble" object is. Of particular cause for concern would be the mistaking of alabaster for marble. Made of gypsum rather that calcite, **alabaster** is somewhat soluble in water, and while water cleaning is generally acceptable for calcite rocks, it might attack the surface of alabaster.

Igneous Rocks

Igneous rocks are formed from highly siliceous molten material during vol-canic activity. Because of the silica, igneous rocks tend to be relatively resistant to chemical attack. Those that formed inside volcanoes can be difficult to cut and form but are generally durable. Probably the most common igneous rock of this type used for artistic purposes is granite, often employed for sculpture bases. Although highly resistant to weathering, granite can be damaged from use of deicing salts, as, for example, you can see at the base of pillars at the front of Union Station, in Washington, D.C. Compared to granite, igneous rocks like **pumice** or tuff, formed after the molten magma leaves the volcano, can be very porous, readily carved, and much more easily damaged. The enormous statues on Easter Island were made of this type of stone, but it has been less commonly used for artifacts found in collections.

Common Problems and Accepted Treatment Solutions

Cleaning

Cleaning is one of the most common activities for stone. The extent of cleaning may be debatable and a matter of taste. What may appear to one viewer as "filthy dirty" may be the "**patina** of age" to another. Hence, you should make clear the extent of cleaning you desire to the conservator. If there is any doubt, request that a test patch be cleaned for approval. You need to be aware, however, that some types of unwanted materials are virtually impossible to remove, such as iron stains, and they may have to be accepted as part of the object. After the type of stone has been ascertained, the next step prior to cleaning is to determine the nature of the material to be removed.

Dirt

Removal of dirt is a common treatment for stone objects, especially for light-colored stones on which it is particularly visible. Water can be an effective cleaner, enhanced by use of a wetting agent. Nevertheless, cleaning with water is not always harmless in itself, as water etches the surface of alabaster and **deionized water** can etch polished marble if it is not buffered. Steam cleaning is currently a popular method for cleaning stone. Care must be taken, however, to ensure that pressure does not dislodge loosely bound crystals and that cleaning is even. Pressurized water is a technique applied mainly on outdoor stone. It should also be used with caution because it can cause significant losses on deteriorated stone, even when applied at low pressure. Abrasive **blasting** with materials like sand is too aggressive for use on most stone.

Not only does sandblasting remove stone from the surface, but it also increases surface area, thus promoting further deterioration. Organic solvents may be useful for cleaning, especially when dirt is greasy, as it may be when a stone piece has been handled or touched frequently. Application of cleaning solutions in **poultice** form may be more effective for removal of ingrained dirt. The cleaning solution is mixed with a thickening material to make a thick paste, which is applied and left on the stone for a period of time ranging from half an hour to days. During that time, dirt is put into solution and, if the poultice is allowed to dry, sucked into it. Many materials have been used as thickeners, including paper pulp, clay powders like attapulgite and sepiolite, and methylcellulose. Erasers can also be remarkably effective in removing dirt from polished stone surfaces. Lasers can be used to remove dirt from light-colored stone by vaporizing it, but the equipment is expensive and may not be available to the conservator.

GRAFFITI. Graffiti removal is a common treatment, whether the graffiti was applied by spray can or scribbled on the surface with ink or magic marker. If the surface of the stone is smooth, graffiti might be easily removed with an organic solvent or eraser. If it is not, application of solvents in poultice form may be necessary. It should be noted, however, that the entire object may require cleaning in order to match the graffiti-cleaned area; otherwise, there may be "graffiti ghosts."

STAINS. Stains derived from rusting iron dowels (orange-red) or adjacent corroding bronze statues (blue-green) can be very disfiguring on light-colored stone. A conservator may test various chemicals, perhaps applied in poultice form, but minimization of the stain may be the best that can be achieved. Again, the entire area may require cleaning to achieve an even appearance after stain removal.

OUTDOOR STONEWORK. Outdoor stonework presents special cleaning problems, particularly when stone has been attacked by air pollutants. In the case of limestone and marble, black crusts can be formed, which contain soot and calcium sulphate, the latter an alternation product of calcite. There is difference of opinion about the removal of black crusts, and a decision on removal may depend on the particular case. Black crusts can be very disfiguring and they may exfoliate, but the original sculpture form may be present in the black crust and its removal may increase the rate of deterioration on newly exposed surfaces.

BIOLOGICAL GROWTH. Biological growth frequently disfigures stone objects displayed outdoors, and it is a common problem on tombstones. Much of the growth can be removed by cleaning with water, but use of commercial biocides may be necessary. Solutions containing sodium salts (including household bleach) should be avoided as they introduce deleterious material into stone. It should be noted that while chemicals may remove biological growth, they are rarely prophylactic. Consideration should be given to prevention, such as elimination of the conditions that promote growth, like trimming overhanging branches and redirecting sprinklers that water sculpture as well as flower beds.

Rejoining

Rejoining broken stone artifacts is a common treatment for stone. Reversible adhesives often employed in conservation, like Acryloid B-72, can be used to adhere broken elements when artifacts are small; the broken element does not present a structural problem, such as an outstretched appendage; and the artifact is to be kept indoors. Often, however, stronger adhesives are required, and these are limited to two types: **epoxy** and polyester **resins**. Epoxy resins are generally considered the more durable of the two, but polyester resins may be more easily removed in the future, should that prove necessary. When used on stone outdoors, adhesives formulated specifically for outdoor stone should be used. Dowels made of metal, Teflon, or nylon are often used to strengthen joins, especially when join surfaces match poorly. If metal is used, it should be metal that does not corrode easily, such as high-quality stainless **steel**; if plastic, it should be threaded or scored. Use of steel pins should be carefully considered, however, as they can cause serious fracturing of stone if pressure is placed on a joint in the future.

Loss Compensation

Loss compensation in stone is often done with the same adhesives used for repair of broken stone, incorporating powdered stone to imitate the original stone. Because even the best organic **binders** (including epoxy and polyester) do not hold up well outdoors, fills made with them discolor and alter in gloss relatively quickly. As a result, in outdoor stone, fills are frequently made with cementitious materials. Mixtures that contain Portland cement may contain deleterious soluble salts; hydraulic cement mixtures, now available custom-matched, may be preferable. Replacement of stone losses with stone, known as dutchmen, is sometimes done on buildings, but it is more rarely appropriate for sculpture. Replacement of missing or badly damaged features such as arms or other limbs should be considered carefully, as it is difficult to do satisfactorily and may misrepresent the condition of the artifact. On the other hand, historic repairs, like eighteenth-century plaster repairs on antique statues, might be retained, as they may be considered historic in themselves.

Removal of Efflorescing Salts

Efflorescing salts will be encountered principally on outdoor sculpture or by the collector of archaeological artifacts; such salts are notoriously problematic for Egyptian stone pieces. Borne by **rising damp** from the ground up into exposed stone or absorbed from groundwater during burial, soluble salts may crystallize on the surface, indicated by the presence of white powder (actually small crystals) and/or surface damage, ranging from granular surface losses to large **spalls**. Removal of salts by soaking an object repeatedly in water baths until the conductivity of the water has returned to normal (the presence of salts in water raises its conductivity) is a common technique for salt removal. However, this method should only be done if any loose stone has been effectively secured prior to immersion of the object in water, and it should be avoided if the stone contains substantial quantities of clay or other water-sensitive material. In the latter case, consideration should be given to controlling the **relative humidity** at a level that will preclude further damage. Outdoor stone sculptures should always be separated from and slightly above ground level to prevent salt damage from rising damp. Separation with lead sheet is the traditional method; neoprene rubber has been used more recently.

Consolidation

Consolidation of the surfaces of friable stone objects kept indoors can often be done with common resins used in conservation, such as Acryloid B-72. For outdoor stone, however, these organic resins will not hold up over the long term. Outdoor stonework may cry out for treatment, in part because of dramatic increases in rates of deterioration during the twentieth century from industrial and automotive pollution. It cannot be stated strongly enough, however, that there are no chemical panaceas and that historically the result of application of various liquids to stonework has generally been failure. The only consolidants used with any degree of success outdoors have been those of the alkoxysilane family (such as ethyl silicate), which deposit inorganic silica in the stone, and they have been most effective when used on sandstones. Any proposals for consolidation should be viewed with considerable scrutiny, and when possible, consideration should be given to placing the sculptures indoors. Repair of structural defects, such as poor drainage, wintertime covering of stone sculptures, and maintenance of stone pointing often can be better uses of resources than consolidation.

Surface Coating

Surface coatings used on stone artifacts kept indoors include hard waxes, resins, or wax-resin mixtures; soft coating materials are avoided as they attract dirt. Surface coatings are often employed on white marbles to prevent them from retaining dirt or to provide some gloss to the surface when the stone has been etched by overzealous cleaning or outdoor exposure. Their use may be particularly advisable on easily stained items like tabletops, but to some extent application of a coating is a matter of taste, as many people do not like a "coated" appearance. On outdoor stonework, protective surface coatings should be viewed with the same skepticism as consolidants. While silicone resin coatings may provide some water repellence (and water is a principal agent of deterioration), they might also produce unsightly streaking on the surface, and their positive effect will last a few years at best.

Stone that was originally painted should be carefully cleaned so that paint is not damaged. Any loose paint should be secured. If the problem is limited to paint, this type of object is sometimes treated by a painting conservator, rather than a stone conservator. It is inadvisable to leave painted stonework outdoors.

Resetting stones, such as gravestones, present special conservation problems. A gravestone specialist should be sought.

Questions To Ask a Stone And Sculpture Conservator

- Have you worked on a similar type of object before?
- Have you dealt with a similar problem before?
- How should I display and care for my object?

Questions To Be Prepared To Answer

- What is the origin and provenance of the object?
- Do you know what type of stone has been used?
- Describe the problem and your goal for treatment as specifically as possible. (For example, don't just say that you want to clean a piece. Rather, describe exactly the color, nature, and location of "dirt" or other material you want removed.)
- Have you tired to clean or repair the object yourself, and what did you do?

Further Reading

Ashurst, John, and Francis G. Dimes. *Conservation of Building and Decorative Stone.* London: Butterworth-Heinemann, 1990.

Strangstand, Lynette. *A Gravestone Preservation Primer.* Nashville, Tenn.: American Association for State and Local History, 1998.

Sub-specialties

Analysis, architectural stone objects, architectural stonework, consultation, fountains, gravestones, painted sculpture, stone sculpture displayed indoors, stone sculpture displayed outdoors

Conservators

Conservation Solutions, Inc. 147–150
John Scott Conservator of Art and Architecture 181
Stromberg Conservation, LLC 187
Catharine Valentour 194

CHAPTER 13

Outdoor Sculpture

O UTDOOR SCULPTURE, ERECTED AS MONUMENTAL TRIBUTE TO WAR dead, historic events, or great citizens, often has come to be regarded as pure art, for aesthetic and decorative purposes much like indoor sculpture, but usually on a larger scale.

Along with **archaeological objects** and architecture, outdoor sculpture differs from other art objects by the simple, but critical, characteristic of being placed outdoors, excluded from even the most basic controls and protections given to art housed indoors. Although apparently robust, materials commonly used outdoors, such as **stone** and metal, are fragile when confronted with aggressive elements of the environment. Exposure to the various forms of water is the major factor in the deterioration of outdoor sculpture. In cold climates, rain and snowmelt can penetrate into voids and fissures and cause subsequent cracking during **freeze/thaw cycles**. Standing water holds dissolved pollutants that become dilute baths of corrosive chemicals. Dew, fog, or a misty rain can turn surface pollutants into a bath of corrosive chemicals repeatedly, even on a daily basis for long periods of time. Wind-driven particles can abrade sculptural detail. Strong, bright, unfiltered sunlight accelerates the breakdown of paints and coating materials. Heat ages adhesives, reducing their useful life.

Often heavy and large, outdoor sculpture may develop problems caused by a specific site, such as shifting ground, **rising dampness**, bird guano, structural disruption by tree roots, or surface encroachment from vines or overhanging limbs. Bases may begin to give way over time due to crumbling masonry mortar; the destructive action of salts on stone, brick, or **ceramics**; or wood rot. In many cases, the large size and elevated placement of outdoor sculpture make it inaccessible for monitoring and maintenance, and its very appearance of solidity may deceive caretakers into "benign" neglect. Large, complex, or "interestingly shaped" sculptures become a challenge to be climbed, played on, or used as the background for photographs, with people sitting in laps or on backs.

The outdoor environment is hostile to buildings, cars, boats, bicycles, roads, bridges—and sculpture. Unfortunately, the best place for outdoor sculpture is indoors; and in some cases, moving a sculpture indoors may be the only means to minimize its deterioration. Several Italian civic monuments determined to be of irreplaceable cultural value, such as Michaelangelo's David, the *Marcus Aurelius* equestrian sculpture, and the four horses of Saint Mark's Cathedral in Venice, have been moved indoors to slow their deterioration. When an outdoor sculpture must be moved inside, a replica can be fabricated for the original site, with the original object resituated indoors, but nearby. Nevertheless, there is a long tradition of creating and siting sculpture in outdoor public spaces. When moving a sculpture inside is not acceptable, conservation must "hold the fort." With informed oversight and frequent maintenance, most sculpture can survive an extended lifetime outdoors, depending on the inherent durability of the **medium**, the environment, suitable **conservation treatment**, and frequent maintenance.

Why You Need an Outdoor Sculpture Conservator

Because of the complex and potentially aggressive outdoor environment, outdoor sculpture conservators must deal with problems of a nature, degree, and scale almost never encountered by other conservators. In a badly deteriorated metal sculpture, the surface may be largely lost, subsumed, or completely converted to **corrosion** products. In these instances, removing corrosion products means removing the radically altered original surface. This process demands an experienced, thoughtful approach, mindful of the cumulative consequences of frequent corrosion removal—loss of the sculpture's details and form—and the benefits of frequent, regular, less-invasive low-level maintenance.

In a relatively undamaged area the conservator may be able to discover evidence of the original surface. The more likely path to discerning the original appearance is through research into foundry, artist, or owner records containing descriptions and photographs of the original condition. In this way, collaborating with a curator or owner, the conservator may arrive at a treatment that attempts to reclaim the appearance of the original, though not of course the original itself. A more conservative approach would focus on efforts to stabilize that which is there at present and to try to control future loss rather than attempting **restoration**.

Through examination of the existing sculpture and collaboration with owners or curators, the conservator will find a treatment that is aesthetically appropriate to the object and practically attainable, and that can be continued or maintained while also advancing the likelihood of preserving the sculpture despite persistently adverse conditions.

Inaccessibility and large surface areas make the care and treatment of many outdoor sculptures logistically challenging. Good access to all surfaces, which even basic maintenance operations require, may call for rigging, cherry-picker-type lifts, or scaffolding, or a combination of these. Most conservators do not own such specialized equipment but rent it when necessary for large-scale maintenance or repair projects. Other heavy-duty equipment may also be required for large cleaning or corrosion-removal projects, such as pressure-washers and air-abrasive equipment (technology borrowed from the fields of architectural and aeronautical maintenance). Gas-powered torches and electrical buffing devices may be used for surface treatments. The conservator's sensitivity, experience, and skill using these kinds of equipment will greatly affect the success of a treatment.

The experienced conservator may also have developed a network of supporting staff or contractors such as scaffolding erectors, welders, masons, and engineers and an understanding of when these adjunct fields are needed. Other craftspeople such as foundry workers, fabricators, or mold makers skilled at replicating lost parts may also be required.

The informed outdoor conservator will be aware of any legal responsibilities to the artist or artist's estate regarding the aesthetic aspects of the treated sculpture's final appearance.

What Can I Expect From an Outdoor Sculpture Conservator?

Below is a summary of major operations that might be involved in a **conservation treatment** on outdoor sculpture. For more specific information, refer to the chapters in this directory that address specific materials such as metals (see Chapter 10), or stone (see Chapter 12), or ceramic materials (see Chapter 11).

Conservation treatment should always be preceded by an examination of existing conditions, documented in writing and with photographs and a **treatment proposal**. Tests may be performed at this stage to obtain information pertinent to treatment, and a test patch may be created to demonstrate the effect of cleaning methods or coating materials intended for use; if possible, such tests should be completed in an inconspicuous location. Further tests may be performed during treatment if the need arises.

Structural stability is a primary concern and may involve assessing the site (for marshy, shifting ground, perhaps), **stabilizing** a deteriorating base, reinforcing or replacing a rusted or broken **armature**, repairing or filling cracks, replacing lost parts, and assuring good drainage by clearing existing **weepholes** or drilling new ones if standing water is actively contributing to deterioration.

Once the sculpture is determined to be stable, surface problems can be addressed. Proposed treatments might range from **washing**, waxing, or **lacquering** to more complex surface treatments involving graffiti or stain removal, anticorrosion treatment, removal or reduction of disfiguring corrosion products or deteriorated lacquers, and **repatination** or **regilding**. These operations will differ widely in type and extent depending on the sculptural medium. Treatment decisions are made from an informed perspective, drawing on experience and whenever possible, knowledge of a given artist's working methods and aesthetic intent.

A long-term maintenance plan should be designed that might include landscape control, bird abatement, and periodic monitoring and maintenance. In many cases, a conservator can train a technician to perform routine inspections and maintenance procedures.

Issues About Which Competent Professionals May Disagree

As new technologies emerge, there are evolving ideas about what treatments are appropriate for outdoor sculpture. Some technologies such as blasting with sand have been completely abandoned as unduly harsh. Other methods such as glass-bead peening to remove corrosion products have mostly fallen into disuse, supplanted by other materials such as ground walnut shells, plastic blasting media, or pressurized water washing. Of an experimental nature are techniques such as carbon dioxide pellet abrasives and laser technology for coatings removal. These newer methods are currently beyond the repertory of all but the most cutting-edge conservators but may eventually come into wider use as costs decrease and techniques are more widely understood. Ultimately, any treatment method must work in tandem with the sensitive pursuit of established treatment goals. Current trends favor the philosophy of "less is more," because some effects of treatments are seen only after long periods of time.

Choice of protective surface coatings is another area where different means may be used to approach the same problem. Clear synthetic coatings are the usual choice for protecting most metal sculptures outdoors (matte painted surfaces and weathering **steel** are notable, but not the only, exceptions). For ease of application some might choose a paste-wax mixture, applied at ambient temperature (cold). This low-tech method does not enhance the penetration of wax into pores and other voids in the metal structure and is, therefore, considered by some to be more **reversible** than using the heated wax method. The latter method requires initially heating the sculpture with a torch, brushing one or two coatings of a wax mixture, and reheating the surface to distribute the wax evenly and facilitate flow into any voids. Although believed to exclude water more effectively, the deeply embedded wax is harder to reverse should it degrade or discolor. Different practitioners view this trade-off differently.

Many conservators of outdoor bronze sculpture apply a chemical inhibitor, benzotriazole (BTA), prior to applying synthetic Incralac lacquer, which contains the same chemical. According to a well-known manufacturer of clear coatings, the chemical additive does not prevent corrosion of the metal but preserves the coating itself (by shielding it from contamination by copper salts), protecting it from cross-linking, and becoming insoluble and resistant to removal. The metal benefits indirectly from this additive. Others believe that this procedure does not counter corrosion effectively. Still other conservators contend that a scratched lacquer coating endangers a sculpture by concentrating the galvanic potential of the entire sculpture into a very small area, causing it to corrode rapidly at the site of any accidental voids in the coating. Some are wary of the safety and environmental issues involved in removing a lacquer coating and will prefer to use wax. Sometimes a combination of these materials will be employed, with wax applied over lacquer.

Another kind of dilemma arises when severe metal corrosion disfigures the surface of a sculpture. When metal corrodes, it becomes a nonmetallic crust of roughly the same shape as the original metal but a different color. Corrosion of a metal sculpture's surface converts the microscopic upper design layers to a corrosion crust. Removing these corrosion layers to get back to the metal surface will obliterate the original **patination** layer as well as those beneath that subtle detailing. This loss is analogous to that which occurs on silver-plated objects whose thin coating of corroded silver has been rubbed away in many bouts of **tarnish** removal, taking with it the sculptural detail and revealing the base metal below. Although corrosion products can be quite disfiguring, some conservators might opt to guard some or all of the corroded original surface. In any case, the original material cannot be retrieved by even the most careful conservation treatment at the present time. Selective in**painting** with durable paints can make the appearance more acceptable while retaining the original material in its altered state.

Despite differences in opinion as discussed above, on one subject outdoor conservators will all agree: adherence to a steady maintenance program is the major determinant in prolonging the life of outdoor sculpture. Careful maintenance can give new life to a work of outdoor sculpture, bringing it closer to its original state and prolonging that condition so the art can be enjoyed for many years. Even more important, maintaining a sculpture from the time of its installation may prevent or effectively postpone the need for major intervention or treatment for many years.

Maintenance: Practical Suggestions

- Keep plants cut back from outdoor sculpture. The biological processes of ivy, for example, create **acidic** by-products that can dissolve stone, and grappling for a hold, the roots may penetrate and displace mortar. Ivy also keeps the surface wet almost constantly, promoting biological and chemical activity. Algae may be temporarily abated by gentle scrubbing using clean water and a soft brush.
- Keep sculpture guano-free by hosing off when necessary.
- Do not use granular chloride compounds to melt snow on walkways or patios in the immediate area of the outdoor sculpture or in other areas where salt-containing splash or mist could easily contact them.
- Grass mowers can damage the bases of sculpture by scratching or abrading paint, stone, metal, or finishes. They will often leave small fragments of steel imbedded in the stone, resulting in significant rust staining. Tire marks are almost impossible to remove. Cut the grass closest to the sculpture by hand, or prop protective boards against the bottom parts when using a mechanical or gas-powered mower.
- Never use metal or other scratchy brushes to clean outdoor sculpture. Use only plastic or natural bristle brushes for maintenance, and test a small area first to make sure no scratch pattern is being introduced by scrubbing. Vigilance is required to avoid picking up grit (i.e. sand or gravel from the sculpture); if a brush is dropped on the ground do not use it until it is very well rinsed!

Questions To Ask an Outdoor Sculpture Conservator

- How did you acquire your expertise with outdoor sculpture? How long have you been doing conservation work on outdoor sculptures? How many sculptures like mine (size, material, age, and problem) have you treated? What materials do you normally work with? Can you provide references?
- Have you performed structural work on outdoor sculpture as well as surface work?
- What are the treatment options for the work and the reasons for each option?
- Will the treatment attempt to retain the original patina?
- Will the treatment prolong the sculpture's life outdoors as well as improve its appearance?
- Will a long-term maintenance plan be part of the final report on the sculpture?

Questions To Be Prepared To Answer

- What material is the sculpture made of?
- Does it have a pedestal or plinth? What material?
- When was the sculpture made or installed outside?
- How large is the sculpture? How tall?
- What appears to be the problem?
- Are there mounting, site, or location problems?
- Are there problems with the patina?
- Has the sculpture ever been treated before? What is the maintenance history, if any?
- Is a coating present?
- Are photographs or slides available?
- Why do you want to have this sculpture conserved, and what outcome do you expect from the process?

Further Reading

Montagna, Dennis R. *Conserving Outdoor Bronze Sculpture.* Preservation Tech Notes, National Park Service, U.S. Department of the Interior. Washington, D.C.: National Park Service, 1989.

Naude, Virginia Norton, ed. *Sculptural Monuments in an Outdoor Environment.* Philadelphia: Pennsylvania Academy of Fine Arts, 1985.

Naude, Virginia, and Glenn Wharton. *Guide to the Maintenance of Outdoor Sculpture.* Washington, D.C.: American Institute for Conservation of Historic and Artistic Works, 1993. Available by downloading an order form from the AIC website at **http://:www:palimpsest.stanford.edu/aic/**.

Ruell, David. *No Stone Unturned: Saving Outdoor Sculpture—A Handbook.* New Hampshire SOS. Desktop publishing by the New Hampshire State Council on the Arts. Additional copies may be obtained from the New Hampshire Division of Historical Resource, Department of Cultural Affairs, P.O. Box 2043, Concord, N.H. 03302-2043; tel. 603/272-3483.

Van Zelst, Lambertus, and Jean-Louis Lachevre. "Outdoor Bronze Sculpture: Problems and Procedures of Protective Treatment." *Technology and Conservation* 8, no.1 (Spring 1989): 18–28.

Veloz, Nicholas F. "Practical Aspects of Using Walnut Shells for Cleaning Outdoor Sculpture." *Association for Preservation Technology Bulletin* 25, (1994): 70-6.

Veloz, Nicholas F., W. Thomas Chase, and A. W. Ruff. "Successful Use of Soft Abrasives (Walnut Shells) for Cleaning Outdoor Sculptures by Air Jets." Symposium Papers Subthemes 1&2, U.S./ICOMOS, 1:492–98. Washington, D.C.: 1987.

Weisser, Terry Drayman, ed. *Dialog / 89: The Conservation of Bronze Sculpture in the Outdoor Environment—A Dialogue among Conservators, Curators, Environmental Scientists, and Corrosion Engineers.* Houston: National Association of Corrosion Engineers, 1992.

Zycherman, Lynda A., and Nicolas F. Veloz, Jr. "Conservation of Monumental Outdoor Sculpture: Theodore Roosevelt by Paul Manship." *Journal of the American Institute for Conservation.* (1980): 24–33.

Conservators

Conservation Solutions, Inc. 147–150
Albert Marshall Conservation, LLC 170
John Scott Conservator of Art and Architecture 181
Stromberg Conservation, LLC 187

CHAPTER 14

Furniture and Wooden Artifacts

URNITURE AND WOODEN ARTIFACTS HAVE SERVED BOTH FUNCTIONAL and decorative purposes for thousands of years. These objects represent both the functional and decorative characteristics of the region and time period in which they were produced as well as the individuality and skill of the craftsman. These objects were produced from a variety of materials using many systems and techniques to produce a variety of forms and decorative treatments. The objects may have been constructed utilizing solid **wood** or a frame-and-panel system or by applying a thin decorative wood surface (**veneer**), on a wood substrate. This thin veneer could be in the form of **marquetry**, which utilizes different woods and other materials (ivory, **metals**, mother-of-pearl, and bone) to form floral, *arabesque,* and figurative patterns, or by parquetry, which uses thin veneer applied in a geometric pattern. In addition, pieces of contrasting wood or other materials may be inlaid into a wood surface to highlight areas rather than to form a complete decorative surface.

Many other materials are used to decorate wooden objects and furniture: metals for hardware and ornament, **marble** for tabletops, and leather and **fabrics** for writing surfaces and upholstery. The furniture or wooden artifacts can be finished with natural or synthetic **resins**, coated with an **oil** or wax, **gilded** (applying a metal leaf), or painted in an overall monochrome fashion or in a polychrome decorative pattern. Some objects may be decorated with a combination of these materials to achieve a desired appearance. A conservator who works with furniture and wooden objects must be trained to deal with all these materials, both separately and together.

Unlike purely decorative objects, furniture is used, necessitating more maintenance and subjecting objects to damage and sometimes to uninformed repairs. Furthermore, as furniture becomes unfashionable, it often is relegated to the attic, basement, or barn, where accelerated degradation can occur. Oftentimes its owners or unscrupulous dealers alter the piece of furniture or wooden artifact to resemble the newest fashion and the whims of the marketplace. These alterations might be uninformed repairs, refinishing, or redecorating of the surface, or even modifications of the object's original form. Therefore an object may have several generations of alternations and/or presentation surfaces. You must consider these issues when reviewing a conservator's **treatment proposal**, with particular regard to which physical state in the object's history should be preserved.

How we maintain and treat objects today has much to do with how long they will survive and in what state. As a steward of the furniture in your collection, you can affect its **preservation** by altering how objects are used, maintaining proper environmental conditions, and making informed treatment decisions.

The Primary Causes of Damage to Furniture and Techniques for Avoiding Them

Exposure to Light

Both **visible** and **ultraviolet (UV) light** rays fade the natural colors of wood as well as applied **pigments** in paints, stains, and **dyes**. Light also can accelerate the chemical and physical breakdown of coatings, adhesives, and applied materials such as upholstery, **paper**, and leather.

To prevent exposure to light, move the objects away from direct light, avoid high-intensity spotlights, and lower light levels. For highly sensitive objects, appropriate lighting should be selected. Close the shades and curtains when a room is not in use and light exposure would damage the furnishings. Filter out ultraviolet rays by having a professional coat windowpanes with UV-filtering film, or placing UV-filtering glazing over flat, exposed surfaces such as tabletops.

Exposure to Extreme Changes in Temperature and Relative Humidity

Wood expands and contracts in response to fluctuations in **relative humidity** causing cracks and warping in solid wood construction system when the panels are not allowed to move, **delamination** of veneer and inlays, and instability of applied components such as molding. Placing a wooden object in direct line with heating and air conditioning vents can cause extreme damage, particularly if the object is painted, veneered, or gilded, or has an unstable coating. Direct, untreated heated air dries the wood and coatings, producing cracks and splits in the wood; delamination of the veneer, paint, and gilding; and degradation of the coatings and adhesives.

Monitor the temperature and relative humidity immediately around the object using a **hygrothermograph**. If necessary, install humidification and dehumidification systems by contracting a heating and air conditioning professional. Move the most sensitive objects to a more stable humidity and temperature environment within the home or institution. Ideally, temperatures should be kept at about 70°F and the relative humidity in the range of 40–50 percent, allowing for fluctuations to occur slowly over a longer period of time (seasonal). However, objects incorporating marquetry or parquetry may require a relative humidity maintained closer to 50 percent, and sensitive wooden objects should be kept away from an exterior door or frequently used window to avoid blasts of untreated, uncontrolled air. If it is possible, avoid placing furniture adjacent to heating and air conditioning vents, and if that is not possible, deflectors can help divert the air away from direct contact with the object.

Wood Boring Insect Infestation

Wood-boring insect larvae burrow through the wood causing damage via wood fiber loss that results in both cosmetic and structural damage. The mature insect, primarily a beetle either of the Lyctid (powder post beetle) or the Anobiid exits through the wood surface, leaving a small hole. Active infestation may be indicated by light-colored *frass* (powdery undigested wood) in or around light-colored fresh exit holes. Other types of insects can harm upholstery materials (see Chapter 7).

If you suspect active insect infestation, consult a conservator with experience in pest control. **Fumigation**, oxygen deprivation (**anoxic** treatment), or other types of treatment may be required to eradicate the active infestation.

Improper Handling, Use, and Maintenance

A significant percentage of damage to furniture is the result of mishandling and improper use and maintenance. Moving furniture without the proper help or lifting the object from a fragile, nonbearing applied element can severely damage the object. Overloading drawers in case pieces can result in damage to the drawer bottoms and sides and excessive wear to the drawer runner and guide system, and exert too much pressure on the case itself. Overusing a fragile seating piece can damage its frame and upholstery. Improper or ill-advised use of commercial or homemade polishes and cleaners on various decorative surface materials can result in irreversible loss of **patina** and separation or loss of fragile paint, finish, or gilded layers, or an inappropriate change in the surface appearance of an object.

Lift furniture from rigid location such as the lower edge of the sides of a case piece and not by the applied molding, the seat rails of a chair, or the crest rail or arms. Do not drag objects across a floor; lift and carry them to avoid snagging their legs or feet on carpets or obstructions. Eliminate excessive weight from drawers by removing heavy materials, and consider having a conservator apply a protective film over drawer runners. Avoid continued use of seating furniture suffering from adhesive failure or weakened joints to minimize the possibility of fractures.

Before dusting with a soft cloth or brush, make sure that inlay, paint, or gilding surfaces are intact. If not, consult a conservator for proper maintenance procedures. The dusting cloth can be very slightly dampened with water to increase its ability to attract dust or remove food spillage or drink from a stable clear coating only.

Specific Problems and Conservation Treatments

Structural Components

Large, flat expansions of wood from a single board such as tabletops and chests can warp or crack as the wood responds to change in atmospheric moisture. Joint members are susceptible to adhesive failure. Case joinery should be secured to support the weight of the object and be capable of functioning for its proposed use or display. The treatment of an object should include providing secure and stable joinery and panels, particularly if the object will be used or if its weight causes stress within the joinery systems. Cracks should be inspected to see whether they have stabilized, and their cause should be corrected (e.g., poor environment conditions or properly applied metal fasteners). Cracks may need to be consolidated, and if they are visually disturbing, they can be filled with a colored, flexible, and **reversible** material.

Applied Moldings and Carvings

Components can detach fully or partially if adhesive or metal fasteners fail. In treatment, loose components should be resecured using appropriate systems considering the use, display, and method of construction. Missing sections can be reconstructed using the same type of material or cast in a synthetic material molded from a like component.

Veneer, Inlay, and Marquetry or Parquetry

The veneer, inlay, or marquetry is attached to a wood substrate, often in opposing positions. During humidity and temperature fluctuations this wood substrate shrinks and expands at rates that are different from the rates of the decorative veneer, inlay, marquetry, or parquetry. This causes the adhesive to degrade, which in turn can cause the decorative surfaces to partially or fully delaminate from the substrate. Also cracks and separations can form in the veneer. In treatment, partially or fully delaminated veneer and inlay should be reattached using reversible adhesives. Losses can be replaced with like or synthetic materials. If breakage does occur, save all fragments so they can be reattached later.

Coatings, Finishes, and Patina

Decorative surfaces are very susceptible to damage by abrasion, food spillage, and ultraviolet light. Repeated expansion and contraction of the underlying wood can cause surface coatings to crack, flake, and delaminate. Historically correct or older coatings can be preserved by cleaning, consolidating degraded areas, and incoating or infilling losses. If necessary, a reversible coating can be applied to protect a historic surface. If tests determine that upper layers of paint and/or coatings are inappropriate, they can often be removed safely utilizing solvent and mechanical systems, thereby exposing an original decorative surface. Because of varying solvent solubility parameters, custom solvent gels can be formulated to remove one or more specific layers while rendering the original layers unharmed.

Objects should never be subjected to "dip stripping" or finish-removal techniques involving large quantities of water or spray-on finish remover because these treatments can cause irreversible damage to the object and eliminate original decorative surfaces. Completely damaged or deteriorated finish coatings can be replaced with a finish type and to a tonal and sheen level that represents a balance between what would be historically appropriate and what is practical in terms of its current use, while remaining reversible. A barrier system between the older coating materials and the new coating being applied can be employed to isolate and protect the original coating layers.

Painted and Gilded Surfaces

Painted and gilded surfaces are very delicate, requiring careful handling, display, and treatment. Often gilding is applied over multiple layers of **gesso**, a mixture of glue and chalk (whiting) and as the wood substrate moves in response to humidity fluctuations, the gesso layers may separate from the wood substrate. These same problems can also occur with various painted surfaces.

The conservator will stabilize the structure prior to reattaching lifting paint or gilded surfaces to the substrate. Losses may be infilled and toned to blend visually with their surroundings by **inpainting** or ingilding the fill material with easily detectable and reversible materials. Additional care should be taken to prevent ill-advised applications of cleaning, polishing, dusting, or wax products to the surfaces of painted or gilded objects. Particular attention should be paid to the handling of gilded objects since the pressure exerted on that decorative surface may in fact damage it.

Upholstered Objects

By definition, upholstery in seating furniture is subjected to wear. Over time a frame is likely to receive multiple applications of decorative fabric and underupholstery (webbing, springs, and padding). The many nail, tack, and staple holes that result contribute to the deterioration of the wood tacking rails, which in turn leads to deterioration of the wood frame and can often lead to quick fixes by a nonconservation trained upholsterer.

If you are considering having antique furniture reupholstered, have the frame inspected by a furniture conservator and if necessary have it treated prior to reupholstering. Inquire about alternative upholstery systems, which may eliminate further deterioration of the frame by minimizing the use of metal fasteners. These nonintrusive upholstery systems often combine modern materials and techniques with traditional upholstery craft.

Innovation and Tradition

Furniture conservators constantly balance practical and purist approaches and need to devise a treatment that will allow an object to be used while ensuring its preservation as a valued decorative artifact. Craft traditions are the backbone of the cabinetmaking profession and an integral part of furniture conservation, but conservators may differ on the role of tradition in the repair of damaged objects. For example, one approach to replacing missing decorative moldings or carvings would be to carve the matching elements from wood similar to the original. A nontraditional approach would be to make a mold of the original and then cast a replacement with the synthetic material. In the latter case, using a material different from the original prevents confusion about which part of the object is original and which is not. Also, the insertion of a metal nail or similar material into a newly fabricated wood element in an area where such an element would not normally be found can ensure easy detection through x-ray examination. This procedure will in turn aid future scholars in determining that the decorative element is not original. A traditional approach to replacing old seating upholstery would be similar to the original utilizing existing fastener types and holes as well as foundation materials and systems. An alternative to this approach would be a nonintrusive upholstery system, which uses separate platforms and foam panels to form the foundation, with the show covers attached with a removable system such as Velcro. This system would no longer cause damage to the frames while allowing for simplified show cover replacement and access to the frame for study and examination.

Today a partnership between scientists and conservators has broadened the knowledge of wood technology and the chemistry of coating materials and adhesives and many conservators regularly seek laboratory assistance before designing a treatment. For example, analytical technique can tell us the exact number, general composition, and colors utilized in a coating sample, enabling the conservator to remove unwanted layers without harming the original surfaces. These systems can also determine whether the existing coating layers may be original by comparing them to the methods and materials used in the period in which the object was produced.

Selecting a Conservator

Since wooden objects are used in so many ways and exposed to a multitude of environments, preservation treatments can be simple or complex, traditional or experimental. These treatments can range from simply moving the object away from the window, which is exposing the top to ultraviolet light, to a complex experimental treatment to preserve its paint-decorated surface. An important factor in preserving your object is exercising good judgment when choosing someone to treat it. In addition to the guidelines for choosing a conservator in the introduction, here are some things to discuss with the conservator so that the treatment can be tailored to your particular desires as well as the needs of the object.

- How is the object going to be used, and to what extent?
- Where is the object going to be stored or displayed?
- What are the environmental conditions within the area?
- What are the expectations as to the appearance of the decorative surfaces?
- What do you know about the object's history and possible previous repairs?

Your conservator should:

- Fully examine the object and answer all of your questions to your satisfaction.
- Design and submit a treatment proposal as detailed in the introduction to this directory.
- Identify the materials of which the object is made and evaluate its condition.
- Evaluate the object's environment.
- Suggest maintenance and display criteria.
- Remain flexible in the treatment of the object in regards to information uncovered during the course of the treatment.

Further Reading

Aronson, Joseph. *Encyclopedia of Furniture.* New York: Crown Publishers, 1965.

Bigelow, Debra, Ellizabeth Cornu, Gregory Landry, and Cornelius van Horn. *Gilded Wood Conservation and History.* Madison, Conn.: Sound View Press, 1991.

Dorge, Valerie, and Carey Howlett. *Painted Wood: History and Conservation.* Los Angeles: Getty Conservation Institute, 1994.

Florian, Mary-Lou E., Dale Paul Kronkright, and Ruth E. Norton. *Conservation of Artifacts Made from Plant Materials.* Los Angeles: Getty Conservation Institute, 1990.

Conservators

CHAPTER 15

Frames

FRAMES ARE BOTH DECORATIVE AND FUNCTIONAL: THEY PROTECT ART and provide a means for its display. A well-suited frame enhances the art object, establishes a border between the art and the room around it, and harmonizes with surrounding architecture and furnishings. In recent years there has been renewed interest in period frames. Italian Renaissance paintings are being removed from nineteenth-century frames and rehoused in period and reproduction Italian frames. American Victorian frames are being retrieved from basements and reunited with nineteenth-century paintings, which during the mid-1900s had often been placed in eighteenth century French frames. Although changing a frame is sometimes justified, in most cases the integrity and value of a work are increased by maintaining the original frame. If an original frame must be removed from artwork, the frame should be saved and the change documented. Even frames with little aesthetic appeal have value if they are original to the art or through their craftsmanship provide information about the date and origin of a family treasure. Paintings that retain their original frames are rare, and frames signed by the designer or frame maker are even more scarce. Most frames were made anonymously or remain unidentified. Their dual roles as decorative and functional objects combined with the variety of materials used to make them render frame conservation a complex undertaking.

Materials and Fabrication Techniques

Frames have been made from a variety of materials, including **metal**, ceramics, plastics, and **stone**; but the vast majority are made from wood. Most of those are made by combining moldings, which are strips of wood shaped into decorative profiles. Frames are usually described by the *molding profile* (e.g., the S-shaped ogee or C-shaped cove molding) and finish (gold leaf, stained wood, etc.). More detailed descriptions include ornament (leaf, beads, floral), country of origin, and historic period. Ornamentation may be carved from or applied to the molding, and the finishes vary greatly.

Structure

Simple moldings are made from a single piece of wood, more elaborate ones from several small moldings attached to a larger form. In the nineteenth-century, moldings were often set inside each other to create deep profiles. The most common corner joint is the miter, where moldings meet at 45 degree angles. Miter joints are reinforced with wood splines, nails, bolts, or pegs. Other joining methods include lap, mortise-and-tenon, and butt joints. An important part of every frame is hidden behind its face—a recessed channel called a **rabbet**. The artwork and glass or acrylic glazing sit in this channel.

Ornamentation

Three-dimensional decorative elements may be carved from the wood molding or applied to it. Applied elements can be made of wood, plaster, **compo** (a mixture of chalk, rosin, linseed oil, and glue), and sometimes even **papier-mâché**. Once the ornamentation is in place, the frame is often coated with **gesso**, a mixture of ground chalk, animal skin glue, and water. Additional details are sometimes carved or punched into the gesso. Ornament may also include wood **veneers**, glass, precious and semiprecious stones, tortoiseshell, ivory, horn, cast or stamped metal, leather, **textiles**, and found objects. Some frames are embellished with a combination of materials and ornamentation techniques.

Surface Finishes

The finishing coat on frames can range from a simple wax or **varnish** to complex painted and **gilded** decorations.

Gilded Surfaces

Gilding is the art of applying thin sheets of metal, called *leaf,* to a prepared surface. Gold, silver, or alloys of gold, silver, and copper provide the best results;

but **bronze** or aluminum, often called *metal leaf,* may be used. Gold ranges from 12 to 24 karats and usually is alloyed with silver and copper: the more silver, the cooler or paler the color. 12K gold looks like silver, while more copper makes a warmer, redder gold. Gold leaf is manufactured in sheets 3 3/8 x 3 3/8 x 1/250,000 in., while metal leaf is made in much thicker and larger sheets.

Gilding techniques have remained essentially the same throughout time. Leaf is applied in two ways—by oil or water gilding. In **oil gilding** a slow-drying oil varnish is applied to the frame. When the varnish is almost dry, the leaf is laid on. Oil gilding cannot be burnished to the luster that is so appreciated on water gilding. To water gild, the wood base is coated with protein glue, followed with layers of gesso and then with **bole**, a fine, colored clay mixed with animal skin glue. After the surface has been smoothed, the glue in the bole layer is reactivated by brushing with water; then the leaf is laid on. Once the bole has dried, the gold can be burnished. Because water gilding requires more preparation, some frames are largely oil gilded, with burnished water gilding used only for highlights.

Tones or Changing Varnishes

A gilded surface is often coated to protect or modify its appearance. Liquids such as oil varnish, lacquer, **shellac**, and even dilute animal skin glue may be used by themselves or tinted with **dyes**, **resins**, or **pigments** to alter the apparent color of a gilt surface or emphasize ornaments as the tone settles into their recesses. Often a tinted coating is used to make silver leaf imitate gold. Like other silver objects, silver leaf **tarnishes** without a protective coating: the black spots that often appear on silver leaf frames result from failure in a protective coating. Besides clear coatings, toning materials include tinted waxes and dilute **washes** of paint.

Paint

Picture frames were often painted, sometimes directly on the wood and other times after coating the wood with gesso. Faux finishes resembling exotic woods, stone, tortoiseshell, and even carved ornaments are not unusual. Combining paint with gold or metal leaf was also a regular practice. Applying a layer of paint over gilding and then scratching through to make a decorative pattern is called *sgraffito.* Powdered metals carried in a paint binder also have been used. Bronze powder paint (radiator paint) was used frequently in **restora-**

tions and on lesser frames to imitate gold, but unfortunately even if it initially looks like gold, it darkens over time.

Textiles

Frames may incorporate textiles such as linen- or velvet-covered liners between the molding and the picture.

Common Problems

Most often damage to a picture frame is caused by well-intentioned, but uninformed, repair. For example, when dirt is removed improperly, gold and toning coats can be washed or rubbed away. Repairing a loose joint by adding more nails and glue will only aggravate the problem.

Structural Weakness and Damage

In addition to problems caused by inappropriate cleaning or repair, extreme changes in heat and humidity can harm both the structure and surface finish of a frame. Fluctuations in humidity cause wood to expand and contract, eventually loosening frame joints. Low **relative humidity** can cause glue to desiccate and then fail, while high humidity encourages insect and fungal attacks. Many structural problems arise from poor construction and inferior or incompatible materials. Of course careless handling also causes damage.

Coating Damage

In our area relative humidity can fluctuate from 20 percent in winter to 80 percent in summer. Wood, gesso, and paint all react differently to these changes, causing paint and gesso to separate from the wood. Toning coats and paint can be discolored or faded by harsh light. Both the light and heat generated by frame lights (fitted over the top edge of the molding) are damaging. Without regular housekeeping, frame surfaces darken and grime becomes ingrained. On the other hand, improper cleaning with household cleaners, especially water, harms toning, gilding, and gesso. Sometimes surface damage begins when a frame maker uses incompatible materials.

Ornament Loss and Damage

Decorative elements frequently become damaged or dislodged as a result of careless handling or humidity fluctuations that lead to glue failure. If an ornament does break, carefully save all the pieces for a conservator.

Improper Restoration and Alteration

As mentioned previously, most frame damage is caused by misguided restoration attempts. In the past heavy-handed restorations were the norm, and it was not uncommon to entirely strip and **regild** frames. Frame makers' advertising labels declared "Old frames regilt." As fashions changed, gilded frames were painted and painted frames were gilded. Sometimes gesso was applied over an existing finish, obscuring or obliterating original details. When the size of a frame is altered, aesthetic balance, structural integrity, and financial value are lost. Repairs that attempt to strengthen a frame with excessive glue or fill material can cause serious damage if the frame cannot expand and contract as the humidity changes.

Treatment

A **conservation treatment** plan should stabilize structure, ornaments, and coatings while preserving original materials and respecting fabrication techniques. A conservator will consider many factors. Is the frame stable structurally? Has it merely acquired a **patina** over the years, or is it disfigured by heavy grime? Patina is an overall look rather than specific, obvious, and distracting areas of loss and damage. Are missing ornaments and old repairs noticeable? Is it strong enough for the art it will house?

Examination and Analysis

Careful examination should precede treatment to clarify the problems needing attention. Very discreet solvent testing can reveal whether coatings are historic or later additions and if the frame can be cleaned safely. In some cases it may be necessary to take very small samples for examination under a microscope in order to understand the multiple layers of gesso, gold, paint, or varnish from past alterations. X-rays assist in identifying hidden structural problems.

Treatment Proposals

From the information gathered by careful examination, and considering the intended use of the frame, treatment proposals can range from minimal to major. For example, minor treatments may include light surface cleaning; **stabilization** of structure, ornaments, coatings; and **inpainting** small nicks, while major treatments may include injecting synthetic resins into degraded wood and replicating lost decoration. Loose joints may call for disassembling the frame and removing thick glue deposits and overly large nails before re-aligning and readhering the members. Layers of restoration gesso, gilding, and toning may need to be removed to reveal the original surface.

The historic integrity of the frame should be addressed, and the original finish should be preserved and incorporated into the final presentation surface if at all possible. If it is impossible to preserve the original surface while removing a disfiguring alteration, alternate approaches should be considered. For example, applying a **reversible** surface coating over a past restoration may offer a temporary solution until new techniques make uncovering the original surface possible. The sacrifice of original material and coating should be avoided. When original materials must be altered or sacrificed, the work should be undertaken only after careful consideration and written agreement between client and conservator.

In the past, frames were restored with the same materials and techniques that the frame maker had used, thereby making it difficult and sometimes impossible to remove restorations without damaging the frame. Advances in materials and techniques have made irreversible restoration unacceptable except in unusual situations. Modern conservation calls for stable and reversible materials, such as synthetic materials, that can also replicate the appearance of traditional materials. Applying a reversible isolating layer of varnish between original and new materials can make procedures with traditional materials reversible and provide clear differentiation between original and added materials.

Altering Frame Sizes

It is important to keep an original frame with its art. When frames and objects become separated, the frames often are recycled to other objects, decreasing the likelihood frame and object ever will be reunited.

In addition, changing frames and objects usually requires an alteration in size. Minor changes include enlarging the rabbet to accommodate a larger artwork or adding a liner to size down to a smaller one. However, if the proportions of the frame are different from the new artwork, reducing or enlarging the molding would be required; and this irreversible alteration would reduce the historic and monetary value of the frame and weaken it structurally. The more intrusive alternations such as extensive routing out of the rabbet and enlargement or reduction of the frame profile should be avoided. Indeed, some frames are so important historically that they should never be altered.

Care and Maintenance

Handling

Handle and move frames only when necessary. Before moving a framed object, check that both the frame and artwork are stable. If you find flaking coatings, loose ornaments, or weakened joints, contact a conservator. Prepare a safe, padded place to rest the frame. Always lift with two hands and on two sides: never lift a frame by the top molding alone. Avoid pressing on decorative elements. Make sure your hands are clean and dry or wear clean gloves to protect sensitive surfaces.

Placement

When deciding where to place a framed work of art, look for a moderate, stable environment. Avoid locations near heat and cooling ducts, over fireplaces and radiators, and on uninsulated exterior walls. Art should not be hung in bathrooms or kitchens since humidity and cooking grease will harm both the frame and object inside. Avoid direct sunlight and intense artificial light. Be sure the hanging hardware is sufficiently strong and tightly secured to both the frame and the wall.

Maintenance

Examine a frame at least annually: look for fresh cracks or flaking on the surface. Check for loose ornaments or joints. If everything appears secure, the frame may be dusted.

Use a soft, natural bristle brush. Do not clean frames with a feather duster or coarse cloth. Feathers can catch in the ornaments, and harsh cloth will abrade the surface. Start at the top of the frame and gently move loose dust away from the art and toward a vacuum cleaner held near—but not—touching the frame. Stretching a nylon stocking over the vacuum nozzle will catch any fragments that may come loose.

Further Reading

Grimm, Claus. *The Book of Picture Frames*. New York: Abaris Books, 1981.

Mitchell, Paul, and Lynn Roberts. *Frameworks: Form, Function and Ornament in European Portrait Frames*. London: Merrell Holbertson Publishers, 1996.

Wilner, Eli, with Mervyn Kaufman. *Antique American Frames: Identification and Price Guide*. New York: Avon Press, 1995.

Conservators

FRAMES
Archival Art Services, Inc. 133
Gold Leaf Studios 158–159
Nick Greer, Antiques Conservator 161
Roberta Dolores Gregor Painting Conservation 162
William A. Lewin, Conservator LLC 166–167
Page Conservation, Inc. 175–177
John Scott Conservator of Art and Architecture 181
South Royal Studios 183

FRAMING AND MATTING
Archival Art Services, Inc. 133
Brierwood Consultants /Stephen A. Collins 141
Fulton Framing Services 156
Gold Leaf Studios 158–159
Andrei N. Kuznetsov Painting Conservation 165
South Royal Studios 183

CHAPTER 16

Plastics

PLASTICS INCLUDE OBJECTS COMPOSED OF BOTH SYNTHETIC AND NATURAL materials. All **plastics** are **polymers** made up of a large number of small molecules called monomers. Polymers can be grouped into three broad headings: (1) natural (including horn, amber, gutta-percha, **shellac**, and bitumen); (2) semisynthetic (including casein, ebonite, cellulose nitrate, cellulose acetate, and the trademark Celluloid); and (3) synthetic (including phenol formaldehyde, urea formaldehyde, polyethylene, polyvinyl chloride [PVC], polyester, and the trademark Bakelite). Most semisynthetics tend to be older, dating from the late nineteenth to the early twentieth century, and were replaced by synthetics, particularly after World War II. Earlier plastics often were more experimental, produced with less quality control than the synthetic polymers manufactured today.

Plastics can broadly be grouped into two categories based on how they are manufactured. **Thermosetting** materials are heated and stay in a fixed shape when heated again. **Epoxies**, PVC, polyester, and urea formaldehyde are all thermosetting **resins**. **Thermoplastic** materials are heated, become firm when they are cold, and then can soften again upon heating. Nylon, polypropylene, and polyethylene are examples of thermoplastic resins. Additives added to polymers help to form the final shape and characteristic of the plastic. Fillers, colorants, fibers, antioxidants, **ultraviolet** absorbers, and **dyes** are all added to modify the plastic and obtain the desired result.

Plastic objects are all around us and are part of our everyday life. They have become an integral part of the medical field, transportation, the fashion industry, and everything from diapers to baby bottles to Barbie dolls. It is not surprising then, that many museums collect and preserve plastic objects in their collections. Additionally, collecting plastic objects has become part of the ever-growing antiques industry, and many private individuals have collections of Bakelite, Celluloid, and Civil War period gutta-percha and vulcanite.

Degradation of Polymers

Although plastics may seem like they will last forever, polymers break down and deteriorate with age just like other materials such as metals, leather, and wood. Even materials made to survive extreme environments, such as space-suits and nonstick Teflon-coated frying pans, have already begun to show signs of degradation. Several factors contribute to the breakdown of plastic objects. The compositions of plastics and their methods of manufacture are factors. Additionally, the environments in which they were used and are stored and exhibited play a role. Temperature, **relative humidity**, ultraviolet radiation, and **pollutants** all can cause chemical and physical changes in plastics.

- Higher temperatures cause chemical reactions to proceed at a faster rate. Excess heat causes polymer chains to break, affecting the mechanical properties of the plastic.
- Fluctuations in relative humidity can be harmful to plastics. Large fluctuations can cause objects to crack, split, and warp. Excess moisture can cause chemical changes.
- Elevated temperatures and relative humidity may also stimulate **mold** spores and fungal colonies to grow.
- Ultraviolet radiation and excessive levels of daylight will cause some plastics to change color (usually yellow) and can also cause a polymer to **cross-link**, so that a chemical bond joins two or more polymer chains. With cross-linking, a plastic may become inflexible and brittle, often resulting in mechanical failure if dropped or flexed.
- Pollutants such as sulfur dioxide, nitrogen dioxide, and **ozone** are harmful to plastics and may cause off-gassing of volatile components, leading to further degradation of the synthetic matrix.
- Physical damage can result if fragile plastics are dropped, handled improperly, or packaged improperly during transit and long-term storage.

Common Problems

Degradation of polymers can result in visible changes to plastic objects. These changes occur for a variety of reasons, as stated above, and may occur in stages over time. Chemical degradation may not always happen rapidly, and then suddenly the plastic object may crack, discolor, or change dramatically overnight. Some signals that indicate degradation are listed below.

Odors

One indication that plastic materials are degrading is a very discernible odor. Cellulose acetate, for example, produces acetic acid upon deterioration, emitting a vinegar smell; the condition is called **vinegar syndrome**. Other plastics, such as polyvinyl chloride, produce hydrochloric acid, which has a very sharp and acidic smell.

Color Change

Many plastics change color when undergoing a chemical change. The most common color change occurs when clear plastics are exposed to ultraviolet radiation, which causes a yellowing over time. Yellowing can occur in a variety of materials, but it is most noticeable in polyvinyl chlorides, nylon, and clear adhesives such as epoxy resins and cyanoacrylates.

Other color changes can occur in which clear and colored objects become more opaque. Occasionally a white **bloom** can be seen on the surface of the plastic. This bloom, common with both cellulose acetate and cellulose nitrate, is most likely the result of plasticizer (or other additives) being leached to the surface of the object.

Weeping

Many plastic materials begin to **weep** as they degrade. This term refers to tiny droplets of liquid that become evident on the surface of objects. The droplets, often acidic in nature, are commonly sticky and oily. This phenomenon is a direct result of the loss of plasticizer in the material. It is most common with polyvinyl chloride, which produces fine droplets of phthalates on the surfaces. These droplets are harmful not only to the object or material but also to those handling the object or material.

Chemical Changes

Chemical changes in some plastics may cause distortion in the object over time. The appearance of small bubbles or **crazing** beneath the surface is an indication that degradation is occurring. These changes may cause such physical instability that the object may crumble when touched. Chemical changes are most often found in cellulose acetate and cellulose nitrate materials.

Physical Damage

Physical damage to plastic materials can occur in a variety of forms. If a plasticizer off-gasses or leaches from the object over time, softer, more flexible plastics such as rubbers and resins will become inflexible and brittle. Embrittlement can result in physical breaks and cracks. In more rigid plastics, such as polystyrene or polymethyl methacrylate (Lucite), cracks may also be the result either of an internal stress in the materials initiated in the manufacturing process or of an outside force (i.e., dropping the object). Crumbling of plastics such as polyurethane foams is the result of chemical breakdown due to exposure to oxygen and ozone. Other damage resulting in physical changes may include warping, flaking of layered materials, and fraying of fibers.

Consulting a Conservator

If you notice any of the problems described above, you will probably want to consult a conservator. Before a conservator can treat a plastic object, its condition must be assessed and the type of plastic correctly identified. Many synthetics, including rubbers, appear to be similar materials, but they can vary both in chemical formulation and in manufacturing technique. It is very important to determine the material of an object prior to treatment.

Several types of analytical equipment available to conservators can correctly identify the type of plastic and sometimes even the additives present (such as a plasticizer). Chemical spot tests and tests in which the synthetic is either burned or probed with a heated copper wire to indicate composition present hazards and may be detrimental to the object. Unknown substances, such as dirt, dust, paint, or a gummy residue, that may need to be removed for aesthetic reasons or because they are harming the object should also be analyzed prior to removal.

The conservator should record all available information, such as what the object was used for, what materials are present, and what damage exists, either from use or unintentional. Photographic documentation will also help record the condition of an object. All cleaning methods, no matter how minor or small, should be documented, and the materials and techniques of **conservation treatment** used should be recorded. This **treatment report** should be kept with the object.

Treatment Options

It is difficult to deal with plastic objects, because each class is unique. Because these materials are relatively recent, conservators are just beginning to understand how different plastics age and what treatment is best for their long-term preservation. A single solution for each type of material simply does not exist. Synthetic materials also are easily misidentified: what appears to be horn or ivory may in fact be Celluloid or urea formaldehyde. The importance of identifying a material by testing, before any treatment is performed, cannot be overemphasized.

Because conservation treatment methods for plastics are still being developed, a conservative approach is recommended: less is definitely better. But careful attention to the environment in which objects are stored and exhibited can help prevent damage and degradation. Some simple rules apply to all plastics.

Handling Plastics

All plastics should be handled wearing gloves. White cotton gloves or disposable gloves (made of latex or vinyl) should be worn at all times. Plastics are very sensitive to the acids in human hands and can be damaged if handled too often. Gloves also protect the handlers. If decay products are noticeable on the plastic's surface, especially on polyvinyl chlorides, then disposable gloves should be worn and disposed of immediately after use.

Cleaning

Conservators can perform light cleaning of plastic surfaces using a museum-quality HEPA (high-efficiency particulate air) filtered vacuum with variable speed control. Harder plastics, such as polycarbonate, polystyrene, and acrylics can be cleaned using a dry, electrostatic cloth. Usually minimal cleaning is all that is necessary, unless the object is needed for an exhibition or it is deteriorating so severely that total loss is feared.

A conservator should be the only one to undertake any **wet-cleaning** on plastics. Wet-cleaning involves the use of water, solvents, detergents, or waxes. Some porous plastics will be permanently damaged by water, and solvents can soften plastics. Proprietary auto body polishes, nonabrasive paste cleaners, gum erasers, and scratch cleaners can irreversibly abrade surfaces and should never be used.

Repairs

Conservators have had some success using **adhesives** to repair broken plastic objects. Off-the-shelf adhesives are generally not suitable for the adhesion of historic plastic objects because they often contain solvents that can soften, and even melt, the plastic. While a variety of technical adhesives are available, finding the right adhesive for a specific plastic is much more difficult than it appears, so professional advice is recommended.

Preventive Conservation

Plastics benefit greatly by being stored and exhibited in stable environments. Temperature and relative humidity extremes should be minimized. While temperatures should be cool, freezing is not recommended, because exceeding cold can irreversibly embrittle some plastics. A drier environment of approximately 35–45 percent relative humidity is ideal. Good air ventilation is recommended to avoid a buildup of harmful fumes that can off-gas from plastics. Conditions also should be free of ultraviolet radiation, pollutants, dust, and insects. Plastics should be stored and supported using only museum approved **acid-free** materials.

Some plastic materials cannot be stored in contact with other objects because they will chemically interact. Plastics such as polyurethane foam, silicone rubber, and cellulose nitrate can break down in storage, producing acidic by-products that may harm other objects or storage materials. No object should be stored in close contact or proximity to polyvinyl chloride. Some particularly valuable plastic objects could be stored with oxygen and pollutant scavengers, materials that absorb and trap chemical molecules, which will help remove or reduce chemical off-gassing.

Questions To Ask a Conservator

- Have you worked on plastics or polymers?
- Can you identify my plastic? If so, will the identification be destructive to the surface?
- How big of a sample is necessary to undertake analysis of my plastic?
- What will the plastic look like after treatment?
- Will there be any follow-up work required on my part, such as monitoring the plastic?

- Is the treatment absolutely necessary?
- How should I store my plastic object before and after treatment?
- Is it harmful to continue to use my plastic object?
- Should I be wearing special gloves to handle my plastic object?
- How much will the conservation treatment cost?

Questions To Be Prepared To Answer

- How was the plastic object used and stored in the past?
- What is the intent of the treatment?
- Is there more than one of the same object available?

Further Reading

Blank, Sharon. "An Introduction to Plastics and Rubbers in Collections." *Studies in Conservation* 35 (1990): 53–63.

Grattan, David W., ed. *Saving the Twentieth Century: The Conservation of Modern Materials.* Ottawa: Canadian Conservation Institute, 1993.

Morgan, John. *Conservation of Plastics.* London: Museums and Galleries Commission, 1991.

Quye, Anita, and Colin Williamson, eds. *Plastics: Collecting and Conserving.* Edinburgh: National Museums of Scotland Publishing, 1999.

Shashoua, Yvonne. "A Passive Approach to the Conservation of Polyvinyl Chloride." In *ICOM—Modern Materials Working Group,* 961–66. London: James and James, 1996.

Shashoua, Yvonne, and Clare Ward. "Plastics: Modern Resins with Ageing Problems." In *SSCR Resins: Ancient and Modern,* 33–37. Edinburgh: Scottish Society for Conservation and Restoration, 1995.

Winsor, Peter. "Conservation of Plastics Collections." Museum and Galleries Commission Fact Sheets, September 1999.

Young, Lisa, and Amanda Young. *The Preservation, Storage and Display of Spacesuits.* Collections Care Report 5, National Air and Space Museum, Smithsonian Institution. Washington, D.C.: Smithsonian Institution, 2001.

Subspecialities

Animation cels, materials analysis

Conservators

CHAPTER 17

Home Movies, Videotape, and Audiotape

A RELATIVELY NEW AREA OF CONCERN FOR PRESERVATION IS THE REALM
of moving image and audio materials. Though motion picture film,
videotape, and audiotape are modern materials, they actually have a
known shorter lifespan than many important personal documents on paper.
This chapter addresses the most common twentieth-century moving image and
sound materials used by families and nonprofessionals and those most likely
to be in personal collections; items such as wax cylinders, unusual experimental film formats, vinyl recordings, broadcast videotape, and the like, are beyond
the scope of this chapter. Professionally produced film, video, and audio collections such as vintage movies (e.g., *Gone with the Wind*), prerecorded tapes
(e.g., VHS copies of *Saturday Night Fever*), and music collections (e.g., discs
and tapes of professional musicians like the Rolling Stones) are usually covered
by copyright and are also beyond the scope of this chapter.

Motion picture film, videotape, and audiotape are made with materials
that are known to deteriorate within decades, and their content is accessible only through machinery that may rapidly become obsolete. This
"machine-readable" issue separates these materials from conventional collectibles and personal artifacts. Deterioration and format obsolescence go
hand in hand to create some of the most vulnerable artifacts of our society.

The specific materials that make up moving image and most sound
materials (also known as audiovisual or a/v materials) are contemporary
plastics and **dyes**. They were not intended to last. The machines that "read"
and project these materials evolve to become faster, less expensive, and eas-
ier to produce, but leave behind formats and standards that become obsolete. Motion picture films may be on an unstable base or use unstable dyes,
which make them unreadable or unprojectable. All videotapes and audiotapes have a polyurethane binder that will become unstable in ten to thirty

years. Format obsolescence is a common experience: it is rare to find a working 8 mm film projector, an 8-track tape player, or a BetaMax videotape player.

An audiovisual conservator will be able to advise you about the content and preservation needs of your collection, be it film, video, or audio. Most conservators will, however, refer the important work of transferring the content of the film, video, or audio to a new, contemporary format to a vendor who has the specialized electronic equipment to do this work.

Motion Picture Film

Most motion picture film found in personal collections are "home movies." Since the 1920s, parents have pulled out a cumbersome camera and captured important events in life, such as a trip to the beach or a birthday party. Early home movies tend to be 16 mm wide; these are simply known as "16 millimeter." In 1932, Kodak introduced the 8 mm film, and in 1965 the Super 8 film, which is 8 mm wide, but the image is widened on the film. Only rarely are home movies made on a professional film such as 35 mm, which requires expensive equipment and is costly to develop, edit, and cut into a projectable item. (Note: if you have 35 mm film made prior to 1957 in your collection, you may have a particularly fragile and potentially hazardous nitrate film; seek the help of a vendor or conservator immediately.) One of the charming aspects of home movies on film is that they are short; a typical 8 mm film is three minutes long.

The Nature of Film

Motion picture film is very similar to photographic negatives. Film is not to be confused with videotape (see below): you should be able to hold the film up to the light and see a succession of images, each one known as a frame. Both 16 mm and 8 mm films are manufactured on a cellulose acetate clear plastic base film, with a gelatin coating and silver or organic dyes.

Strategy for Maintaining "Home Movie" Collections on Film

Proper storage and handling are essential to maintaining motion picture films. Cool and dry storage (not the attic or basement) will go a long way to keeping **vinegar syndrome** from occurring. Cellulose acetate film deteriorates in the presence of water, forming and releasing acetic acid, which smells like vinegar. Elevated temperature and relative humidity will accelerate this reaction, and the acetic acid contributes to continuing deterioration. One irreversible and unfortunate aspect of some motion picture materials is that the dye changes or fades, so that there may be an unusual red, yellow, or blue cast to the picture. A vendor may be able to "color correct" this shift in hue at additional cost.

The most common preservation strategy for film is to duplicate it onto a contemporary format, such as VHS videotape or DVD for the purposes of access, and to rehouse and maintain the original film. More than one duplicate can be made, either for safeguarding purposes or to distribute to friends or relatives. It is never recommended that original home movies be destroyed just because they have been duplicated, unless the original has been damaged beyond the ability to view or handle it in the future. Copies may not, in fact, capture all of the detail of the original film. The benefit of having an access or viewer copy on VHS or DVD, however, is that you and your family can watch the movie easily without fear of damaging the original.

The vendor who duplicates your film should be familiar with handling older, archival materials. He or she should suggest a direct duplication by running the original film through a "telecine" machine using either a "wet-gate" or "digital wet-gate." The telecine is an elaborate piece of equipment that will allow your original film to be properly registered onto videotape (which has a different "frame ratio"). The wet-gate squeegees a fluid onto the film that reduces the incidence of visible scratches on the duplicate (it will not permanently remove scratches from the original). The digital wet-gate uses a complex digital recognition program to reduce scratches on the duplicate. A duplicated film should be placed on a wide-aperture plastic core, four inches in diameter, and stored in an acid-free labeled box. Be sure to tell the vendor what kind of titles ("slates") or other identifying information you want on the copy. Some vendors offer compilation videotapes or DVDs, on which several films are duplicated together. Some vendors will also, at your request, place background music on the duplication, especially if the movies are silent.

Once the vendor has returned your original and duplicate home movies, store them separately. The originals may be served by using a special "freezer storage kit," which was developed by a Smithsonian scientist and is sold by Metal Edge, Inc. This kit is only for use with motion picture film; never use videotape or audiotape in a freezer storage kit. Follow the instructions completely, or you will irreparably damage your film. Your access copies on videotape will last for as long as the videotape does not deteriorate (see below) and the playback machine does not become unusable and obsolete. DVDs have a published longer lifespan, but because this format is evolving it is likely that the machinery will become obsolete before the format physically deteriorates.

Videotapes

More and more family moments are captured on videotape. The portable video camera does not require special lighting; unlike film, the videotape does not have to be chemically developed; and the sophisticated videotape can shoot images for hours, not minutes. In the mid-1970s the cassette-format videotape became the home movie alternative. Prior to the introduction of the VHS tape cassette in 1977, some "portable" videotape was available in a reel-to-reel format, but the equipment was bulky and the picture was not as good as film. Several consumer videotapes have been developed in the years since, and while the tape is essentially the same, each requires a different machine to read the encoded information on the tape surface.

The Nature of Videotape

One misperception is that all videotape is digital; in fact, until the late 1990s the majority of consumer videotape was analog, meaning that the signal was laid in linear tracks analogous to the colors and light that was being shot. One shortcoming of analog videotape is that subsequent copies have a lower-quality resolution, a deterioration of the image that is known as generational loss. It is therefore important to make duplicates from the earliest copy of a videotape (or from the original).

Videotape is a flexible, laminated tape consisting of a stable polyester plastic base, a polyurethane binder, and the "pigment," which is typically black or red iron oxide (other pigments include "metal evaporated," and "metal particle" tapes, which apply primarily to high-end broadcast formats or to miniaturized tape cassettes such as DV Cam). The oxide holds the magnetic information that will be translated by playback machines into images and sound.

Strategy for Maintaining Videotape Collections

The polyurethane binder in videotapes reacts with moisture in the air over time and becomes "sticky," leading to **sticky-shed syndrome**. In other words, the binder loses the chemical properties that hold it to the polyester base and that hold the pigment, too. The binder literally falls off of the tape base when played back on your tape deck; on the monitor or television, this damage may be noticeable as bright flashes, known as "dropouts," or a periodic snowy image. Other sources of the dropouts may be a dirty tape deck, so consider having your machine cleaned prior to playing back older, vulnerable tapes. A high-humidity and dusty environment accelerates sticky-shed syndrome, so keeping videotapes in a cool (never freezing) and dry environment and in an enclosure (preferably a plastic shipping container) is important. Sticky-shed syndrome, which may appear within ten to thirty years, is thus far irreversible.

Videotape can be duplicated by a knowledgeable vendor onto a preservation/access format such as a contemporary VHS tape or DVD, like motion picture film. The vendor who duplicates your videotape should do it in real time, using cleaned machines and minimal electronic intervention. Do not use high-speed dubbing. Some very damaged tapes may need to be cleaned using inert tissue wipes (a fairly noninvasive procedure) or heated in a convection oven ("baking") to temporarily eliminate sticky-shed; neither of these techniques has been tested independently, and they may accelerate more deterioration in the original videotape. Nonetheless, an experienced vendor may have better success in getting the image off the tape by employing these methods. Because tapes are long (sometimes six hours) and vendors charge by the hour, duplication is expensive. Make sure you know what is on your tapes, and eliminate or edit extraneous information in the duplication process. The original tape is usually kept unless it is damaged beyond usability. It should be returned to you in a fully wound or rewound position, with the "record tab" removed, and in a slipcase or protective box. It is now ready to be stored for long-term preservation.

Unfortunately, there is no "archival" (meaning long-lasting) electronic media format. Typically several copies are made, one for access and one to become the "preservation master." These should be stored separately when they are returned to you and carefully labeled. Because there are many excellent high-end, broadcast videotapes available, it is sometimes recommended that the preservation master be in an expensive broadcast format such as the digital Digital Betacam or analog Betacam SP, while the access copy should be in a format that you can play at home such as VHS or DVD. You probably will not be able to play the broadcast copy at home (tape decks for these tapes are in the $5,000–15,000 range), but its purpose is to be a high-resolution copy that will carry the information for a decade or so. In a decade's time the preservation master will have to be copied again onto a contemporary format of your choosing.

Audiotapes

Many will remember family gatherings and personal recollections recorded onto audio reel-to-reel tape or audiocassette formats. Recordings ranging from oral histories to piano recitals to letters on tape may be part of your collectible heritage. Audiotape in a reel-to-reel format became available commercially shortly after World War II, and the audiocassette was introduced in 1963.

The Nature of Audiotape

Audiotape is similar to videotape (see above) in construction, with the one exception that reel-to-reel tapes from 1947 to the late 1950s may be on a cellulose acetate base and can suffer, like film, from vinegar syndrome. Otherwise, all audiotapes will deteriorate because the polyurethane binder becomes sticky. This damage frequently manifests itself as a high-pitched squeal during playback, or the tape may come to a complete halt while running through the tape deck.

Reel-to-reel tapes and compact cassettes are analog. More recently, digital audiotape (DAT) has become a preferred audio recording material. DAT tape tends to be more fragile than analog tapes; making duplicates of material recorded on DAT is important.

Strategy for Maintaining Audiotape Collections

Like the other machine-readable formats, audiotape is best preserved by duplicating by a knowledgeable vendor onto a contemporary format such as CD or audio-DVD, both of which are digital formats. The procedures, cautions, and storage recommendations are the same as those described above, for videotapes. As the duplication formats recommended are digital, the basic reformatting should be in WAV files with 16 bit sampling rate, 44.1 KHz output onto CD-R (not audio-CD) or audio-DVD. Some vendors may prefer other types of encoding. Never bake DAT tapes. Store originals in a box or handling container that fits snugly so that the original tape cannot be jostled.

Further Reading

Blasko, Edward, Benjamin A. Luccitti, and Susan F. Morris, eds. *The Book of Film Care.* 2nd ed. Kodak Publication H-23. Rochester, NY: Eastman Kodak Company, 1992.

Boyle, Deirdre. *Video Preservation: Securing the Future of the Past.* New York: Media Alliance, 1993.

Van Bogart, John. *Magnetic Tape Storage and Handling.* Washington, D.C.: Commission on Preservation and Access [now National Council of Library and Information Resources], June 1995.

Wilhelm, Henry, and Carol Brower. *The Permanence and Care of Color Photographs: Traditional and Digital Color Prints, Color Negatives, Slides, and Motion Pictures.* Grinnell, Iowa: Preservation Publishing Company, 1993.

Please see advertising section for vendors who handle duplication and restoration of home movies, audiotape, and videotape.

CHAPTER 18

Explanatory Notes

The entries that follow were written by the conservators themselves in response to questions about their background, services, and facilities. Each conservator was also invited to provide additional information the readers of the directory might find useful. Conservators have verified the accuracy of these entries as presented. All the contributing conservators are members of WCG.

The entries are arranged in alphabetical order. In cases where the business name is that of the conservator, the entry appears under the first letter of the surname; that is, John Smith Conservation Associates would be found under "S", whereas Art Restoration, Inc., would appear under "A".

ABBREVIATIONS
Professional Associations

AIC	American Institute for Conservation of Historic and Artistic Works
CIPP	Conservators in Private Practice (AIC Specialty Group)
IIC	International Institute for Conservation of Historic and Artistic Works
WCG	Washington Conservation Guild

Other

CAL	Conservation Analytical Laboratory, Smithsonian Institution (now SCMRE)
CAP	Conservation Assessment Program, funded by IMLS and administered by Heritage Preservation
GSA	Government Services Administration
ICOM	International Council of Museums
ICCROM	International Centre for the Study of the Preservation and Restoration of Cultural Property
IMS/IMLS	Institute of Museum Services/now the Institute of Museum and Library Services

NEA	National Endowment for the Arts
NMAH	National Museum of American History
SCMRE	Smithsonian Center for Materials Research and Education (formerly CAL)
SOS!	Save Outdoor Sculpture! A joint project of Heritage Preservation and the Smithsonian American Art Museum

AIC MEMBERSHIP CATEGORIES

ASSOCIATE Associate membership is open to anyone who is working in the field or is interested in and would like to learn more about conservation. The Associate category includes practicing conservators as well as museum curators, administrators, librarians, archivists, and art historians.

PROFESSIONAL ASSOCIATE Professional Associates (PAs) are conservators, conservation scientists, educators, or others professionally involved in conservation who through training, knowledge, and experience have shown a commitment to the purposes for which the AIC was established. The PA category was established in 1980. Effective January 1997, a conservator who has earned an undergraduate university degree (or the international equivalent) may apply for PA status after completing two years of basic conservation training and acquiring at least three years of experience in his/her special field. Applications for PA must be supported by three Fellows or PAs. Candidates must agree in writing to abide by the *Code of Ethics and Guidelines for Practice*.

FELLOW In addition to the qualifications required for election to Professional Associate membership, a candidate for Fellow must have a minimum of three years of graduate-level education (including an internship) in a conservation-related field or the equivalent in a formal apprenticeship plus a minimum of seven years of experience after the three years of conservation training. Moreover, evidence must be submitted of sustained high-quality professional skills and of ethical behavior. Applicants for Fellow status must also demonstrate that they have participated in an exchange of ideas regarding methods. Professional recommendations from five AIC Fellows must be included with the application.

AIC does not at present certify conservators. However, a few paper conservators were certified by the AIC Board of Examiners in the 1980s.

Clarification

The Cooperstown Graduate Program, State University of New York at Oneonta, is now the art conservation program at the State University College at Buffalo, N.Y.

CHAPTER 19

Conservator Listings

AIKEN & RAMER
1725 Linden Avenue, Baltimore, MD 21217-4312
Tel 410 383-9867 *Fax* 410 383-9867 *Email* carol.aiken@verizon.net or
brian.ramer@verizon.net
Business hours By appointment
Established 1989

CAROL AIKEN, Conservator
1977–present Conservator in private practice, portrait miniatures
1974–76 Conservator of Decorative Arts, New York State Division of
    Historic Preservation
1992–98 Ph.D. in Art Conservation Research, University of Delaware

BRIAN RAMER, Consultant
1989–present Conservation consultant, preventive conservation
1986–88 Project Coordinator, Scottish Museums Council, nationwide
    conservation survey of collections in Scotland
1984–85 Conservator, International Center for Study of Preservation and
    Restoration of Cultural Property, Rome, Italy
1974–77 B.Sc. in Conservation of Archaeological Materials, Institute of
    Archaeology, University of London, England

Two conservators. Available full-time

Services Facility and general collection assessments, environmental surveys,
consultations on climate and lighting control, and planning for exhibitions
and storage facilities. Evaluation and treatment of portrait miniatures.

Facilities Treatment of portrait miniatures in dedicated studio space with climate control and central security/fire alarm system. Full insurance coverage
for objects on premises. Collections also treated in situ.

Mr. Ramer evaluates the state of collections and facilities, advises on environmental controls and monitoring, and plans storage and exhibition improve-
ments. His expertise encompasses the care and management of collections in
modern buildings and historic structures. He often collaborates with architects,
engineers, and exhibit designers.

Albro Conservation

822 South Taylor Street, Arlington, VA 22204
Tel 703 892-6738 *Fax* 703 892-1985 *Email* salbro@aol.com
Business hours Monday–Friday 10–3
Established 1976

Thomas C. Albro II, Rare Books Conservator
Conservator of Rare Books at the Library of Congress, Washington DC from 1972–2000. Head of the Rare Books Conservation Section from 1980–2000. Acting Chief of Conservation Division from 1995–1999. Conservator Apprentice from 1972–1978. Graduated in 1972 from American University with a B.A. in American History. Treated a wide variety of high profile and high value materials at the Library of Congress including incunabula, printed and manuscript volumes and diaries, Asian and Middle Eastern bound collections, maps, atlases, musical scores, individual manuscripts, and photograph albums. Retired from the Library of Congress in 2000 and continued with private practice at home studio, doing similar work for many local museums, rare book libraries, and collectors.

Sylvia Rodgers Albro, Paper Conservator
Senior Paper Conservator, Library of Congress 1984–present. Part-time contract Paper Conservator with The Phillips Collection since 1998. Assistant Paper Conservator for the Yale Center for British Art 1982–84. Assistant Paper Conservator for the Fine Arts Museums of San Francisco 1982. Graduated with a M.A. and a Certificate of Advanced Study in the Conservation of Historic and Artistic Works from the Cooperstown Graduate Program, State University of New York, 1982. B.A. magna cum laude in Fine Arts and Italian from Santa Clara University, Santa Clara, CA.

Two conservators

Services Conservation of rare books, documents, works of art on paper, parchment and vellum, maps, musical scores, photograph albums, and three-dimensional paper artifacts. Treatments, exhibition advice, object storage, storage advice, matting and framing, written documentation and photo documentation.

→

Facilities Well-lit dedicated studio space in quiet residential neighborhood with easy parking. Climate control, alarm system, and fire extinguisher. Fine Arts insurance coverage of objects on the premises. Historic antique finishing tools and equipment for books, reference library, and photographic equipment for documentation.

Thomas C. Albro II has thirty years of experience in the field of rare books conservation. Sylvia Albro has twenty years of experience in the field of conservation of works of art on paper. The practice has completed a wide variety of conservation treatments for museums, galleries, libraries, and private collections in the Washington, DC area. Conservators abide by the AIC Code of Ethics and Guidelines for Practice and participate regularly in local and international educational conferences and forums. Since 1983 both conservators have served annually as guest faculty at the European School for the Conservation of Library Materials in Spoleto, Italy.

ALEXANDRIA CONSERVATION SERVICES, LTD.
5001 Andrea Avenue, Annandale, VA 22003
Tel 703 503-5346 *Fax* 703 503-5346 *Email* conserveit@earthlink.net
Website http://home.earthlink.net/~conserveit
Business hours Monday–Friday 9–5, part-time
Established 1997

LISA YOUNG, Objects Conservator, AIC Professional Associate
February 2000–2004 Project Conservator and Project Manager, National
    Air and Space Museum, Smithsonian Institution, Save America's
    Treasures, Apollo spacesuit conservation project and Saturn V, Johnson
    Space Center, preservation project
October 1997–present Principal and Owner, Alexandria Conservation
    Services. Clients include National Air and Space Museum, National Park
    Service, Historic St. Mary's City, Mount Vernon, Poplar Forest, Alexandria
    Archaeology Museum, National Museum of Civil War Medicine
1995–97 Conservation intern: National Air and Space Museum; Cynon
    Valley Museums Service, Aberdare, Wales; the American School of
    Classical Studies, Agora Excavations, Athens, Greece
1990–95 Archaeologist (part-time), Maryland-National Capital Park and
    Planning Commission, History Division
1990–94 Conservation Assistant: Alexandria Archaeology Museum; Mount
    Vernon Ladies Association; Jefferson Patterson Park and Museum;
    National Museum of Natural History, Smithsonian Institution

Education
1996 B.Sc. in Archaeological Conservation (First Class Honors), University
    of Wales, Cardiff, United Kingdom
1989 B.A. in Anthropology, Mary Washington College, Fredericksburg, VA

Additional Training
2000 Plastics Damage and Analysis (AIC)
1998 Preservation of Plastics (Smithsonian Institution)
1998 Special Techniques for Waterlogged Organic Materials (Canadian
    Conservation Institute)

→

Services Conservation of archaeological, historical, and space history objects. Treatments, object surveys, environmental surveys, exhibition advice, storage advice, written documentation, photo documentation, packing/shipping, archaeological field services, wet and dry sites.

Facilities Laboratory work performed on-site at clients' location; laboratory for the conservation of small archaeological and historical objects, including wet collections, in Annandale.

Alexandria Conservation Services, Ltd., is a woman-owned and operated company that specializes in the conservation and preservation of historical and archaeological objects. Lisa A. Young, President, has more than ten years of experience performing active and preventive conservation of objects as well as conservation surveys, speaking, and conducting professional seminars. Lisa Young has worked primarily in the Mid-Atlantic Region of the United States as well as overseas in Wales, England, Egypt, and Greece. She is an active member of AIC and WCG, as well as a number of local and national archaeology societies.

ANTIQUE RESTORATIONS LTD./BRUCE M. SCHUETTINGER

17 North Alley, P.O. Box 244, New Market, MD 21774
Tel 301 865-3009 *Fax* 301 865-3009 *Email* bschuettinger@erols.com
Business hours Monday–Friday 8:30–5
Established 1981

BRUCE M. SCHUETTINGER, Conservator
Bruce M. Schuettinger received a B.Sc. with a Fine Arts major from Towson
State University, graduating cum laude with honors in art. He attended "Wood
Technology for Furniture Conservation" in 1992 given by the Smithsonian
Institution and "Regionalism in American Furniture" at the Winterthur Mu-
seum in 2001. He also has attended numerous lectures, seminars, and classes
concerning conservation and historic furniture issues during the past twenty
years. He has successfully completed personal property appraisal courses from
Indiana University and The University of Maryland from 1985–1995. Mr.
Schuettinger has lectured on furniture conservation and numerous aspects
of historic furniture to institutions, organizations, and the public. He was a
faculty member of the Appraisal Studies and Connoisseurship programs of
the George Washington University from 1995 to 2003. He was granted Professional Associate status in AIC in 1993.

RICHARD FARMER, Associate Conservator
Richard Farmer is an Associate Conservator and has been employed by Antique Restorations Ltd. since 1985. He is skilled in structural consolidation
and all aspects of wood loss replacement, including veneer, inlay, marquetry,
and carved and turned elements.

Services Conservation of wooden artifacts. Treatments; object surveys; consultation on environmental, usage, and display issues; authentication; lectures; and emergency response. Treatments performed on-site as well as at
our conservation facility.

Facilities Antique Restorations Ltd. is housed in a 2,500 square foot commercial building with complete climate control and 24-hour monitored fire/
security system. Housed in this facility is an extensive array of stationary machinery and historic hand tools as might be required to fabricate all types of
elements used in historic wooden artifacts. Also part of our equipment are
35 mm cameras, digital cameras, stereo microscope, and an extensive reference library of approximately 350 books. Full fine arts insurance coverage is
supplied as part of our service.

→

Antique Restorations Ltd. has been in business for nineteen years, serving the conservation needs of the museum, institutional, and private communities. Antique Restorations Ltd. is experienced in all aspects of wooden artifact conservation, specializing in original surface preservation, structural consolidation, and historical and sensitive loss replacements, including turned, carved, inlaid, gilded, and marquetry elements. Treatments utilize traditional craft methods and materials, often combined with innovative state-of-the-art conservation materials and techniques. Antique Restorations Ltd. has treated wooden artifacts from the seventeenth through twentieth centuries. All of the treatments are considered individually and are based on the historical and analytical research available. Various forms of analysis are conducted including cross-sectional microscopy for coating identification. Extensive historical research is also performed in an effort to ensure sensitive and accurate treatments. Treatments attempt to be as minimally intrusive to the object as possible while meeting the display, usage, and environmental factors imposed by the client. The treatments are designed to be in compliance with the Code of Ethics and Guidelines for Practice of AIC. Thorough photographic and text documentation is supplied upon completion of the treatment. Antique Restorations Ltd. regularly treats objects for major museums and government institutions, house museums, historical societies, embassies, and private collectors.

Accepts interns.

Archival Art Services, Inc.

P.O. Box 21399, 2412 18th Street NW, Rear Alley, Door C, Washington,
   DC 20009
Tel 202 667-3575 *Fax* 202 265-2818 *Email* safeart@erols.com
Website www.archivalartservices.com
Business hours Tuesday–Friday 10–6, Saturday 10–3
Established 1977

William Butler, President
Bill Butler has thirty five years of professional framing experience and has owned
framing businesses since the age of nineteen. He has invented and holds patents
for framing systems and tools. Provides on-site consultation and design advice
to museum conservators and exhibition designers and oversees a staff of eight.

Seven technicians
Two office staff

Services Conservation picture framing and three dimensional displays for
paintings, works on paper, textiles, books, sculptures, photographs. Object
surveys, exhibition advice, matting/framing, shipping advice, packing/ship-
ping, written documentation, installation advice.

Facilities Free-standing, 4,500 square foot commercial building with central
security alarm system and climate control. Separate woodworking shop and
art storage. Full insurance coverage for all artwork on premises.

Archival Art Services provides custom framing and a variety of exhibit related
services to museums, galleries, institutions, and private collectors. It takes pride
in a strict adherence to the use of archival methods and materials while providing unique and elegant presentations. A full woodworking shop with a staff of
three full time employees produces custom milled and hand finished frames,
display pedestals, custom expansion canvas stretchers, and shipping crates. Other
capabilities include on-site matting, framing, and installation, custom book cra-
dles, text labels, and panels and three dimensional displays. Archival Art Services has been privileged to create frames and displays for some of America's
most treasured documents and artworks including the Emancipation Procla-
mation, the Louisiana Purchase, paintings by Picasso, Matisse, Pollack, and Cas-
satt, and vintage photos by Ansel Adams, Man Ray, and Walker Evans.

Accepts interns.

ART CARE ASSOCIATES

P.O. Box 4141, Frederick, MD 21705
Tel 301 845-1010 *Fax* 301 845-8265 *Email* nrpollak@aol.com
Business hours By appointment
Established 1996

NANCY R. POLLAK, Conservator
1991 M.Sc. Winterthur/University of Delaware Program in Art Conservation,
majoring in Painting Conservation, special emphasis in painted textiles. 1987
B.F.A. graduate of Seton Hill College, majoring in Painting. Prior to establishing private conservation practice in 1996, worked as Assistant Conservator
at the Williamstown Art Conservation Center, Williamstown, MA. Internships
include the Pennsylvania Academy of Fine Arts, Textile Preservation Associates
of Keedysville, MD, and the Capitol Preservation Committee in Harrisburg,
PA. Continues advancing skills and knowledge through attendance at workshops and courses. Teaches painting and textile appreciation classes to adult
learners and provides lectures on various conservation topics at professional
meetings and to school students and public groups. Published papers include
subjects such as treatment of an Arthur B. Davies painting, and various aspects
of the study and treatment of painted textiles. Clients include government institutions, small museums and historical societies, and private individuals.

Services Conservation of paintings (canvas and panel) and painted textiles.
Treatments, object surveys, written documentation, photo documentation,
lectures.

Facilities Dedicated studio space with controlled climate and central secu-
rity/fire alarm systems. Full insurance coverage for objects on premises. Work
done on premises or at site, as necessary.

The philosophy of Art Care Associates is to plan and undertake treatments
that ensure the structural integrity of an object and improve its appearance,
while honoring its historical and artistic qualities. Nancy Pollak, Conservator,
is experienced in the treatment of both painted textiles, including Thangkas,
flags and banners, and traditional paintings on panel and canvas. She has a
working relationship with conservators of other specialties, which enables
her to offer well-rounded treatments of all aspects of complex objects. She
seeks to find an agreeable balance among the preservation needs of the object, its history, and the desires of the client, and enjoys helping her clients
to learn about and care for their valued and treasured objects.

ARTEX Conservation Laboratory
ARTEX Fine Art Services
8712 Jericho City Drive, Landover, MD 20785-4761
Tel 301 350-5500 *Fax* 301 350-6620 *Email* bramsay@artexfas.com
Website www.artexfas.com
Business hours Monday–Friday 9–5:30 by appointment
Established Artex 1990, Conservation Laboratory 1999

Barbara A. Ramsay, Director of Conservation Services/Chief
  Painting Conservator
Barbara Ramsay is a Certified Professional Conservator of the Canadian Association of Professional Conservators (CAPC), Professional Associate of AIC, Fellow of IIC, and Member of the Canadian Association for Conservation (CAC) and WCG. Ms. Ramsay graduated in 1976 with a Master of Art Conservation degree (Paintings and Paper) from Queen's University, Kingston, Canada, and has over twenty eight years of specialized experience in painting conservation. Former Senior Conservator of Fine Art in the Restoration & Conservation Laboratory of the National Gallery of Canada (NGC) in Ottawa, Ms. Ramsay worked there as a painting conservator for eighteen years, treating Canadian, American, and European paintings from the 16th through 20th centuries. She also managed the NGC Sculpture & Decorative Arts Laboratory for five years. In addition, she worked as Exhibition Project Manager and Head of Traveling Exhibitions at the NGC. Ms. Ramsay taught graduate students as Associate Professor of Painting Conservation at Queen's University in 1983–84 and 1996–97. She served as President of the IIC-Canadian Group and Chairman of the Board of Directors of CAPC. Ms. Ramsay was Director of Ramsay Conservation Services in Ottawa, Canada, before moving to Washington, DC in 1999 when appointed Director of Conservation Services at ARTEX.

Peter N. Nelson, Senior Associate Conservator
Peter Nelsen has more than twenty five years of experience in treating paintings. He has provided consultation, conducted condition surveys, and treated works for private and public collections in the United States and has worked on both antique and modern/contemporary paintings from the diverse cultures of Russia, East and South Asia, Africa, and Western Europe, as well as America. Mr. Nelsen has worked extensively as a visiting conservator in major museums in Washington, DC and Baltimore, MD since 1983, including the international museums and galleries of the Smithsonian Institution and the Walters Museum of Art. He holds both undergraduate and Masters degrees
→

from the Columbian College of Art and Sciences of the George Washington University. Mr. Nelsen is a Professional Associate of AIC and member and past Director of WCG. He joined the ARTEX Conservation Laboratory in 2001.

MARIE-HÉLÈNE GUGENHEIM, Associate Conservator
Marie-Hélène Gugenheim was a conservator in private practice in Washington, DC for fourteen years before joining ARTEX in 2002. Her prior contract work was primarily on easel paintings on canvas or wood, for a variety of public and private collections. Mural paintings include subcontracting for projects for the U.S. Treasury, the U.S. Capitol, the Federal Reserve, the Hillwood Museum, the Capitol in Harrisburg, PA, the White House, the Carnegie Institution in DC, GSA, and the Custom House in Baltimore. From 1984 to 1988, Ms. Gugenheim worked in France as assistant to Claire Brochu, Chief of the Department of Mural Paintings at Institut Français de Restoration des Oeuvres d'Art, and Olivier Nouailles, liner for Musée du Louvre and Musées Nationaux, Paris. From 1982 to 1984, she was apprentice to the late Louis Pomerantz, Conservator of Paintings, Chicago, and in 1981, apprentice to Ada Kazarnovskaya, Conservator of icons and paintings at the Grabar Academy, Moscow. Ms. Gugenheim studied at the Institut d'Art et d'Archéologie, École Nationale Supérieure des Beaux Arts, Paris, the Institut National des Langues et Civilisations Orientales, Paris, and at Northeastern Illinois University, Chicago. She is a Professional Associate of the AIC and member and past Director of WCG.

ELIZABETH MEHLIN, Assistant Conservator
Elizabeth Mehlin graduated from Queen's University, Kingston, Canada, in 2002 with a Master of Art Conservation Degree (Paintings). She worked on paintings and wall paintings as Assistant Paintings Conservator for Peter Malarkey Painting Conservation in Seattle, WA, from 1995–2000. Ms. Mehlin held internships at Legris Conservation in Montreal, Quebec, Canada in 2001, and at the Restoration and Conservation Laboratory of the National Gallery of Canada in 2002. She worked as Paintings Conservator and Productivity Supervisor at Legris Conservation in Ottawa, Canada from 2002–2003. In 1991, Ms. Mehlin received a B.A. in Art History from Williams College, Williamstown, MA. She is a member of AIC and WCG.

Four conservators
One office staff

→

Services Conservation of easel paintings and mural paintings of all kinds. Examination, written and photographic documentation, preventive conservation and restoration treatment, surveys, UV and normal light photography, scientific analysis including pigment and fiber analysis, technical studies, expert witness, lectures, emergency response. Advice on care of paintings, preparation for exhibition or loan, framing, storage, and transport. Management of conservation projects involving all types of objects; subcontracting of sculpture and paper conservation projects. Collaboration with other conservators and related professionals. Professional art handling, crating, and storage available on site. Installation and transport available nationally and internationally. Services provided for museum, gallery, government, corporate, and private collections, in both English and French. Conservation project management for paintings and objects of all kinds. Rental of conservation laboratory by conservators for special projects.

Facilities Spacious, modern studio in the Washington, DC area. Museum standard environmental controls, security system, fire protection, excellent storage capabilities, and adjacent crating workshop. Nederman fume extraction system, 6 x 9 foot heated suction table, surgical microscope, 35 mm and digital cameras, UV light units. Adjacent loading dock, large access doorways, and north-facing light exposure.

ARTEX Fine Art Services has provided professional art handling, crating, storage, installation, and transportation services since 1990. ARTEX expanded its services to include art conservation in February 1999 when it established the ARTEX Conservation Laboratory (ACL) in Landover, MD. Barbara A. Ramsay, Director of Conservation Services, manages the Conservation Services division, directing her staff of professional painting conservators. ACL provides conservation examination, documentation, research, and treatment services for paintings, as well as conservation project management for objects of all kinds. Ms. Ramsay brings to ARTEX her more than twenty eight years of experience in the painting conservation field, along with her extensive project management experience. All four painting conservators on staff have considerable conservation experience and adhere to the Code of Ethics and Guidelines for Practice of AIC. The highest possible standard is applied to all treatments, making use of materials and methods appropriate to each individual object and in accordance with currently accepted practices.

BOONE CONSERVATION SERVICES, INC.
4103 College Heights Drive, University Park, MD 20782
Tel 301 213-0355
Business hours By appointment
Established 1980

TERRY BOONE, Paper and Rare Book Conservator
1989–present Senior Rare Book Conservator, Library of Congress
1983–89 Rare Book Conservator, National Archives
1979–83 Bookbinder, Newberry Library
1978 University of Washington, B.F.A. Printmaking
Fellow AIC

Two conservators
One half-time intern

Services Conservation of rare books, parchment, manuscripts, archive collections, and works of art on paper including drawings, watercolors, prints, and maps. Custom bindings and housings for presentation materials and special collections. Treatments, object surveys, environmental surveys, exhibition advice, storage advice, matting/framing, shipping advice, packing/shipping, written documentation, photo documentation, lectures.

Facilities Dedicated laboratory space located within a residential structure with central HVAC and security systems. Surfaces and sinks for oversize materials, paper suction table, book suction platen, binocular microscope, digital and 35 mm photography.

Boone Conservation Services provides private clients and private and public institutions throughout the Eastern Seaboard region with a range of fine binding and conservation services.

Accepts interns.

JULIA M. BRENNAN, TEXTILE CONSERVATION SERVICES

209 N. Edgewood Street, Arlington, VA 22201
Tel 703 276-1681 *Fax* 703 276-7422 *Email* julia@caringfortextiles.com
Website www.caringfortextiles.com
Business hours By appointment
Established 1994

JULIA M. BRENNAN, Textile Conservator
Julia Brennan trained as a conservator at the Philadelphia Museum of Art
and for six years in a private atelier specializing in the treatment of sixteenth-
through twentieth-century tapestries, Oriental carpets, Asian textiles, and
American samplers and quilts. Her education has been supplemented through
independent course work in chemistry, dye, and fiber analysis. She helped
establish the treatment and storage space for collections at the Philadelphia
College of Textiles and was the recipient of a Getty Research Grant in 1989.
She worked at The Textile Museum, Washington, DC, as Assistant Conservator for Exhibitions until 1994. She has conducted public outreach programs
and lectured on the identification, care, and display of textiles. Extensive projects within the last five years include treatment and consultation for traveling exhibitions of tapestries for the Embassy of Australia and costumes for
the Andy Warhol Museum, Pittsburgh, PA, and surveys and treatments of
the textile collections at The John F. Kennedy Center for the Performing Arts,
George Washington's Mount Vernon, The Kaiser Family Foundation, and
The Turkish Embassy. In 2003, Ms. Brennan received a grant from the Getty
Grant Program in conjunction with The Friends of Bhutan Culture to lead
the first textile conservation training and preventative conservation programs
in Bhutan.

One conservator
One technician

Services Conservation of antique and contemporary textile artifacts, including flat, three dimensional, and costume. Treatments, exhibition and storage
advice, written reports and photo documentation, fiber analysis, matting/
framing, lectures.

→

Facilities Home based studio space with rolled and flat storage capacity and flexible dry and wet cleaning capacity. Local fire, smoke, and security alarms.

Julia Brennan is the owner of Textile Conservation Services, which provides a complete service for the conservation and presentation of a wide variety of antique and contemporary textile arts. Her specializations include wet and dry cleaning and repair of textiles. She particularly enjoys the challenges of exhibition and display in order to present textiles in the safest and most appealing manner. She has served museums, galleries, private institutions, foreign governments, and collectors since 1990. She often collaborates with other professionals, such as architects, art consultants, designers, framers, and conservators, in order meet the specific needs of each client.

Accepts interns.

Brierwood Consultants/Stephen A. Collins
4905 Pole Road, Alexandria, VA 22309
Tel 703 799-2577 *Fax* 703 360-2599 *Email* brierwood@aol.com
Business hours By appointment
Established 1988

Stephen A. Collins, Conservator
1988–present Contract conservation services, primarily textiles, to federal, state, and local museums, archives, and private clients
1989–90 Postgraduate Intern, CAL, Smithsonian Institution. Research on conservation of fabrics, exhibition materials, dyes, wet- and dry-cleaning, stain removal
1988 International Centre for the Study of the Preservation and the Restoration of Cultural Property (ICCROM), "The Scientific Principles of Conservation," course on the chemical and physical make up and the deterioration of stone, metals, paint pigments, ceramics, textiles, and paper
1986–88 Master-Apprentice Intern in textile conservation, the Textile Conservation Workshop, Main Street, South Salem, NY
1984–91 Center for Museum Studies, John F. Kennedy University, San Francisco, CA, M.A. in Museology with concentration in conservation, interned DeYoung Museum
1975–77 Southeastern Massachusetts University, North Dartmouth, MA, course work towards a B.Sc. in Textile Technology, emphasis design and structure, testing, and identification
1968–72 Tyler School of Art, Temple University, Philadelphia, PA, B.F.A. Crafts major, junior year Rome, Italy

Services Our services include assessment, stabilization, consolidation, cleaning, rehousing, mounting, surveys, written proposals, and photographic documentation. We specialize in mount and form building, conservation framing, treatments of the highest quality using up-to-date materials and techniques for textiles, and provide minimal treatment such as flattening, cleaning, minor stabilization, and framing for works on paper. All the work is done at our studio using only proven conservation-safe and acid-free materials.

Facilities Dedicated studio space with separate wet and drying areas.

Chase Art Services

4621 Norwood Drive, Chevy Chase, MD 20815
Tel 301 656-9416 *Fax* 301 656-4103 *Email* TChase4921@aol.com
Business hours By appointment
Established 1997

William Thomas Chase, III, Conservator

Tom Chase now runs Chase Art Services, specializing in archaeological metals and metal sculpture. From 1968 to 1997 he was Head Conservator of the Department of Conservation and Scientific Research of the Arthur M. Sackler Gallery and the Freer Gallery of Art, Smithsonian Institution, Washington, DC. He majored in Conservation of Art at Oberlin College and then studied at the Conservation Center of the Institute of Fine Arts of New York University. He took his student internship at the Freer Technical Laboratory under Rutherford J. Gettens and returned to the Freer after completing his degree in 1966. A Fellow of IIC and AIC, he has traveled much in Europe and the Far East and examined many famous Chinese bronzes. He organized and taught a short course on archaeological bronze conservation at Peking University in 1997. In the 1999–2000 academic year he was Visiting Professor in the Conservation Science Department of the Tokyo National University of Fine Arts and Music. Mr. Chase's primary research interest has been technical study of ancient Chinese bronzes. In 2003, Mr. Chase became President of AIC.

Services Conservation of archaeological bronzes, metal artifacts from all periods. Treatments, object surveys, storage advice, written documentation, photo documentation, expert witness, lectures, research projects, technical studies leading to determinations of authenticity and age.

Facilities Small workshop, photographic area, microscopes, metalworking shop, research library, and computers.

Chase Art Services specializes in the examination and treatment of ancient Chinese bronzes and other archaeological metals, but also works on modern sculpture. Services range from quick examination of the object's surface under the microscope (to find added parts or suspicious restoration) up to full-scale technical examination using x-radiography, metal analysis, cross-sectional analysis, lead isotope analysis, and carbon-14 testing. Research projects can be undertaken to solve involved and difficult questions. Because of the limitations on our staff and space, Chase Art Services contracts to use other facilities as necessary. Client list includes Christie's, Sotheby's, National Archives and Records Administration, the Office of the Architect of the Capitol, the Nelson-Atkins Museum of Art, the Cleveland Museum, and many dealers and private collectors.

CLEVELAND CONSERVATION OF ART ON PAPER, INC.

Conservation of Archival Documents, Works of Art on Paper and Historic
Paper Objects

7701 Alloway Lane, Beltsville, MD 20705

Tel and Fax 301 210-3731 *Email* conservationofpaper@erols.com

Website www.conservationofpaper.com

Business hours By appointment

Established 1995

RACHEL-RAY CLEVELAND, President

Rachel-Ray Cleveland, President, has been a member of AIC since 1990 and
ranks as a Professional Associate. She holds two degrees—one in Paper Conservation and the other in Collection Management. She holds a Master's degree in Conservation of Works of Art on Paper from the State University of
New York at Buffalo (1993) as well as a Graduate Certificate in Collection
Management from the Chicago Art Institute (1986).

Services Cleveland Conservation of Art on Paper, Inc. provides conservation
treatment of archival documents and works of art on paper—including prints,
watercolors, gouache, drawings, maps, architectural drawings, ephemera, wallpaper, parchment, seals, Middle Eastern calligraphic works, and Asian paper
objects. All conservation services are personally carried out by Ms. Cleveland.
No services are carried out by associate conservators, interns, or technicians.
Ms. Cleveland has extensive training, not only in conservation treatment but
also in needs assessment surveys, preservation planning, exhibit preparation,
and disaster preparedness. We invite clients to investigate treatments carried
out at Cleveland Conservation by referring to images "Before" and "After"
conservation on our website www.conservationofpaper.com.

Facilities The most up-to-date conservation techniques and technologies are
employed at the Cleveland Conservation lab. Conservation treatments are
based on knowledge of the chemical nature of archival documents and works
of art on paper. Chemical and physical stabilization of the paper object is always the main goal of treatment, in accordance with the AIC Code of Ethics
and Guidelines for Practice. The conservation lab and office are a dedicated
facility measuring 800 square feet. The four thousand pound Mozlar Vault
storage system is Underwriter's Laboratory approved and carries a TL15 bur-
glar-resistive rating. There is a CV Security System with motion detectors.
Additional Fine Art Insurance is available.

→

Ms. Cleveland has worked a great deal with historic American documents and continues a special interest in handwriting inks of the eighteenth and nineteenth centuries. She contributed a chapter on early American handwriting inks in the book *Before Photocopying*, by Barbara Rhodes (Oak Knoll Press, 1999). In 2000, she was invited to speak at the international Iron Gall Ink Meeting in Newcastle, England. The company serves major museums in the Washington metropolitan area, small museums along the eastern seaboard, and private collectors. A partial list of clients includes the Smithsonian Institution, the University of Maryland, the Maryland Historical Society, the U.S. National Park Service, the United States Holocaust Memorial Museum, the National Institutes of Health, National Library of Medicine, the International Baha'i Archives in Haifa, Israel, and the White House.

Visa, MasterCard, and Government Charge Cards welcome.

CONSERVATION ANTHROPOLOGICA
1083 Oakdale Road NE, Atlanta, GA 30307
Tel 404 373-0995 *Fax* 404 373-3827 *Email* singley@mindspring.com
Business hours Monday–Friday 9–5
Established 1990

KATHERINE SINGLEY, Principal
1983–present Self-employed conservator, establishing Conservation
Anthropologica in 1990
1977–83 Conservator, Institute of Archaeology and Anthropology,
University of South Carolina, Columbia, SC
1977 B.Sc. Conservation of Archaeological Materials, Institute of
Archaeology, University of London
1973 A.B. Classical and Near Eastern Archaeology, Bryn Mawr College,
Bryn Mawr, PA

One conservator

Services Conservation of archaeological, ethnographic, and historic objects,
with a specialization in waterlogged organic materials. Treatments, object surveys, exhibition advice, object storage, storage advice, written documentation, photo documentation, emergency response, freeze-drying.

Facilities Fully insured and alarmed, the 1000 square foot laboratory contains a binocular microscope, taxidermy freeze-drier, freezer, heated ultrasonic tanks, electrolytic reduction equipment, HEPA vacuum, nebulizer, air-
brasive unit, and pneumatic airscribe pen.

The laboratory largely serves universities, state agencies, historic houses, and
private collectors in the Southeast. With fifteen years of experience in freeze-
drying waterlogged organics, Ms. Singley is also available for disaster response
and insurance consultation. Member of AIC, IIC, United Kingdom Institute
for Conservation, Society for the Preservation of Natural History Collections,
as well as the Southeastern Museums Conference, the Society for Historical
Archaeology, and ICOM's working group on waterlogged organics.

CONSERVATION OF ART ON PAPER, INC.
2805 Mount Vernon Avenue, Alexandria, VA 22301
Tel 703 836-7757 *Email* consartpap@earthlink.net
Business hours Monday–Friday 10–6 by appointment
Established 1984

CHRISTINE SMITH, President
After receiving an M.Sc. from the Winterthur/University of Delaware Program in Art Conservation (1978), Ms. Smith served as Paper Conservator at the Smithsonian Institution's Conservation Analytical Laboratory (1978–80) and National Portrait Gallery (1980–84). She founded Conservation of Art on Paper, Inc. (CAPI) in 1984, where she serves as President and Chief Conservator. Her continuing education ranges from treatment of traditional Japanese prints to microscopy. She is a Fellow of AIC, an active member of both U.S. and international professional organizations, and writes and lectures professionally. She earned an A.B. in art history from Vassar College (1972) and served as Technical Assistant to the Curator of Prints and Drawings at the Cleveland Museum of Art (1972–75). Recent treatments include drawings, paintings, and prints by L. Bourgeois, G. Braque, A. Giacometti, E. Munch, P. Picasso, J.S. Sargent, and J.A.M. Whistler as well as collections of Japanese ukiyoe and American fraktur.

Services Treatment of fine art on paper, including ukiyoe, and rare manuscripts. Surveys, exhibition and storage consultations, written and photo documentation, research and writing, lectures and seminars, prepurchase consultations, vault storage, expert witness, publications, and supplies for collectors.

Facilities 1,700 square feet dedicated to paper conservation in a secure professional building twenty minutes from downtown Washington, DC. CAPI has areas for treatment, analysis, photography, research, client conferences, and documentation. All objects are stored in a room-size vault, there is a centralized security system, and insurance coverage is available. Parking lot, loading dock, freight elevator.

CAPI is a full-service paper conservation center providing the highest quality work for a world-wide clientele of institutions and individual collectors. In a field without licensing or standardized education, the quality of conservators' training and experience is critical: at CAPI objects are treated only by professionals with graduate degrees in art conservation. Thorough examination and testing precede written proposals and cost estimates, and all treatments comply with AIC's Code of Ethics and Guidelines for Practice. We are happy to provide a tour of our facility and give professional references.

CONSERVATION SOLUTIONS, INC.
503 C Street NE, Washington, DC 20002
Tel 202 544-3257 *Fax* 202 544-3229 *Email* info@conservationsolution.com
Website www.conservationsolution.com
Business hours Monday–Friday 7–5
Established 1999

JOSEPH SEMBRAT, President & Senior Conservator, Professional Associate, AIC
In 1999, as a conservator and passionate advocate for historic preservation, Joe
Sembrat founded a unique conservation firm designed to serve the expanding
needs of the historic preservation field. Sembrat has been immersed in the conservation field for eleven years, achieving his Professional Associate status in AIC
in 1996. He has worked on a wide range of historic structures, monuments,
sculpture, and industrial artifacts, from the "Big Piece" recovered wreckage from
the RMS Titanic to the colossal carrara marble Barnard Statuary Groups at the
Pennsylvania State Capitol. Not only is Sembrat passionate about testing, design, and implementation of conservation treatments, but he is equally enthu-
siastic about research and writing. He has written and lectured internationally
on various conservation topics, including his research on reliable methods for
the application and monitoring of protective barrier coatings for outdoor monuments which introduced a new treatment method to the field. He has also published many articles in *Traditional Building,* such as "Planning, Performing, and
Managing the Conservation of Outdoor Monuments," which serves as a guide
for property owners on how to successfully work with a conservator.

Education
1993 M.Sc. Historic Preservation. Research and Thesis: *The Conservation of
    Outdoor Bronze Statuary,* Columbia University, New York, NY
1990 B.A. Art History, University of Pennsylvania, Philadelphia, PA
1990 Art History Studies, University College, London

JULYA SEMBRAT, Vice President & General Manager
Julya Sembrat is co-founder of Conservation Solutions, Inc. and oversees the
general management of CSI including finance, sales & marketing, human
resources, and administration. She has provided leadership and strategic planning resulting in a 400% increase in the company's sales from the first year
of incorporation to the third year. Additionally, she increased the visibility
of the company through sales and marketing efforts while achieving organizational and financial stability resulting in the hiring of ten additional full-
time employees and ten seasonal employees.

$\rightarrow$

Education
1995 M.A. Arts Management, Columbia College, Chicago, IL
1992–93 Graduate Fellow, Graduate Studies in Arts Management Program,
    Brooklyn College, Brooklyn, NY
1991 B.A. Theatre, Ohio University, Athens, OH

MARK RABINOWITZ, Vice President & Senior Conservator, Professional
    Associate, AIC
Mark Rabinowitz, former President of Conservation and Sculpture Company
in Brooklyn, NY, initiated and directed the Central Park Conservancy monuments conservation and historic preservation programs, since 1991 focusing his
efforts exclusively on the treatment and management of outdoor monuments.
The Central Park programs and others he founded at the City Parks Foundation and Hispanic Society of America received numerous awards and successfully treated nearly 200 significant outdoor sculptures in New York City. Rabinowitz and Sembrat have been colleagues over the past ten years and in July
2003, Rabinowitz joined Conservation Solutions, Inc. as a partner.

Education
1975 B.A. Sculpture, Rhode Island School of Design, Providence, RI
1971–72 Tyler School of Art, Elkins Park, PA

ROBIN GERSTAD, Conservator, Professional Associate, AIC
Robin Gerstad relocated from New York to join Conservation Solutions, Inc.
in August of 2003. Gerstad brings her varied experience in architectural and
sculpture conservation from Ehrenkrantz, Eckstut & Kuhn Architects, Conservation and Sculpture Company, and the City Parks Foundation Monuments Conservation Program, where her primary project was the restoration
of the Washington Square Arch. Her expertise includes condition assessment
reports and specifications, treatment reports, and historic documentation, as
well as hands-on conservation skills, such as corrosion removal, patination,
coating application and removal, and masonry patching and pointing. Gerstad's talents extend to managing projects, programs, and people. Her professional affiliations include the Association for Preservation Technology (APT),
Preservation Alumni (Columbia University), National Trust for Historic Preservation, and Society for Industrial Archeology.

Education
1998 M.S. in Historic Preservation from the Graduate School of
    Architecture, Planning, and Preservation, Columbia University, New
    York, NY. Research and Thesis: *Petrographic Analysis of Historic Mortars*
    →

1988 B.A. Latin American Studies, New York University, NY
1983 The Brearley School, New York, NY

PATTY MILLER, Conservator, Professional Associate, AIC
Prior to joining Conservation Solutions, Inc. in 2003, Miller was senior staff conservator at Jablonski Berkowitz Conservation where she performed assessments of numerous eighteenth through twentieth century structures and laboratory analysis for a variety of historic materials including masonry, mortar, plaster, decorative finishes and metals. Noteworthy projects completed include a condition assessment of three thirteenth-century early French Gothic limestone windows installed at The Cloisters, Metropolitan Museum of Art, New York; an investigation into decorative plaster ceiling failure in the City Council Chamber, City Hall, New York; and an historic materials investigation for the Matthew Persen House in Kingston, NY, a pre-Revolutionary Dutch stone house that was built in five phases over a 300 year period. Her investigation included period wallpaper research and interior and exterior finishes analysis to assist in the authentication of construction materials. Miller came to the field of architectural conservation from a background in fine arts and five years experience as an outdoor sculpture conservation technician at the Chicago Parks District and at Conservation Technical Associates, LLC, in Connecticut.

Education
2000 M.S. Historic Preservation. Research and Thesis: *An Analysis of Plastic Media for the Air Abrasive Cleaning of Marble*, Columbia University, New York, NY
1993 B.F.A. Sculpture & Art History, School of the Art Institute of Chicago, Chicago, IL
1992 Semester Abroad: Glasgow School of Art, Glasgow, Scotland

Four conservators
Eight technicians
Five office staff

Services Conservation of Historic structures, monuments and sculptures, industrial artifacts, decorative metals, and fountains. Treatments, object surveys, pigment analysis, object storage, shipping advice, packing/shipping, written documentation, photo documentation, lectures, emergency response.

Facilities Conservation Solutions, Inc. (CSI) has its corporate office ideally situated on Capitol Hill and within walking distance from Union Station. In close proximity to the office is the 4,000 square foot conservation studio of

→

CSI, which is located at 2100 Oakwood Lane in District Heights, MD. The secure facility is suitable for the conservation of large-scale sculptures, monuments, and industrial artifacts, and includes a testing laboratory for mortar and finishes analysis. It is 1.5 miles from the Washington, DC beltway, one hour driving distance to Baltimore and Annapolis, MD, and two hours driving distance to Richmond, VA. The facility is suitable for the conservation of large-scale sculptures, monuments, and industrial artifacts. The studio is housed in a masonry structure that has two loading docks, ten ton and two ton overhead cranes, sixteen foot high ceilings, a 400 square foot secured, outdoor workspace, and an 800 square foot lab/office space. The facility is also equipped with a variety of equipment and tools that make it well suited for the conservation of various kinds of metal, stone, wood, and terra-cotta artifacts.

Established in July 1999, Conservation Solutions Inc. is a unique firm, tightly focused on delivering innovative answers to the expanding needs of the fields of conservation and historic preservation. We blend extensive expertise in the hands-on treatment of historic structures, monuments and sculptures, industrial artifacts, decorative metals, and fountains with a thorough scientific understanding of the materials of their construction and the often complex interactions that lead to their deterioration. Our staff includes experts in analysis, planning, treatment, and documentation of a wide variety of materials including terra-cotta, stone, metals, wood, concrete, and modern synthetics. Our flexible organizational structure allows us to apply our staff expertise and skills within a network of world-renowned specialists. Project teams are assembled according to the client's specific needs, guaranteeing that the highest and most current standards of care are delivered in a timely and cost-effective manner.

The broad range of our projects, which have included artifacts recovered from the RMS Titanic wreck site, an 1851 lighthouse on an isolated island off the coast of New Hampshire, the Johnson Space Center Saturn V rocket, a 1711 English wrought iron gate from New York State, a 1911 Arkansas cotton gin, the Confederate Monument in Montgomery, AL, and the Barnard Statuary Groups at the State Capital of Pennsylvania, demonstrates the diversity of projects we encounter. Our growing client list includes governmental agencies, museums, and important institutions, all of which attest to the success we have had in treating this wide variety of objects and structures. Conservation Solutions, Inc. provides the following services: assessment, testing and analysis, treatment design including the development of contract documents, all phases of implementation, project management, documentation, and training. Depending on the client's needs we can perform any or all of the steps towards achieving their conservation goals.

ANN CREAGER
65 I Street SW, Washington, DC 20024
Tel 301 238-2008, *Home* 202 543-1733, *Studio* 202 898-1309 (weekends)
Email creagera@saam.si.edu
Business hours By appointment
Established 1973

ANN CREAGER, Conservator of Paintings
Is presently conservator of paintings at the Smithsonian American Art Museum
and has been since 1977. She apprenticed (1973–77) in paintings conservation
with the conservator who began the conservation labs at the Smithsonian Institution. She has an A.A. and a B.A. (1965) in Art History and Fine Arts. Since
1978 has maintained a private practice providing conservation work to museums, historical societies and houses, embassies, private galleries, and institutions.
Her clients have included the Ohio and New York Historical Societies, Dallas
Museum of Art, South Carolina Senate, Blair House, Belmont, Georgetown
University, Montgomery Museum of Fine Arts, Lauren Rogers Museum, the
Cosmos Club, and private collectors. She is available on a part-time basis.

Services Conservation of oil paintings on canvas and panel. Treatments, exhibition advice, storage advice, shipping advice, written documentation,
UV/IR photography, lectures.

Facilities Dedicated, well-equipped studio space located in downtown Washington with centrally monitored security/alarm system. Equipment includes
binocular microscope, vacuum hot table, 35 mm camera, ultraviolet light
stands, enclosed separate storage area within studio space. Insurance coverage for objects on premises.

Ann Creager provides complete conservation services, including examination, full written and photographic documentation, and treatment, for paintings on canvas and panel. All work is done by Ann Creager, and treatments
are carried out with sensitivity to the painting using appropriate materials
and methods. Her twenty-seven years in conservation have provided significant experience in the treatment of both American and European paintings.
Her special expertise includes nineteenth-century American portraits, such
as works by Gilbert Stuart, Thomas Sully, and the Peale family, as well as
Hudson River paintings by Thomas Cole, Thomas Moran, and Albert Bier-
stadt. She has also had significant experience on twentieth-century American paintings. She has published and lectured in this country and abroad.
She holds Fellow status in AIC and is a Director of WCG.

Creative Metalworks, Michael Schwartz

10501 Wheatley Street, Kensington, MD 20895
Tel 301 933-1500 *Fax* 301 933-9070 *Email* ms@creativemetalworks.com
Website www.creativemetalworks.com
Business hours Monday–Friday 9–6 and by appointment
Established 1978

Michael R. Schwartz, Conservator
Thirty years of professional experience as a metalsmith, gemologist, conservator, and educator in the metals field. Owner of Creative Metalworks®, a precious metals conservation and design studio specializing in large precious and nonferrous metals conservation and restoration services as well as original presentation art. Born and raised in the Washington metropolitan area, Mr. Schwartz resides in Montgomery County with his wife and son. Mr. Schwartz earned his Bachelor of Science degree in 1978, concentrating in jewelry fabrication and casting, and received his Master of Education degree in 1982 from the University of Maryland.

One conservator
One intern
Two technicians
Two office staff

Services Creative Metalworks offers conservation and restoration services specializing in large precious metal, gilded, and nonferrous metal decorative art objects. Objects are kept in high security safes and can be fully insured. Treatments, object surveys, exhibition advice, object storage, storage advice, shipping advice, packing and shipping, written documentation, photo documentation. In addition to metals conservation work for the museum industry, Creative Metalworks designs and manufactures presentation art objects in precious metals that can be seen on our website.

Facilities Creative Metalworks is located on the corner of Metropolitan Avenue and Wheatley Street in the heart of historic Kensington, MD. The 7,200 square foot building has been totally renovated to house the company. The facilities include a complete machine shop, smithing studio, foundry, design studio, photography studio, and showroom/gallery.

→

Clients include: the White House, Blair House, Freer Gallery of Art, the American Legislative Exchange Council, the Asia Society, the National Council on U.S.-Arab Relations, the American College of Cardiology, the American Farmland Trust, the Catholic University of America, Columbia Union College, U.S. Department of Agriculture, the Embassy of Oman, the United States Holocaust Memorial Museum, the Embassy of Greece, Intergem Corporation, the National Center for Education and the Economy, National Biomedical Research Foundation, Ottenberg Bakery, the National Parks Association, the Postal Museum, the Salvation Army, the U.S. Supreme Court, Temple Micah, the National Cathedral, Basilica of the National Shrine of the Immaculate Conception, National Air & Space Museum, World Wildlife Fund, Partners for Livable Places, the Business-Higher Education Forum, Bowie State University, the University of Maryland, Clark Atlanta University, Chase Manhattan Bank, the International Electrical and Electronics Engineers Society, and numerous other foundations, corporations, associations, and individuals.

References and portfolio available upon request.

Accepts interns.

KATHERINE G. EIRK/CONSERVATION SERVICES

5523 Oak Place, Bethesda, MD 20817
Tel 301 571-9764
Business hours By appointment
Established 1985

KATHERINE G. EIRK, Conservator

Katherine G. Eirk has been a practicing conservator since 1970. She holds a Master's degree from The George Washington University in Museology (1972). The first fifteen years of her career were spent as a conservator at the Smithsonian Institution, where she treated works of art on paper, objects, and portrait miniatures. Since establishing her private practice in 1985, Ms. Eirk has surveyed and treated works of art on paper on a contract basis for the Corcoran Gallery of Art, and portrait miniatures and small composite objects incorporating cellulosic materials on a private basis. She has taught, supervised interns, and mentored numerous now-prominent conservators. Particular interests are eighteenth-century American portrait miniatures and the works of Joseph Cornell.

Services Conservation of portrait miniatures and composite objects. Treatments, object surveys, exhibition advice, storage advice, written documentation, photo documentation, lectures.

Facilities Exclusive use home space with central security and fire alarm system, and climate control.

All work is performed by Katherine Eirk. She focuses on the history of objects in her care in addition to their treatment. Her collection of through-the-microscope slide details of portrait miniatures facilitates comparisons and often aids in forming attribution possibilities. She has served numerous private collectors as well as institutional clients such as the Corcoran Gallery, the Metropolitan Museum of Art, the Yale University Art Gallery and Center for British Art, and Historic Hudson Valley. She has written about and lectured on paper and miniature conservation and care as well as the technical examination of American portrait miniatures.

LIZOU FENYVESI
16501 Comus Road, Dickerson, MD 20842
Tel 301 972-8974 *Fax* 301 349-5558 *Email* lfenyvesi@aol.com
Business hours By appointment
Established 1991

LIZOU FENYVESI, Conservator
1997–present Textile Conservator at the United States Holocaust
    Memorial Museum
1992–96 Consultant at the Textile Museum and at the United States
    Holocaust Memorial Museum
1989–91 Textile Museum, Washington, DC
1983–84 Consultant at the Smithsonian Institution

Education
1991 University of Alberta, Canada (Andean Textiles)
1989 National Center for Museums, Budapest, Hungary (Chemical
    background of textile conservation)
1985–86 University of Maryland (Degradation of fibers; textile
    conservation)
1967–70 Graduate courses at The George Washington University,
    Washington, DC
1965 Teaching certificate from Paris, France
1962 B.A. in Theater from Budapest, Hungary
Also studied weaving, lace making, embroidery, Navajo weaving, and other
    textile techniques in the 1970s and 80s.

Services Conservation of textiles, ethnographic textiles, Judaica, costumes.
Treatments, object surveys, environmental surveys, exhibition advice, storage advice, shipping advice, written documentation, photo documentation, fiber analysis, lectures, and identification and/or authentication of some types of textiles.

Facilities Dedicated laboratory/studio space in my home, equipped for examination, documentation, and treatment of textile artifacts.

FULTON FRAMING SERVICES

516 C Street NE, Washington, DC 20002
Tel 202 544-8408 *Fax* 202 544-8410 *Email* ffs@fultonframing.com
Website www.fultonframing.com
Business hours Monday–Tuesday 12–6, Wednesday–Saturday 10–6, other
   hours by appointment
Established 1989

Laura Neal began her first framing job in 1984 and created Fulton Framing
Services in 1989. She began working at the National Gallery of Art as a contractor in matting and framing in 1995 and continues to work there in that
capacity. Greg DeFelice began framing in 1986 and began working for Fulton Framing Services in 1995.

Services We handle all types of objects including works on paper, paintings
on board or canvas, textiles, photographs, memorabilia, and more...

Facilities We are located on two floors of a small building on Stanton Park
on Capitol Hill.

We are a small shop that specializes in the preservation of art, documents,
and objects by providing:
   Appropriate matting and framing
   Archival storage packages
   Referrals to conservators

We have relationships with many conservators and institutions and strive to
provide, for a range of customer requirements, many of the techniques and
materials in use in museums, galleries, and archives.

CORNELIA STEWART GILL CONSERVATION
1191 Crest Lane, McLean, VA 22101
Tel 703 522-4328
Business hours By appointment
Established 1975

CORNELIA GILL, Conservator
Attended Smith College, Pre-Med, from 1953–54. Graduated from the Corcoran School of Art in 1975, apprenticing with Robert Scott Wiles in the conservation studio at the Corcoran Gallery for five years. Also apprenticed with the late Peter Michaels in Baltimore for three and a half years. Completed Richard Wolbers' course on the cleaning of paintings at the University of Delaware. Part of the team treating the ceiling mural of the Salon Doré at the Corcoran Gallery. Clients include government institutions, small historical societies, commercial galleries, and private individuals. Available part-time.

Services Conservation of oil paintings on canvas, board, or panel through the first half of the twentieth century. Minor touch-up of frames. Treatments, written documentation, photo documentation, condition surveys.

Facilities Dedicated studio space in my home with climate control and a central security/fire alarm system. Fine art insurance for paintings on premises and in transit with me.

All work is done by Cornelia Gill, who seeks to preserve the original intent of the artist while conserving the painting for future generations. She especially enjoys working on family portraits and has worked on many by prominent American artists. Other experience includes icons, religious subjects, still lifes, and land/seascapes. She is willing to "make house calls" if the owner needs assistance in transporting reasonably sized works.

GOLD LEAF STUDIOS

Rear 1523 22nd Street NW, Washington, DC 20037
Tel 202 833-2440 *Fax* 202 833-2452 *Email* gls@goldleafstudios.com
Website www.goldleafstudios.com
Business hours Monday–Friday 8:30–5:30
Established 1982

WILLIAM ADAIR, Conservator and Principal
Holds a B.F.A from the University of Maryland. He began his career as a
frame conservator with the National Portrait Gallery. He studied frame history and gilding techniques in England and Italy and is a recipient of the
Rome Prize in Design/Arts. He curated and wrote the catalogue for the exhibition, "The Frame in America 1700–1900," at the American Institute of
Architects. In 1982 he formed his own company, Gold Leaf Studios, to specialize in the conservation and restoration of gilded antique picture frames,
furniture, and decorative objects. The studio has offered gilding and frame-
related services to private collectors, museums, and designers for over twenty
years. Clients have included the White House and the Department of State.
Mr. Adair continues to write and lecture widely on frame history, forming
the International Institute for Frame Study as a public archive in 1992.

Six conservators. Three office staff

Services Conservation of frames, gilded furniture, architectural ornament on
ceilings, domes, columns, statuary. Treatments, object surveys, exhibition advice, matting/framing, packing/shipping, written documentation, photo documentation, emergency response, curatorial consultation.

Facilities Historic carriage house located two blocks west of Dupont Circle
with ample spaces for studio, exhibition rooms, and offices. Central secu-
rity/fire alarm system. Full insurance coverage for objects on premises.
Gold Leaf Studios uses traditional techniques to conserve and restore frames
and other gilded objects. Skilled craftsmen reproduce wood and composition antique frames, as well as create new designs and contemporary styles
complementary to the art they will surround. The gilding team accepts a wide
variety of projects involving the gilding of architectural ornamentation on
ceilings, domes, columns, statuary, and lettering. Museum standards of mat-

→

ting and mounting protect and enhance artwork done on paper; special treatments include archival hinging, French mats, wrapped silk mats, gilded bevels, and églomisé.

Antique frames are available for sale or reproduction. The collection of period frames, reproductions, and custom contemporary frame designs are displayed throughout the Studios. Consulting services are supported by comprehensive reports including a wide range of photographic and digital documentation. Gold Leaf Studios also sells various limited edition and out-of-print publications on the history of picture frames and gilding techniques.

Accepts interns.

Graham Conservation
Radcliffe Lane, Glen Echo, MD 20812
Tel 301 320-7719 *Fax* 301 320-7719 *Email* GrahamCon@aol.com
Established 1983

Alec Graham
Educated and trained in the United States and Europe, Alec has twenty-five years of experience as a furniture conservator. He was a furniture and wooden objects conservator at the Museum of Fine Arts, Boston, and the Charleston Museum in South Carolina before establishing Graham Conservation in 1983.

Services Conservation of furniture and wooden objects. Treatments, object surveys, exhibition advice, storage advice, shipping advice, written documentation, photo documentation, lectures.

Facilities Dedicated secure studio space.

Graham Conservation specializes in the preservation and restoration of furniture and wooden objects, serving museums and individual collectors.

Nick Greer, Antiques Conservator
37627 Allder School Road, Purcellville, VA 20132
Tel 540-338-6607 *Fax* 540-338-6604 *Email* greersant@aol.com
Business hours Monday–Friday 9–5 and Saturday by appointment
Established 1974

Nick Greer
Nick Greer learned the trade through his grandfather who was an experienced woodworker specializing in sculpture, relief carving, and French polish finishes.

Fifteen conservators
One office staff

Services Antique conservation of furniture including repair, rebuilding, restoration of original finishes, French polishing, marquetry, and upholstery. Custom furniture design and reproductions.

Facilities Work performed in restored barns on Nick Greer's property in rural Loudoun County, Virginia.

A majority of our employees have B.A.s or Master's degrees in various fields and have been trained in antiques conservation by Nick Greer over the past 30 years. Our average employee has approximately 10 years of experience in antiques conservation. Our clients include museums, decorators, dealers, and private collectors.

Accepts interns.

ROBERTA DOLORES GREGOR PAINTING CONSERVATION

1413 Audmar Drive, McLean, VA 22101
Tel 703 288-0088 *Email* r.d.gregor@att.net
Business hours By appointment
Established 1982

ROBERTA DOLORES GREGOR, Conservator
Apprenticed with Charles H. Olin of Great Falls, VA, in 1979. Course work in art history and gallery management at Northern Virginia Community College. Apprenticed with C. Gregory Stapko of McLean, VA, from 1982–84, studying conservation, old master techniques, and old master copies. Seminar with WCG in 2000. Projects of note: Assisted C. Gregory Stapko with a copy of Benjamin West's *John Wilmont and the Federal Land Grants*, commissioned by Paul Mellon. Also assisted Stapko with copies of Gilbert Stuart's paintings of George and Martha Washington owned by Fred Bradlee of New York, commissioned by Sally Quinn and Ben Bradlee. Sole conservator for restoration of murals in the National Academy of Sciences building in 1990. Applied gold leaf to all the doors and their trim in the U.S. Capitol's House of Representatives' chambers in 2000. Clients are from government, non-profit, commercial, diplomatic, and private sectors. Professional affiliations: Member AIC, WCG.

One conservator

Services Conservation of easel paintings, paintings on panels, painted wooden objects, murals in situ, gilded frames and objects, enamels, and plique-à-jour. Treatments, object surveys, exhibition advice, storage advice, written documentation, photo documentation.

Facilities Dedicated studio space with climate control, central security system, and dead bolt locks. Access to 4 x 6 foot and 6 x 8 foot vacuum heat tables.

All work is done by Roberta Dolores Gregor, who always seeks to preserve the beauty and integrity of the object and to retain the artists' original intentions. She uses the minimal treatment necessary to maintain the art object. She feels strongly that original intent should not be altered, only assistance given to offset the damage of time.

KRUEGER ART CONSERVATION

621 Beverley Drive, Alexandria, VA 22305
Tel 703 684-9325 *Email* petekrueger@starpower.net
Business hours By appointment
Established 1992

JAY KRUEGER, Conservator of Modern and Contemporary Paintings
1992–present Senior Conservator of Modern Paintings, National Gallery
   of Art
1984–92 Conservator of Modern and Contemporary Paintings, Perry
   Huston and Associates, Fort Worth
1983–84 Conservator, Kimbell Art Museum
1982–83 Conservator, San Francisco Museum of Modern Art
1982 State University of New York, Cooperstown Graduate Program, M.A.
   with a Certificate of Advanced Study in Painting Conservation
1981–82 Internship, San Francisco Museum of Modern Art
1978 Washington University, St. Louis, B.A. in Art History
1978 B.F.A. in Printmaking
Fellow, AIC; recent past President, AIC; Board of Directors, Heritage
   Preservation

HOLLY KRUEGER, Paper Conservator
1992–present Senior Conservator, Library of Congress
1992–present Consulting Conservator, Amon Carter Museum, Fort Worth
1983–92 Senior Conservator, Amon Carter Museum
1983–92 Senior Paper Conservator, Perry Huston and Associates
1982–83 Paper Conservator, Fine Arts Museums of San Francisco
1982 State University of New York, Cooperstown Graduate Program, M.A.
   with a Certificate of Advanced Study in Paper Conservation
1981–82 Internship, San Francisco Museum of Modern Art
1978 University of Texas, Austin, B.Sc. in Biochemistry
Fellow, AIC

Services Conservation of works of art on paper, and modern and contemporary paintings. Treatments, object surveys, exhibition advice, storage advice, shipping advice, written documentation, photo documentation.

→

Facilities 800 square foot dedicated space in a safe, quiet residential setting. Separate entrance, 24-hour monitored security system and hardwired smoke alarms, extinguishers. Insurance coverage is available.

Private practice was established in 1992, and incorporated as an Limited Liability Company in 1999. Two senior-level conservators, working on a contract basis for select clientele including museums, galleries, and individuals. Specialized emphasis on the treatment of works of art on paper, and modern and contemporary paintings and painted sculpture. Both conservators have extensive research and treatment experience in their respective fields and have lectured and published in various professional forums. The treatment of unprimed canvases favored by the Washington Color School painters (Morris Louis, Kenneth Noland, Gene Davis, Tom Downing, Leon Berkowitz, Howard Mehring, etc.) has been a focus of our practice for several years. All treatments are executed with great care and high professional standards, using quality materials and currently accepted practices. Work is documented with photographs and written reports and is carried out in accordance with the AIC's Code of Ethics and Guidelines for Practice.

ANDREI N. KUZNETSOV PAINTING CONSERVATION
239 12th Place NE, Washington, DC 20002
Cell 202 257-0969
Business hours By appointment
Established 1994

ANDREI KUZNETSOV, Conservator
Mr. Kuznetsov graduated from the prestigious Serov Art Institute, St. Petersburg, Russia, in 1984. He obtained a degree in conservation, with specialization in restoration techniques. He was certified by the State Committee as Restoration Expert/Artist in April 1984. From 1986 to 1992, Mr. Kuznetsov was a member of the St. Petersburg City Administration Council. During his tenure, he restored frescoes, murals, plafonds (ceilings), and paintings at the Sts. Peter and Paul Cathedral, the Palace of Grand Duke Vladimir Romanov, the Palace of the Grand Duke Baryatinksy, and other historic collections.

Services Conservation of murals, icons, and paintings on canvas and panel. Treatments, condition surveys, and photographic documentation.

Facilities Dedicated studio space on Capitol Hill.

Andrei Kuznetsov has twenty years of experience in painting conservation. His extensive European education in conservation and restoration makes him uniquely qualified for first-rate, museum-quality restoration. Under the tutelage of professors of restoration from the Hermitage, Andrei Kuznetsov follows the traditional European process, using only natural ingredients and materials and respecting the integrity of the original. He specializes in treatment of European paintings, with a growing familiarity with American and Asian pieces. His clients include auction houses, private galleries, and private collectors.

WILLIAM A. LEWIN, CONSERVATOR LLC

1637 E. Baltimore Street, Baltimore, MD 21231-1510
Tel 410 675-2764 *Fax* 410 675-5605 *Email* wlewin@erols.com
Business hours By appointment
Established 1989

WILLIAM A. LEWIN, Conservator
Seventeen years of experience treating gilded frames and furniture. Apprentice trained for three years, working on American and European gilt frames and furniture for museums and private collections. Enhanced education through lectures and scholastic training. Participant in Jonathan Thornton's workshop, "The Conservation of Picture Frames" at the Intermuseum Conservation Association, Oberlin, OH. Attended the two-year lecture series on furniture conservation at CAL. Interned at CAL and designed an innovative treatment for an eighteenth-century japanned tall case clock. Contract conservator and co-author of a paper on the treatment. Selected as a participant in AIC's *Furniture in France II* study tour. Recently completed onsite treatment of pier mirror frames at Monticello purchased by Thomas Jefferson and a survey of frames in collection of the Barnes Foundation. Emergency disaster consultant to the U.S. Treasury; surveyed period frames and furniture after a building fire. Served on the Board of Directors of WCG. Professional Associate AIC. Clients include museums, public institutions, historic houses, and private individuals.

DAVIDA KOVNER, Conservator
Graduated from Earlham College with a degree in Art-Psychology. Former ceramic artist and professor at Goucher College for twelve years. Taught sculpture, color theory, design, drawing, and ceramics. Apprenticed for five years with Mr. Lewin and trained for two years with an objects conservator concentrating in ceramics. Course work in chemistry. Knowledgeable and skilled in traditional craftsman skills and the latest techniques of wooden and gilt object conservation. Continues her education by attending lectures on current topics in the field of conservation. Past board member and officer of WCG.

One laboratory technician

→

Services Conservation of wooden objects: frames, furniture, decorative art objects, and architectural ornamentation. Treatments, object surveys, exhibition advice, storage advice, written documentation, photo documentation, UV/IR photography, x-ray analysis, cross section analysis of coatings, lectures, emergency response. Fabrication of reproduction period frames.

Facilities Commercial building with monitored security/fire alarm and climate-controlled environment; oversized exterior doors accommodate large objects; treatment lab with microscopes; 35 mm and digital cameras for documentation; separate lab for coating analysis with UV microscope and digital camera with computer interface; and fully equipped woodworking studio. Fine arts insurance for objects on premises.

William Lewin oversees a small, highly trained staff and is involved in the treatment of each object. Mr. Lewin has particular expertise in the identification and recovery of original gilt surfaces obscured by layers of restoration coatings. Each treatment is designed for the individual object, in consultation with the owner, to preserve all original materials using the latest reversible techniques. Objects treated include gilt frames and mirrors, carved furniture, wall sconces, clocks, and architectural ornamentation. Mr. Lewin has worked on the collections of the White House, U.S. Capitol, Walters Art Museum, Baltimore Museum of Art, the Freer Gallery of Art, and Monticello.

NORA LOCKSHIN
Baltimore, MD
Tel 410 340-1630 *Email* noralockshin@mindspring.com
Business hours By appointment
Established 1998

NORA LOCKSHIN, Book and Paper Conservator
Nora Lockshin is a conservator with more than ten years experience in major cultural institutions including libraries, museums and archives, and working with many individual clients on their private collections. She has experience in conservation treatment and preservation management of photographic, architectural, and research archives as well as traditional library collections. Employers have included: the Metropolitan Museum of Art, New York, NY; Preservation Department, General Libraries and the Alexander Architectural Archive, University of Texas at Austin; the Harry Ransom Humanities Research Center of the University of Texas at Austin; the American Museum of Natural History, New York, NY; and the Smithsonian Institution. Ms. Lockshin holds an M.S.L.I.S. from the University of Texas at Austin Preservation and Conservation Studies program, and is a graduate of the Rhode Island School of Design. Her professional practice of conservation includes active participation in AIC, WCG, and the Guild of Book Workers, and adherence to the Code of Ethics and Guidelines for Practice of AIC.

One conservator

Services Conservation of rare book and paper objects, including manuscript and printed works, maps, works on paper, private press books, and artists' books from library, archive and private collections. Treatments, pigment analysis, fiber analysis, object surveys, environmental surveys, exhibition advice, storage advice, matting/framing, shipping advice, packing/shipping, written documentation, photo documentation, lectures, UV/IR photography. Consultation on design, fabrication and production of facsimile editions, and custom design for original book projects.

Facilities Dedicated space in secured private residence.

Background and skills include historical research as pertains to provenance and fabrication of rare book and paper materials; extensive knowledge in historical and modern art techniques, especially livres d'artiste, private press, hand press, hand papermaking, and printmaking; and knowledge and experience in reformatting techniques such as digital and analog facsimile reproduction. She has also collaborated with artists and private individuals on custom design bindings.

Catherine E. Magee

26 14th Street NE, Washington, DC 20002
Tel 202 544-3833 *Email* catherinemagee@hotmail.com
Business hours Monday–Friday 9–6
Established 1999

Catherine Magee, Conservator

February 2000–present Exhibits and Loan Conservator, National Museum of Natural History. Prepares condition assessment and treatments for objects for loan and display. Ensures appropriate packing, transport, and display conditions for objects made from a wide variety of materials.

June 1999–present Private Practice Conservator. Assessments, treatments, and consultations

November 1997–June 1999 Conservator, Maryland Archaeological Conservation Laboratory. Maintained the daily operation of a lab specializing in the treatment of terrestrial and underwater archaeological materials. Supervised staff and interns and developed and implemented professional procedures.

September 1995–November 1997 Conservation Intern, Smithsonian Center for Materials Research and Education. Worked as a conservator on-site on archaeological excavations and supervised local staff and interns. Conducted materials research.

1992–95 Winterthur/University of Delaware Program in Art Conservation, M.Sc. in Object Conservation

1990–92 Conservation Technician, Indiana University Art Museum. Studied art history, ancient jewelry technology, and infrared reflectography.

1989–90 Conservation Apprentice, Cincinnati Art Museum. Studied organic chemistry.

1984–88 Colorado College, B.A. in Studio Art; sculpture, drawing and photography emphases. Minor in Anthropology

Services Conservation of archaeological, decorative arts, ethnographic, and historic objects. Treatments, object surveys, environmental surveys, exhibition, storage advice, shipping and packing consultation, written documentation, photo documentation, x-ray analysis, object storage, lectures.

Facilities Secure workspace dedicated to treatment of objects within home.

Specialize in the conservation, preservation, and restoration of a wide variety of objects and materials including ceramics, metal, glass, wood, leather, basketry, and bone. The work is conducted in my studio, at institutions, or on-site on archaeological excavations depending on the needs of the object or collections.

ALBERT MARSHALL CONSERVATION, LLC

3706 Livingston Street NW, Washington, DC 20015
Tel 202 276-4710 *Fax* 202 244-8295 *Email* albertmarshall@att.net
Business hours By appointment
Established 2000

ALBERT MARSHALL, Conservator
2000–present Private practice conservator, Albert Marshall Conservation, LLC
1993–2000 Director of Conservation, Hillwood Museum
1988–1993 Intern, Mellon Fellow, Contract Conservator, National Gallery of Art
1989 M.Sc., Object Conservation, Winterthur Museum/University of Delaware Program in Art Conservation
1975 A.B. Studio Art, Kenyon College

One conservator

Services Conservation of modern and contemporary sculpture. Treatments, object surveys, exhibition advice, storage advice, shipping advice, written documentation.

Facilities 250 square foot secure studio for small works and ability to rent secure climate-controlled space for larger works.

MARYLAND ARCHAEOLOGICAL CONSERVATION LABORATORY

Jefferson Patterson Park & Museum

10515 Mackall Road, St. Leonard, MD 20685

Tel 410 586-8578 *Fax* 410 586-3643 *Email* seifert@dhcd.state.md.us

Website www.jefpat.org

Business hours Monday–Friday 9–5

Established 1996

BETTY L. SEIFERT, Deputy Chief and Chief Conservator

B.A. and B.Sc. Chemistry and Library Science, Texas Woman's University

M.L.S. Library Science, Rutgers University

Twenty-eight years of experience in archaeological conservation of objects from terrestrial and wet sites; develops state collections programs, policies, and standards; curates and supervises curation of federal and state collections; executes collection assessments and conservation treatments.

HOWARD WELLMAN, Lead Conservator

B.A. Cornell University; M.A. Boston University (Archaeology)

B.Sc.Institute of Archaeology, University College London (Conservation)

Eight years experience in archaeological conservation in terrestrial and marine excavation, museums, and laboratories. Currently oversees object conservation at MAC Lab including collection assessments, photo and x-ray documentation, treatments, material ID, and intern supervision.

Two conservators

One technician

Services The MAC Lab is the State of Maryland's central facility for archaeological research, collections management, and object conservation. We conserve a full range of archaeological materials including ceramics, stone, glass, ferrous and non-ferrous metals, wood, leather, and textiles, specializing in the treatment of organic materials and large metal objects from submerged sites. MAC staff performs surveys, condition assessments, and object documentation and treatment for local, state, and federal agencies, and other institutional clients on a contractual basis.

Facilities Treatment tanks adjustable to any size, electrolytic reduction, two vacuum freeze-driers, stereo and analytical microscopes, two air-abrasives, walk-in refrigerator and freezer, 320kV x-radiograph, FTIR & UV-Vis spectrophotometers.

Accepts interns.

NISHIO CONSERVATION STUDIO

2428 17th Street NW, Morgan Annex #1 NE, Washington, DC 20009
Tel 202 234-0550 *Fax* 202 234-0331 *Email* nishio@ix.netcom.com
Business hours Monday–Friday 9–6 by appointment
Established 1994

YOSHIYUKI NISHIO, Chief Conservator
Mr. Nishio is one of the leading conservators of Asian scroll and screen paintings in the U.S. His background combines traditional apprenticeship and academic training. He received a B.F.A. in studio art from the Nihon University, Tokyo, in 1972, followed by apprenticeships under various conservators
both in Japan and the U.S. He won the John D. Rockefeller III Fund Fel-
lowship to study at the Cooperstown Graduate Program and received a M.A.
and Certificate in Conservation in 1978, with an internship at the Los Angeles County Museum of Art. He worked at the Freer Gallery of Art, Smithsonian Institution from 1984 to 1990 and received the Smithsonian Award in
recognition of his work in 1985. From 1990 to 1993 he worked at the Museum
of Fine Arts, Boston. His responsibilities at both museums included conservation, restoration, and remounting of Japanese and Chinese scroll and screen
paintings. In 1994, he established the Nishio Conservation Studio. He is also
a founding member of Boston Art Conservation (www.bosartconserv.com).
Both studios provide conservation services for public institutions and private
clients throughout the U.S. He is a visiting lecturer at the Conservation Program, State University College at Buffalo, NY, Professional Associate of AIC,
and a member of WCG, IIC, International Paper Conservation (IPC), and
Japan Society for Conservation of Cultural Property. He is the author of several papers on techniques of Asian paintings conservation.

KYOICHI ITOH, Senior Conservator
Mr. Itoh trained for ten years in traditional conservation and scroll and screen
mounting at Harada Studio in Kyoto, Japan. He worked at the Freer Gallery
of Art, Smithsonian Institution from 1986 to 1996 and received Smithsonian
Awards in recognition of his work both in 1990 and 1996. Mr. Itoh joined
the Nishio Conservation Studio in 1996. He has educated many young Western paper conservators and treated various collections, including the Hell
scrolls of Taiwan for the National Museum of National History, Smithsonian Institution, and rare Japanese large-scale maps drawn by Ino Tadataka for
the Library of Congress. He received a Certificate in Conservation from *Bunkacho* (Agency for Cultural Affairs of Japanese Government) and is a member
of the Japan Society for Conservation of Cultural Property.

$\rightarrow$

Keiko Takai, Assistant Conservator
Ms. Takai was trained for seven years in Asian art conservation at the Hyouami Studio in Kanazawa, Japan. Under the supervision of Mr. Hideo Baba, she has treated numerous national treasures and cultural properties of Japan. She received a Certificate in Conservation from *Bunkacho* (Agency for Cultural Affairs of Japanese Government) and is a member of AIC and the Japan Society for Conservation of Cultural Property.

Interns and studio administrator

Services Conservation, restoration, and remounting of Japanese and Chinese hanging scrolls and folding screen paintings. Conservation, matting, and framing of Japanese ukiyoe woodblock prints. Conservation examination/survey of collections and examination/condition reports for insurance claims are available as well as lectures, workshops, and PowerPoint/video presentations. All the conservation treatments are documented by photography (color prints, slides, and digital images). Prior to the conservation treatments, an examination report with art historical research, structural study, and condition assessment with digital images and treatment proposal will be provided.

Facilities A dedicated studio space in Japanese traditional studio environment with climate control and central security/fire alarm system as well as high tech equipment including suction/vacuum table and microscope. All the materials, such as silk brocade and handmade papers, are imported from Japan and are of the highest quality. Full insurance coverage for objects on premises.

Nishio Conservation Studio utilizes highly qualified professional staff to provide conservation of Japanese and Chinese hanging scroll and screen paintings. The conservation approach combines modern science and ethics with traditional aesthetics and conservation craftsmanship/techniques. A partial list of recent clients includes the Herbert Johnson Museum – Cornell University, Virginia Museum of Art, Isabella Stewart Gardner Museum, and major collectors of Asian paintings.

MICHELE PAGÁN
330 12th Street SE, Washington, DC 20003
Tel 202 546-5439 *Email* michele_johnpagan@yahoo.com
Business hours Monday–Friday 9–5
Established 1997

MICHELE PAGÁN, Textile Conservator
Private practice in Washington, DC, and Brookfield, VT
Professional Associate, AIC, 1994
1973 B.S. Clothing & Textiles, University of Vermont
1984 M.A. Textiles & Costume, University of Connecticut

One conservator

Services Conservation of textiles, costumes, quilts, small upholstered items, wedding gowns, flags, and painted banners. Treatments, object surveys, exhibition advice, object storage, storage advice, shipping advice, packing/shipping, written documentation, photo documentation, emergency response.

Facilities Cleaning, stabilization, and custom support facilities, in studio as well at client's site; will travel out of state to accommodate institutional work.

Michele Pagán is in private practice on Capitol Hill, Washington, DC, as well as in Brookfield, VT. She specializes in conservation services for collectors, historic agencies, historical societies, businesses, universities, and individuals in both locations. In addition to conserving textiles and costumes, Michele provides custom reproduction of interior textile furnishings for homes, businesses, and universities which desire a vintage appearance. Vintage wedding gowns and other clothing items are re-sized, renovated, and re-designed for clients desiring to wear them in a contemporary setting.

PAGE CONSERVATION, INC.

1300 Seventh Street NW, Washington, DC 20001
Tel 202 387-2979 *Fax* 202 986-5094 *Email* page3@earthlink.net
Website www.pageconservation.com
Business hours Monday–Friday 8:30–5
Established 1982

ARTHUR PAGE, Chief Conservator
Arthur Page established his private paintings conservation practice in 1982.
The business has expanded to a daily staff of eight working in a permanent
studio facility. As Chief Conservator, Mr. Page executes and directs studio
treatments, interacts with clients, supervises mural field work, and consults
on conservation issues. Since 1990, the firm has actively pursued mural conservation and presently holds multi-year contracts to conserve murals for the
General Services Administration, nationally and locally. Mr. Page is active in
the conservation field. He served two terms as President of WCG (1991–93)
and established the Public Events Participation Program. Arthur is a Professional Associate of AIC and also a longtime member of IIC and WCG.

Education
1982 M.A. and Certificate of Advanced Study, Conservation of Historic
    and Artistic Works, Cooperstown Graduate Program, State University
    of New York at Oneonta
1981–82 Internship at the Walters Art Gallery, Baltimore, MD
1977–79 Formal apprenticeship in paintings conservation
1977 B.A. in Art History, University of North Carolina, Chapel Hill, NC

DEBORAH PAGE, Administrator
Deborah Page has served as Administrator for Page Conservation since 1982.
Deborah's responsibilities extend past normal record keeping and schedul-
ing, to client relations, art historical research, and grants/fundraising consultation. The business functions in an orderly and timely manner with all
projects reviewed at a weekly staff meeting. Page Conservation utilizes Deborah's administrative experience to successfully interact with state and federal governmental agencies as well as private clients. Ms. Page served from
1985–88 as the Administrative Assistant to the Executive Director of the Foundation for AIC. She successfully raised over $100,000 for the 1988 Gilding
Conservation Symposium which was held at the Philadelphia Museum of
Art. Deborah lectures on non-profit fundraising. She is a Professional Associate of AIC and a long time member of IIC and WCG.

→

Education
1982 M.A. in Performing Arts, American University
1978 B.A. double major in Political Science and Parks and Recreation
Administration, University of North Carolina, Chapel Hill, NC

JAMES ZILIUS, Associate Conservator
James Zilius joined Page Conservation in 1999 and is an Associate Conservator of paintings. James has a wide background in furniture, sculpture, and paintings conservation dating from 1984. Mr. Zilius worked specifically on paintings from 1993–96 at the Richmond Conservation Studio. James is a member of AIC, IIC, and WCG.

Education
1995 B.A. in Museum Studies, Virginia Commonwealth University,
Richmond, VA

THOMAS HEFFELFINGER, Assistant Conservator
Thomas Heffelfinger came to Page Conservation in 2001 and is an Assistant Conservator of paintings. Mr. Heffelfinger worked as an objects conservator at Mario's Conservation Services, Inc., of Washington, DC, under Sidney Williston from 1992–2001. His duties included ceramic, glass, and marble conservation, and he was the shop manager and company treasurer. Mr. Heffelfinger is a member of AIC, IIC and WCG.

Education
Attended the University of Maryland, College Park, and the University of
Arizona, Tucson

KATHERINE MOOG, Assistant Conservator
Katherine Moog was hired in March, 2003, as an Assistant Conservator. She is a member of AIC, IIC and WCG.

Education
2000–2002 Conservation Certificate, Scuola Lorenzo de' Medici/Art
Institute of Florence. Studies in conservation of paintings, frescoes,
ceramics, wood, gilding, and museology
1996–1997 Coursework at Art Institute of Philadelphia
1991 B.A. in Literature, Bard College

→

Five conservators
One intern
One technician
One office staff

Services Conservation of easel paintings, murals, painted and gilded objects, modern art. Treatments, x-ray analysis, object surveys, environmental surveys, exhibition advice, object storage, matting/framing, shipping advice, packing/shipping, written documentation, photo documentation, expert witness, lectures, UV/IR photography, emergency response. Artwork protection during construction including design, implementation, and monitoring.

Facilities Page Conservation utilizes a 4,000 square foot downtown studio in a former bank building. Trained personnel, close supervision, proper equipment, and up-to-date techniques are used to conserve paintings to museum standards. Large paintings, including murals, can be accommodated. Facilities include ULA3 security, studio insurance, fire suppression, large vault, microscope, and company van.

Established in 1982 and incorporated in 1987, Page Conservation utilizes a professional staff to respond in a timely manner to the needs of private, institutional, and governmental clients. As of November 2003, total staff is seven full time, two conservators as needed, and one intern. Arthur Page and Deborah Page are Professional Associates of AIC. Clients are received at the studio for an initial consultation at no charge. Treatments are preceded, however, by a written report of examination and recommended treatment with cost estimate.

Accepts interns.

Susan M. Peckham

1600 East Capitol Street NE, Washington, DC 20003
Tel 202 547-9363 *Fax* 202 547-9363 *Email* spec288514@aol.com
Business hours By appointment
Established 1999

Susan M. Peckham, Conservator of Works on Paper and Parchment
2002–present Paper Conservator, National Archives and Records
Administration
2000–2002 Paper Conservator, Smithsonian National Museum of Natural
History
1998–2000 Intern and Marshall Steel Post-graduate Fellow, Colonial
Williamsburg Foundation
1999 M.A. Certificate of Advanced Study in Art Conservation (Paper
Conservation), State University College at Buffalo, NY
1996–1998 Summer internships: Andrea Pitsch, private practice (NYC);
Charles Hosmer Morse Museum of American Art (Winter Park, FL)
1995–1996 Intern and contract conservator, Smithsonian National Museum
of American History
1994–1995 Intern, Indiana University Art Museum, Bloomington, IN
1993–1994 Internships: Rocky Mountain Conservation Center, Denver Art
Museum, Denver Museum of Natural History (Denver, CO); Save
Outdoor Sculpture (Washington, DC)
1990 B.Sc., Biology; Minor, Art History; Indiana University, Bloomington,
IN

One conservator

Services Conservation of works on paper and parchment including fine art
and documents, paper composite objects, and minor book repair. Treatments,
object surveys, pigment analysis, environmental surveys, exhibition advice,
storage advice, written documentation, photo documentation, lectures, emergency response.

Facilities Climate-controlled studio with fire/security alarm.

PRESERVATION SERVICES FOR COSTUMES

4829 27th Road South, Arlington, VA 22206
Tel 703 931-5078 *Fax* 703 931-6629 *Email* pollywillman@erols.com
Business hours Monday–Friday 9–6, Saturdays by appointment
Established 1997

POLLY WILLMAN, Costume Conservator
Polly Willman completed both her degrees at Colorado State University: a
B.Sc. in Textile Sciences and an M.A. in Costume History and Preservation.
She was the Senior Restorer in the Costumes and Textiles Department at the
Brooklyn Museum for eight years. While in New York she was active in the
Textile Conservation Group and served as its chairperson. From 1988 to 1999
she was the Senior Conservator of Costumes at the National Museum of American History at the Smithsonian Institution. Her major projects included the
renovation of the First Ladies Hall, the design and construction of a costumes
and textiles conservation laboratory, and a traveling exhibit celebrating the
Smithsonian's 150th birthday. Throughout her twenty-plus years' career, she
has updated her knowledge and skills by attending professional workshops
and seminars in conservation. She also lectures extensively on costume conservation through professional organizations and academic institutions and is
active in the Costume Society of America, where she has held numerous offices and organized many symposia, both regionally and nationally.

Services Conservation of costumes and textiles. Treatments, object surveys,
exhibition advice, storage advice, shipping advice, object storage, packing/
shipping, lectures, emergency response, custom forms for display.

Facilities The studio for Preservation Services for Costumes is at the home
of the principal. The studio is equipped to support stabilization treatments,
to document (in written and photographic form) treatments, and to build
ethafoam display forms.

Preservation Services for Costumes specializes in designing and producing cus-
tom-fit ethafoam forms for the display of costumes. The client has the option
of sending the costume(s) to the studio and/or having the conservator come
to the client's collection to measure and fit the costumes to the forms.

QUARTO CONSERVATION OF BOOKS & PAPER, INC.

1528 Grace Church Road, Silver Spring, MD 20910
Tel 301 585-2521 *Fax* 301 585-2521 *Email* stagellis@starpower.net
Website www.quartoconservation.com
Business hours By appointment
Established 1998

JANICE STAGNITTO ELLIS, President

Janice Stagnitto Ellis is the President and Conservator for Quarto Conservation of Books & Paper, Inc. She holds a M.Sc. from Columbia University in Conservation of Books and Archives, completed an advanced internship under Anthony Cains, Head of Conservation at Trinity College, Dublin, Ireland, and is a Professional Associate of AIC. Prior to incorporating, she was the Senior Book Conservator at the Smithsonian Institution Libraries, Smithsonian Institution, Washington, DC, for nearly eight years. While there, she provided the conservation treatment for the rare books held in the National Air and Space Museum, Cooper–Hewitt/National Design Museum, the National Museum of American History, and the National Museum of Natural History. She has also worked extensively in the conservation laboratory of the New York Public Library and has completed both short- and long-term contracts for the American Museum of Natural History (New York), the Library of Congress, the National Agriculture Library, the Juilliard School of Music, the Philadelphia Museum of Art, the National Park Service, Rutgers University Special Collections Department, and numerous other rare book collections held by universities and private collectors. She has published articles in the professional conservation literature and lectured at universities, museums, conservation professional meetings, and rare book collector meetings.

Services Conservation of books, documents, parchment, and paper. Treatments, object surveys, exhibition advice, storage advice, shipping advice, written documentation, photo documentation, lectures, emergency response.

Facilities Dedicated laboratory space located within a residential structure (brick, less than a quarter mile from fire station and 100 feet from hydrant). Central HVAC, fire and security system. Full fine art and conservation insurance coverage.

Accepts interns.

John Scott Conservator of Art and Architecture
New York Conservation Center

519 West 26th Street, New York, NY 10001
Forgedale Road, Fleetwood, PA 19522
Tel 212 714-0620, 646 339-6566 *Fax* 212 714-0149
Email jscott@NYConsnCtr.com
Website www.NYConsnCtr.com (business) and www.NYCF.org (educational)
Business hours Monday–Friday 9–5 by appointment
Established 1984

John Scott, Consultant for conservation of architecture and art, Conservator of monuments and sculpture
Principal conservator John Scott is an active conservator-analyst, restorer, investigator, writer and lecturer. He teaches and organizes educational programs through the New York Conservation Foundation and the Eastern Analytical Symposium organizations. Scott has more than twenty five years of experience in conservation, entered through museum work (Spencer Museum of Art, Nelson-Atkins Museum of Art, Hudson River Museum, National Gallery of Art, Philadelphia Museum of Art, and Princeton University Museum of Art) and a university graduate program (M.A. Certificate of Advanced Study in Art Conservation, Cooperstown Graduate Program, State University College at Buffalo, NY). Scott is university trained in humanities, art and science (B.A.), art history/connoisseurship/museology (M.A.) and management (M.B.A.).

Services Conservation of sculpture, objects, and architectural materials; project analysis, planning, and management. Treatments, object surveys, written and photo-documentation, multi-spectral and x-ray imaging, pigment analysis, fiber analysis, expert witness, lectures, materials analysis for art and architecture.

Facilities Two dedicated commercial spaces. Manhattan: studio, analytical laboratory, workshop, and accessible library. Rural southeastern Pennsylvania: studio, workshop. Fully equipped for field operations. Insurance for objects on premises, in transport and in the field.

Firm provides consulting and restoration services for art, monument, and architectural projects nationwide. Scientific analysis specialty for all media: paint, finishes, patinas, materials, and structures. Sculpture and outdoor sculpture specialty for all media, with field services mostly in Central Atlantic and Northeastern United States. Many successful and innovative projects for municipal, institutional, corporate, and private collections, and for the premium art trade.

Accepts interns.

LANDIS SMITH

512 Hawkesbury Lane, Silver Spring, MD 20904
Tel 240 305-7128 *Fax* 301 879-6982 *Email* smthla7@earthlink.net
Business hours By appointment
Established 1985

LANDIS SMITH
Private practice in DC area since 1997: museum contracts, private collections, research, consultations, surveys, treatments, loan, and exhibit conservation. Formerly Head Conservator, Department of Anthropology, American Museum of Natural History, New York, 1981–85: conservation of world collections including examination, treatment, and safe exhibition solutions for major installations, loan exhibits, and storage renovations. Project/Contract Conservator, Museum of New Mexico system, Santa Fe, 1985–97: conservation of American Indian, Spanish Colonial art and history collections, international folk art, and fine arts collections. Contractual work with small museums and private and National Park Service collections. Graduated New York University 1978. Continued education includes microscopy and fiber identification, Institute of Archaeology, London, and ceramics analysis, University of New Mexico, among other courses. She has lectured widely and published primarily on the conservation of Native American objects.

Services Conservation of objects including ethnographic, archaeological, historic, folk, decorative, and fine art. Examination, treatment, object storage, written and photographic documentation. Condition surveys, environmental surveys, facilities assessments, storage, exhibition and shipping advice, grant writing. Lectures, workshops, writing, and teaching.

Facilities Designated studio with climate control, central monitored security/fire alarm system, and insurance coverage. Available to work on-site and/or at institution's conservation lab.

Landis Smith has over twenty years of experience as a conservator for a wide range of museums, historic societies, tribal museums, archaeological repositories, universities, and private collectors. Her work ranges from conservation project director for major exhibits at large museums to the treatment of small collections. Practical solutions and high standards of practice provided.

SOUTH ROYAL STUDIOS

1319 Prince Street, Alexandria, VA 22314
Tel 703 548-5550 *Fax* 703 548-5872 *Email* srsframes@aol.com
Business hours By appointment
Established 1976

TIM KILLALEA, Principal and Senior Designer
Established business after apprenticeships in frame shops and galleries in
Alexandria, VA, and Boston and Cambridge, MA. Areas of expertise include
preservation framing techniques, replicating historic framing treatments, and
reproducing antique gilded and painted finishes. Directs firm's private and
institutional on-site projects and is its chief liaison with Washington area conservators and museums. Available full-time by appointment.

One full-time production manager
One part-time administrative assistant
Two part-time technical assistants

Services Framing and housing of paintings, works of art on paper, manuscripts, textiles, and three-dimensional objects. Repairs of, and modifications
to, existing frames. Treatments, object surveys, exhibition advice, shipping
advice, written documentation, matting/framing, packing/shipping, lectures,
installation design, picture hanging.

Facilities Dedicated commercial space with central security/fire alarm system. Object storage and handling area is climate-controlled and isolated from
manufacturing areas. Full insurance coverage for all customer property. All
work is done on premises.

South Royal Studios is a picture framing business that places a premium on
the proper care and handling of fine art and artifacts. It features handmade,
custom-finished frames and offers a formidable selection of both reproduction period frames and original contemporary frames. The firm is equally
comfortable with one-of-a-kind commissions and major exhibition contracts.
Its clients include private individuals throughout the country, as well as many
Washington area museums, galleries, government institutions, and private
businesses. Mr. Killalea has published and lectured on a variety of topics, including: the role of framers in the conservation community (WCG); creating
a two-way stretcher and frame for a two-sided George Bellows painting (AIC);
framing Picasso's *Reclining Nude* and *Woman in a Green Hat* (Phillips Collection); replicating an Arts and Crafts kiosk (U.S. Treasury); and framing Pierre
L'Enfant's plan of Washington (Library of Congress).

Elizabeth Steele

1835 Phelps Place NW, Washington, DC 20008
Tel 202 328-6182 *Email* esteele123@aol.com
Business hours By appointment
Established 1986

Elizabeth Steele, Conservator
1990–present Conservator, The Phillips Collection
   Management of Conservation Office. Treatment of paintings from the permanent collection. Participation in exhibition and loan programs. Oversight of all preservation activities in the museum.
1986–present Conservator in Private Practice in Washington, DC
Professional Background
1984–86 Fellow, Department of Paintings Conservation, Metropolitan Museum of Art, New York, NY
1983–84 Intern, National Gallery of Art, Washington, DC
1981–83 M.A. Certificate of Advanced Study in Conservation, State University of New York, Oneonta
Pre-Professional Background
1978 B.A. Schiller College, London, England

Services Conservation of paintings. Treatments, object surveys, environmental surveys, exhibition advice, storage advice, packing/shipping advice, written documentation, photo documentation, lectures, emergency response.

Facilities Spacious, well-equipped studio located within a fine arts shipping warehouse complex in Landover, MD. Well-maintained facility has state-of-the-art climate control and security. North light provides an appropriate setting for the treatment of paintings.

Full-time conservator for The Phillips Collection. Freelance practice in paintings conservation. Experience with all periods, from old master to modern paintings.

JOYCE HILL STONER, PH.D.
5105 Kennett Pike, Wilmington, DE 19735
Tel 302 888-4888 *Fax* 302 888-4838 *Email* jhstoner@udel.edu
Business hours By appointment
Established 1976

DR. JOYCE HILL STONER, Professor and Paintings Conservator, Winterthur/
  University of Delaware Program in Art Conservation (and adjunct
  paintings conservator for the Winterthur Museum)
1982–1997 Director, Winterthur/University of Delaware Program
1988–1993 Senior Contract Consultant, Peacock Room, Freer Gallery of Art
June–July 1985 Visiting Scholar, J. Paul Getty Museum
1981–1982 Head, conservation section, Winterthur Museum
March–June 1980 Kress Visiting Scholar, Paintings Conservation,
  Metropolitan Museum of Art
1976–1982 Paintings Conservator, Winterthur Museum
1975–76 Associate Professor, Virginia Commonwealth University
1975–76 Consultant Conservator, Freer Gallery of Art
1976–present Consultant paintings conservator for collectors and museums
  in Richmond, Baltimore, Philadelphia, and the Wilmington area

Education
1995 Ph.D. in Art History, University of Delaware (dissertation on the
  techniques of Whistler)
1973–75 Advanced internship with Bernard Rabin, Newark, NJ
Feb. 1973 Certificate in Conservation, New York University Conservation
  Center
1970 Master's Degree in Art History earned from the New York University
  Institute of Fine Arts
1968 Phi Beta Kappa, summa cum laude, College of William and Mary, in
  fine arts with honors thesis in technical art history

Services Conservation of paintings. Treatments, written documentation,
photo documentation, lectures. Have written over sixty articles and book
chapters on paintings conservation, the history of conservation, the techniques of various American artists (including Whistler, the Wyeth family,
Washington Allston, etc.)

→

Facilities I have an agreement to use space and equipment in the paintings conservation facilities at the Winterthur Museum Research Building. I am, however, responsible for my own freelance treatments.

I teach paintings conservation for one of the three U.S. graduate programs. I take on a small number of freelance treatments, particularly focusing on paintings by the Wyeth family and James McNeill Whistler or on interesting treatment problems to solve with an audience of graduate students. Cannot usually take additional interns because we also have undergraduate interns working in the laboratory.

Stromberg Conservation, LLC
7610 Marbury Road, Bethesda, MD 20817
Tel and fax 301 263-9298 *Email* c.stromberg@verizon.net
Business hours By appointment
Established 2001

Constance Stromberg, Sculpture and Objects Conservator
1998–01 Public Affairs Section (PAS) U.S. Embassy, Lima, Peru, Cultural
    Patrimony Specialist. Organized seminars on conservation,
    archaeological site protection, and illicit trafficking in art.
1996–97 Trateggio Restauración, Conservator for fire damaged wood at La
    Compañía de Jesús (17th C. Baroque church), Quito, Ecuador
1992–94 Conservator in private practice, Barbados. Barbados Museum
    Coordinator, Getty Conservation Project. Barbados National Trust,
    Sugar Machinery Museum Conservation Project
1988–92 Conservator in private practice, Kathmandu, Nepal
1986 National Museum of American Art, Washington, DC, on contract
1986–87 Conservation Analytical Laboratory, Smithsonian Institution,
    Washington, DC, Postgraduate Intern in objects
1986 M.Sc. Winterthur/University of Delaware Program in the Conserva-
    tion of Artistic and Historic Objects. Major: Sculpture Conservation
1978 B.F.A. Carnegie-Mellon University, Pittsburgh, PA. Major: Sculpture
1985–86 Walters Art Museum, Baltimore, MD. Objects Conservation Intern
1981–83 Pennsylvania Academy of the Fine Arts, Philadelphia, PA.
    Assistant in Sculpture Conservation
1980,1982 Art Museum, Princeton University, Princeton, NJ. Conservation
    of 22 outdoor sculptures
1978–80 Johnson Atelier Technical Institute of Sculpture, Princeton, NJ

One conservator

Services Conservation of sculpture, outdoor sculpture, and historic and decorative objects. Treatments, object surveys, exhibition advice, storage advice,
written documentation, photo documentation, technical studies, and insurance reports.

Facilities Dedicated, secure studio space. Work also done on-site.

Ms. Stromberg has twenty years of conservation experience on projects around
the world. She works in the Washington and Baltimore area, specializing in
treatment of sculpture and objects for museums, government agencies, and
private collectors. Professional Associate of AIC, member IIC and WCG.

MARY E. STUDT, PAPER CONSERVATOR

1000 Carlisle Avenue, Suite 212, Richmond, VA 23231
Tel 804 222-7133 *Fax* 804 222-7138 *Email* mestudt@earthlink.net
Business hours By appointment
Established 1998

MARY E. STUDT, Paper Conservator
1998–present Paper conservation services for private clients and
   institutions, Richmond, VA
1998–2001 Fellow and Archives Conservator, Smithsonian Center for
   Materials Research and Education (SCMRE)
1998–99 Contract Paper Conservator, Virginia Historical Society, Richmond
1996–98 Intern and Contract Paper Conservator, Colonial Williamsburg
   Foundation
1996 Intern, Intermuseum Conservation Association, Oberlin, OH
1995–96 Intern, Missouri State Archives, Jefferson City, MO
1994 Intern, Library of Congress
1992–93 Intern, Russell-Marti Conservation Services, Inc., St. Louis, MO
1990–92 Intern, Missouri Historical Society, St. Louis, MO

Education
1998 Completion of course in the "Identification, Preservation and
   Conservation of Photographic Materials," The Centre for Photographic
   Conservation, London, England
1996 M.A. and Certificate of Advanced Study in Art Conservation, State
   University College at Buffalo, NY, specialization in paper conservation
1989 B.A. in English Literature, minors in Photography and German,
   Washington University, St. Louis, MO

Services Conservation of documents, watercolors, prints, drawings, collage, 3-
D paper objects, minor treatment of some photographic material. Treatments,
object surveys, environmental surveys, exhibition advice, storage advice, written documentation, photo documentation, UV/IR photography, lectures, emergency response, preservation housing, digital reproductions.

Facilities The studio space has climate control and monitoring with centralized security and fire alarm systems and full insurance. Facilities include
a water-deionizing system for aqueous treatment and suction table for tape
stain reduction and aqueous treatment of sensitive media. Ability to perform
conventional, digital, ultraviolet, and infrared photography. Washing and lining facilities are available for works up to 4 by 8 feet.

Bruce Hardin Suffield/Conservator of Paintings
18 South Thompson Street, No. 125, Richmond, VA 23221
Tel 804 353-8987
Business hours By appointment
Established 1995

Bruce Hardin Suffield
1994–present Conservator, Virginia Museum of Fine Arts, Richmond, VA
1993–94 Fellow Conservator, Frans Hals Museum, Haarlem, The
    Netherlands. Awarded Samuel H. Kress Foundation Fellowship
1992 M.A. and Certificate of Advanced Study, Art Conservation Program,
    State University College at Buffalo, NY
1991–1992 Conservation Intern, The Art Museum, Princeton University
1991 Conservation Intern, The Radonezh Society, Moscow, Russia.
    Awarded Samuel H. Kress Foundation Fellowship
1991 Conservation Intern, USSR Inter-Regional Special Research
    Restoration Art Department, Moscow, Russia
1990 Conservation Intern, The Detroit Institute of Arts, Detroit, MI
1981–89 Conservation Preparator, Harry Ransom Humanities Research
    Center, Austin, TX
1987 Conservation and Exhibition Intern, The Nelson-Atkins Museum of
    Art, Kansas City, MO
1982 B.F.A. University of Texas at Austin

One conservator
One office staff

Services Conservation of traditional paintings on panel and canvas, icons, modern and contemporary paintings. Treatments, surveys, exhibition advice, storage advice, shipping advice, written documentation, photo documentation.

Facilities Private and secure conservation studio.

Mr. Suffield has written on the materials and techniques of early Italian paintings, seventeenth-century Dutch paintings, and Russian icons, including those from workshops of Carl Fabergé. He has also written on modern acrylic paint media. He has lectured on these areas as well as Dutch Mannerist, French Impressionist, and American painting materials and techniques. He is a member of numerous international and national conservation and art history organizations.

JUDITH WATKINS TARTT

2105 R Street NW, Washington, DC 20008
Tel 202 588-0271 *Fax* 202 588-6370 *Email* Judith@art-care.com
Business hours By appointment
Established 1978

JUDITH WATKINS TARTT, Professional Associate, AIC; Conservator of Paintings
BA in Art History 1973. Certificate of Conservation, International Institute
of Art, Florence, Italy 1974. Work/Apprenticeship Program, H.H. Stewart-
Treviranus, Fellow AIC, Painting Conservator 1974–1980. Painting Conser-
vator in private practice 1980 to present. Contract Conservator of Paintings,
Hong Kong Museum 1983–1984 and during the years of 1992 and 1993. Con-
servator of Paintings, Sotheby's Asia 1992–1995. Conservator of Paintings,
Kreeger Museum 1980 to present. Awarded contracts : U.S. Treasury, GSA,
Art-in-Embassy Program, U.S. Department of State, Air and Space Museum.

One conservator

Services Conservation of paintings and murals, traditional and contemporary. Treatments, object surveys, exhibition advice, object storage, storage advice, shipping advice, packing/shipping, written documentation, photo documentation, lectures, emergency response.

Facilities 800 square foot ground floor of private home; vacuum heat table,
easels, UV light. Parking is provided.

I have a very personal approach to my business. I have a small and secure laboratory. I carry Conservation Fine Art Insurance. I do all of the treatments
on paintings myself. I make sure that my clients understand my recommendations for conservation treatment, and that their expectations of the results
of these treatments are realistic. I adhere to my cost and time estimates. I do
not charge for estimates. I adhere to the principles and ethics outlined in the
AIC Code of Ethics. I provide written and photographic documentation: estimates, examination, and treatment reports. I enjoy my clients and encourage their involvement. I believe that educating the public as to the ethics and
principles outlined by AIC and in conservation in general, the "taking care
of precious objects," is a major part of my job.

TEXTILE PRESERVATION ASSOCIATES, INC.
P.O. Box 60, Keedysville, MD 21756
Tel 301 432-4160 *Fax* 301 432-8797 *Email* tpa@fred.net
Business hours Monday–Friday 8–4:30
Established 1987

FONDA GHIARDI THOMSEN, Director; Fellow, AIC
Fonda started working in conservation in 1968 as Conservator of Organic Materials for CAL, Smithsonian Institution. She worked eight years for the National Park Service as Conservator of Ethnographic Materials and Textiles, then established and managed the Bertrand Conservation Laboratory for treatment of cargo from the sunken steamship *Bertrand*. After studying textile conservation at the Abegg-Stifftung Museum in Berne, Switzerland, Fonda has focused her conservation work primarily on historic textiles. Her research efforts have centered on problems of the conservation and exhibition of flags. This focus has included extensive research on the history of flag conservation and evaluations of the results of earlier treatments. Fonda has been contracted by the states of Alabama, Florida, Georgia, Illinois, Kansas, Kentucky, Louisiana, Maryland, Michigan, Missouri, Ohio, Pennsylvania, South Carolina, and Texas for consultation on the preservation of state flag collections.

CATHY HEFFNER, Conservation Technician
Cathy was introduced to the field of conservation as a participant in the work study program at Brunswick High School in 1975. Assigned to the conservation laboratories of the National Park Service, Cathy immediately showed an aptitude for conservation work that led the National Park Service to employ her as a technician after graduation in 1976. Her projects included working on the traveling Native American exhibit "Indian Pride on the Move," and an exhibit maintenance plan for the Gettysburg National Military Park. Cathy worked on the Bertrand collection of the Fish and Wildlife Service in Iowa in 1978. Cathy joined Textile Preservation Associates in 1987 and has worked on numerous projects including the San Jacinto flag of the state of Texas, the Treasury Guard flag at the Lincoln Museum, the Crestar Bank fiber art sculptures, and the Baltimore Museum of Art's collection of pre-Columbian textiles. Cathy has also worked on state flag collections for Alabama, Florida, Georgia, Michigan, Kansas, Louisiana, South Carolina, Ohio, Texas, and Missouri.

→

One conservator
Six technicians
One office staff

Services Conservation of flags, uniforms, historic textiles, modern fiber arts, samplers, and quilts. Treatments, object surveys, exhibition advice, storage advice, written documentation, photo documentation, fiber analysis, matting/framing, expert witness, lectures.

Facilities We are located in a 1906 building constructed as a bank. The building is equipped with continuous centrally monitored security and fire detection systems, environmental control systems, a computerized office, and two walk-in fireproof bank vaults. Equipment includes a 7 x 7 foot wash table with a deionized water system, a photography area, and a fully automatic binocular zoom surgical microscope.

We offer a wide range of professional conservation services to museums, historic societies, private individuals, and government agencies. Our services include: conservation treatment of textiles, textile analysis, collection conservation surveys, and object exhibit preparation and consulting. Treatments are designed individually based on the composition, condition, and planned use of the object. Treatments are based on a policy of minimum intervention, complete reversibility, and access for research. Extremely fragile objects are often encapsulated between two layers of polyester crepeline, and fragments are fixed in place by sewing through the voids. Most flat objects are prepared for vertical display by sandwiching between a padded panel and Plexiglas in a light pressure mount for support. For exhibit, we have a custom designed two-part aluminum pressure mount frame, wooden frames, and Plexiglas vitrines. Metal, wood or Plexiglas custom exhibit mounts are also available.

ALEXANDRA TICE STUDIOS
162 Quincy Street, Chevy Chase, MD 20815
Tel 301 986-1296 *Fax* 301 215-9097 *Email* ticed@rcn.com
Business hours Monday–Friday 9–5:30, weekends by appointment
Established 1983

ALEXANDRA TICE, Senior Painting Conservator
Alexandra Tice earned an Art History B.A. at Northwestern University (1965) and was an Art History major at Mount Holyoke College (1963–64). She apprenticed in conservation of paintings (1976–79) and was Associate Painting Conservator (1979–83) with the conservator who set up the Smithsonian conservation laboratories, Charles Olin. As a Senior Painting Conservator in Private Practice (1983 to present) she has regularly attended seminars and workshops to update her knowledge in the field. In addition to diagnosis and treatment of paintings, Ms. Tice lectures on conservation issues, surveys collections, and advises on the management and conservation of collections. Ms. Tice has selected, managed, and supervised teams of specialists for treatments of large collections damaged in natural disasters. She has been involved for nearly a decade in public education programs focused on conservation of paintings and care of collections.

Services Conservation of oil paintings: treatments, surveys, advice on exhibition, storage and shipping, written and photo documentation, lectures, emergency response, conservation reframing of paintings, and insurance.

Facilities Dedicated 2,000 square foot studio space with climate control, central-station security/fire alarm, and four principal areas: primary studio/client reception area; photography room; vacuum pressure hot table with suction platen facility; and general work/packing/storage space. Equipment includes binocular microscopic, 35 mm cameras, and special lighting capabilities. Items on premises fully insured.

All work is done by Ms. Tice or by contract senior conservators under her direct supervision. She provides the personal attention that a small private practice can offer. Her specialization is oil paintings of the seventeenth through early twentieth centuries. She works with museums, private clients, galleries, universities, corporations, and historic homes (including Mount Vernon), and has a long client relationship with federal and state painting collections. She is a Professional Associate of AIC and a member and past Board Member and Vice President of WCG.

CATHARINE VALENTOUR
3442 Oakwood Terrace NW, Washington, DC 20010
Tel 202 265-7555 *Fax* 202 265-7666
Business hours By appointment
Established 1987

CATHARINE VALENTOUR, Objects Conservator
I came to conservation through anthropology and classical archeology. I worked for ten years in the Anthropology Conservation Laboratory of the National Museum of Natural History, Smithsonian Institution. I have worked as field conservator in the Middle East and Italy. After leaving the government in 1987, I "went private" and have worked on a wide variety of objects and exhibitions for various museums in the Washington area. Most of my institutional work involves treatment for exhibitions and loans. I work for many local and national associations and provide conservation services to collectors of fine art and individuals with personal treasures.

Services Conservation of objects. Treatments.

Facilities I have a home studio and office centrally located in Washington, DC. I also work on-site in institutional laboratories, collections, and various warehouses, attics and basements.

DIANNE VAN DER REYDEN
10824 Anita Drive, Mason Neck, VA 22079
Tel 703 339-1580 *Email* Dvan@LOC.gov
Website www.si.edu/scmre/about/cv-dvr.html

DIANNE VAN DER REYDEN, Chief of Conservation, Preservation Directorate,
   Library of Congress
Dianne van der Reyden received an MA in Art History ('79) and Diplomas
in Conservation from New York ('80) and Harvard Universities ('81), following conservation internships and training at New York's Museum of Modern Art, Harvard's Fogg Art Museum, Washington's Library of Congress, and
the Rochester Institute of Technology.

She began her career as Acting Head of Paper Conservation at the Bishop
Museum of Hawaii. For two decades she was Senior Paper Conservator at the
Smithsonian Institution's National Museum of American History ('81–'84)
and the Smithsonian Center for Materials Research and Education ('84–2002).
In June, 2002, Dianne became Chief of Conservation for the Preservation
Directorate of the Library of Congress, overseeing a laboratory of forty conservation professionals. She is responsible for the operations of the Conservation Division, advising the Preservation Director on the establishment of
conservation policies and priorities, and overseeing conservation and care of
the collections. She also serves as principal liaison for the Division professionally, nationally and internationally; consults on treatments, research, special preservation activities and emergency preparedness and disaster recovery;
and performs administrative and human resource management functions, including recruitment and evaluation of staff.

Dianne specializes in paper-based materials, such as manuscripts, documents,
photographs, and books, having worked on a wide variety of materials ranging from George Washington's Farewell Address to Joe Lewis' scrapbooks.
She has also examined and treated paper art and artifacts including old and
modern master drawings, watercolors, pastels, and prints; daguerreotypes,
tintypes and ambrotypes; crayon, gelatin, and platinum photographs; maps
and globes; Victorian valentines; Far Eastern fans, folding screens and lanterns;
and papier-mâché furniture. She has published over thirty five articles in international journals on these and other collections materials (such as tracing
and coated papers found in archives and libraries), developing scientific research and conservation treatment projects to address their special needs. She

→

has lectured widely on topics ranging from disaster preparedness, collections care, and scientific research, to forgeries and digitization. Her audiences have included not only the general public, archivists and librarians, but also specialists such as violin restorers, appraisers, museum directors, and scientists. She has served as faculty for high school, university and international programs, including Johns Hopkins University's Material Science Program, and UNESCO's ICCROM program on document preservation. She also designed a six-week curriculum for ICCROM's document preservation program, covering preservation problems (focusing on value, use and risks to collections based on their substrates, media, format and inherent vice) and solutions (based on principles of preservation management, reformatting, environmental control, collections maintenance, treatment, research and training). Her projects have been awarded a half-dozen grants for study and collections care. She has been asked to write a book chapter on conservation treatments, and has created preservation exhibitions, videos, and websites, as well as an international curriculum on preservation principles. She has been in TV programs for "Smithsonian World" and "National Geographic" and consulted on millennium projects for the White House and the New York Times Magazine. Dianne has served as a board member of many professional organizations, including as an Officer for AIC and Chair of AIC's Book and Paper Specialty Group (BPG), and BPG's Education and Training Committee. She is an Assistant Chair of ICOM's Working Group on Graphic Documents, and a Fellow of AIC and IIC. Most recently she served as Chair for Library Materials for the Heritage Preservation Foundation's Heritage Health Index Steering Committee.

Services Conservation of paper-based materials, including books and photographs. Lectures, consultation and curriculum development.

NICOLAS F. VELOZ, OUTDOOR SCULPTURE CONSERVATOR
5 W. Howell Avenue, Alexandria, VA 22301
Tel 703 836-1696 *Fax* 703 836-0847 *Email* nveloz@erols.com
Business hours Available by telephone, other hours by appointment
Established 1983

NICOLAS F. VELOZ, Outdoor Sculpture Conservator
B.A. University of Texas, 1970 (Anthropology/Archaeology); M.A. George Washington University, 1983 (Historic Preservation); a number and variety of related historic preservation and conservation training classes though the National Park Service. A significant amount of independent study and consultation with a variety of experts in conservation, foundries, and other related fields such as scientists at the National Bureau of Standards, regarding corrosion, chemistry, and paint chemistry/removers (related to graffiti), as well as other sculpture conservators, to deal with outdoor sculpture problems resulting from long-term neglect, vandalism, graffiti, accidents, and other similar occurrences. Experience and knowledge from other areas of work/training have also been very useful in developing treatment methods, procedures, and techniques. For example, geology training in mohs hardness scale from anthropology degree was a major factor in the initiation and development of the use of ground walnut shells for the cleaning of outdoor sculpture. Similarly, other interests led to the development of the spray application of wax for a protective coating for outdoor bronze sculptures.

Nicolas F. Veloz began the conservation of outdoor sculpture for a few city and state governments and non-profit organizations on a part-time basis while he was working with the National Park Service (NPS). He started with the NPS after completing studies at the University of Texas as an archaeologist at Mound City Group NM, in Ohio. He then returned to Texas to serve as the Museum Curator for the Lyndon B. Johnson National Historic Park. In 1972, he was transferred to Washington, DC, where he worked for a number of parks within the National Capital Region, and ultimately retired as Regional Conservator of Outdoor Sculpture. Most of his time was at the George Washington Memorial Parkway (GWMP). While at GWMP he conducted several training sessions at a number of other NPS areas, including Valley Forge, Fredericksburg, Shiloh, Andersonville, and Independence National Historic Park, and supervised three Winterthur conservation student summer interns. He consulted and provided assistance to several government agencies, including GSA, Veterans Administration, the Architect of the Capitol, the Smith-

→

sonian Institution's Hirshhorn Museum, Department of the Army, the U.S. Marine Corps, the Rodin Museum in Paris, Parks Canada, and others. Throughout his period of work with the NPS he was able to call on a number of individuals from other government agencies, such as the National Bureau of Standards and the Smithsonian Institution, as well as museums, foundries, and other similar sources of information, for assistance with specific problems or general needs. He also received training in historic preservation/conservation through NPS training courses and a grant to work for a short period in two sculpture/art foundries. Throughout this period his primary interest was in the conservation of outdoor bronze sculptures, but he was involved with other outdoor metal objects and materials as well.

While with GWMP he worked part-time for one year so that he could work with Save Outdoor Sculpture (SOS!), developing and working on the initial pilot project for assessment of sculptures by volunteers. Since then he has served on the Conservation Maintenance Advisory Committee and on occasion has provided other assistance to SOS! as well. He has completed several SOS! assessments for grants as well as sculpture conservation assessments for Lynchburg, VA; Charlottesville, VA; the University of Virginia; the University of Texas at Austin; and, with the assistance of several other conservators, approximately 750 sculptures owned by the City of Philadelphia. The information for the latter project was included in a specially programmed Microsoft Access database, enabling the inclusion of photographs, a record of specific agencies responsible for individual sculptures, past and future treatments, and many other features accessible via a report generator. The survey data included over 3000 images (color slides, black and white prints, negatives, and digital images), and the printed hard copy, requested by the city, took sixteen reams of paper to print.

One conservator
Four technicians

Services Conservation of outdoor bronze sculptures primarily, but also sculptures of other materials and outdoor objects/structures which are metal, or have metal components. Treatments, object surveys, exhibition advice, written and photo documentation, expert witness, lectures, emergency response, training of local personnel in the maintenance of outdoor sculptures.

→

Facilities Work is primarily performed out of a mobile laboratory which is a refurbished ambulance, enabling transportation and storage of tools, supplies, materials, some scaffolding/ladders, and other items necessary for work in situ. Equipment includes a variety of cameras and photographic equipment, microscope, research library, and computers.

Nicolas F. Veloz specializes in the examination and treatment of outdoor bronze sculpture, but has been involved with outdoor metal objects and sculpture made of other materials. Services range from quick examination of individual outdoor sculptures and assessment of their needs, to more detailed studies, examination of individual sculptures, and conservation assessments of large collections of sculptures. Virtually all work is completed in situ, although on occasion work has been removed for more extensive treatment elsewhere. Clients have included the Maryland Military Monuments Commission; Virginia Military Institute; the cities of Philadelphia, Atlanta, and Lexington, KY; the Vulcan Park Foundation; Washington National Cathedral; the Manitoba Department of Transportation Services; and small towns, non-profit organizations, citizen groups, private individuals, and companies. Size of works has ranged from three inch tall bronzes to the 55 foot, 120,000 pound cast iron statue of Vulcan in Birmingham, AL. A complete client list can be provided on request.

Accepts interns.

Sarah S. Wagner llc

7808 Boston Avenue, Silver Spring, MD 20910-4901
Tel 301 587-5569 *Fax* 301 587-5569 *Email* sarahwagner@att.net
Business hours By appointment
Established 1990

Sarah S. Wagner, Conservator
B.A. in Biochemistry from Mount Holyoke College, with extensive course-work in art history and studio art from CUNY Hunter College. Apprenticed for two years at the Hispanic Society of America working in paintings conservation. M.Sc. from the Winterthur Museum/University of Delaware Program in Art Conservation, specializing in paper and photographs. Interned at the Library of Congress Paper Conservation Section. Senior conservator positions held in the conservation divisions of the Library of Congress (three years) and the National Archives (eight years). Participant or lecturer in the series of Mellon Collaborative Workshops in Photograph Conservation, and adjunct lecturer in photograph conservation at the University of Delaware. Private part time practice established in 1990, was expanded to full time business in 2001. Institutional clients have included the National Gallery of Art, Corcoran Gallery of Art, Smithsonian museums, Supreme Court, and the National Library of Medicine. Special projects include treatment of large collections of photographs by Ansel Adams and Alexander Gardner (National Archives), Alfred Stieglitz (National Gallery of Art), Mathew Brady daguerreotypes and Arnold Genthe autochromes (Library of Congress), and traveling exhibit conservator for the eight venues of American Originals Exhibit (National Archives). Fellow of AIC. Member of WCG, AIC/PMG, AIC/BPG, AIC/CIPP.

One conservator

Services Treatments, object surveys, exhibition advice, storage advice, written documentation, photo documentation, emergency response. Custom housing of damaged original photographs; photographic copying and digital restoration for treated items.

Facilities Dedicated, well-equipped, residential studio space. Commercial liability insurance for objects on premises.

Ms. Wagner does all conservation work on-site in institutional facilities, or in her studio. She has extensive experience with the wide variety of photographic processes, and archival paper or mixed-media collections in research institutions.

Code of Ethics of the American Institute for Conservation of Historic and Artistic Works

Preamble

The primary goal of conservation professionals, individuals with extensive training and special expertise, is the preservation of cultural property. Cultural property consists of individual objects, structures, or aggregate collections. It is material which has significance that may be artistic, historical, scientific, religious, or social, and it is an invaluable and irreplaceable legacy that must be preserved for future generations.

In striving to achieve this goal, conservation professionals assume certain obligations to the cultural property, to its owners and custodians, to the conservation profession, and to society as a whole. This document, the Code of Ethics and Guidelines for Practice of the American Institute for Conservation of Historic and Artistic Works (AIC), sets forth the principles that guide conservation professionals and others who are involved in the care of cultural property.

I.   The conservation professional shall strive to attain the highest possible standards in all aspects of conservation, including, but not limited to, preventive conservation, examination, documentation, treatment, research, and education.

II.   All actions of the conservation professional must be governed by an informed respect for the cultural property, its unique character and significance, and the people or person who created it.

III.   While recognizing the right of society to make appropriate and respectful use of cultural property, the conservation professional shall serve as an advocate for the preservation of cultural property.

IV.   The conservation professional shall practice within the limits of personal competence and education as well as within the limits of the available facilities.

V.   While circumstances may limit the resources allocated to a particular situation, the quality of work that the conservation professional performs shall not be compromised.

VI.   The conservation professional must strive to select methods and materials that, to the best of current knowledge, do not adversely affect cultural property or its future examination, scientific investigation, treatment, or function.

VII.   The conservation professional shall document examination, scientific investigation, and treatment by creating permanent records and reports.

VIII.   The conservation professional shall recognize a responsibility for preventive conservation by endeavoring to limit damage or deterioration to cultural property, providing guidelines for continuing use and care, recommending appropriate environmental conditions for storage and exhibition, and encouraging proper procedures for handling, packing, and transport.

IX.   The conservation professional shall act with honesty and respect in all professional relationships, seek to ensure the rights and opportunities of all individuals in the profession, and recognize the specialized knowledge of others.

X.   The conservation professional shall contribute to the evolution and growth of the profession, a field of study that encompasses the liberal arts and the natural sciences. This contribution may be made by such means as continuing development of personal skills and knowledge, sharing of information and experience with colleagues, adding to the profession's written body of knowledge, and providing and promoting educational opportunities in the field.

XI.   The conservation professional shall promote an awareness and understanding of conservation through open communication with allied professionals and the public.

XII.   The conservation professional shall practice in a manner that minimizes personal risks and hazards to co-workers, the public, and the environment.

XII   Each conservation professional has an obligation to promote understanding of and adherence to this Code of Ethics.

The conservation professional should use the following guidelines and supplemental commentaries together with the AIC Code of Ethics in the pursuit of ethical practice. The commentaries are separate documents, created by the AIC membership, that are intended to amplify this document and to accommodate growth and change in the field.

Guidelines for Practice
of the American Institute for Conservation of Historic And Artistic Works

Professional Conduct

1. Conduct: Adherence to the Code of Ethics and Guidelines for Practice is a matter of personal responsibility. The conservation professional should always be guided by the intent of this document, recognizing that specific circumstances may legitimately affect professional decisions.

2. Disclosure: In professional relationships, the conservation professional should share complete and accurate information relating to the efficacy and value of materials and procedures. In seeking and disclosing such information, and that relating to analysis and research, the conservation professional should recognize the importance of published information that has undergone formal peer review.

3. Laws and Regulations: The conservation professional should be cognizant of laws and regulations that may have a bearing on professional activity. Among these laws and regulations are those concerning the rights of artists and their estates, occupational health and safety, sacred and religious material, excavated objects, endangered species, human remains, and stolen property.

4. Practice: Regardless of the nature of employment, the conservation professional should follow appropriate standards for safety, security, contracts, fees, and advertising.

4a. Health and Safety: The conservation professional should be aware of issues concerning the safety of materials and procedures and should make this information available to others, as appropriate.

4b. Security: The conservation professional should provide working and storage conditions designed to protect cultural property.

4c. Contracts: The conservation professional may enter into contractual agreements with individuals, institutions, businesses, or government agencies provided that such agreements do not conflict with principles of the Code of Ethics and Guidelines for Practice.

4d. Fees: Fees charged by the conservation professional should be commensurate with services rendered. The division of a fee is acceptable only when based on the division of service or responsibility.

4e. Advertising: Advertising and other representations by the conservation professional should present an accurate description of credentials and services. Limitations concerning the use of the AIC name or membership status should be followed as stated in the AIC Bylaws, section II, 13.

5. Communication: Communication between the conservation professional and the owner, custodian, or authorized agent of the cultural property is essential to ensure an agreement that reflects shared decisions and realistic expectations.

6. Consent: The conservation professional should act only with the consent of the owner, custodian, or authorized agent. The owner, custodian, or agent should be

informed of any circumstances that necessitate significant deviations from the agreement. When possible, notification should be made before such changes are made.

7. Confidentiality: Except as provided in the Code of Ethics and Guidelines for Practice, the conservation professional should consider relationships with an owner, custodian, or authorized agent as confidential. Information derived from examination, scientific investigation, or treatment of the cultural property should not be published or otherwise made public without written permission.

8. Supervision: The conservation professional is responsible for work delegated to other professionals, students, interns, volunteers, subordinates, or agents and assignees. Work should not be delegated or subcontracted unless the conservation professional can supervise the work directly, can ensure proper supervision, or has sufficient knowledge of the practitioner to be confident of the quality of the work. When appropriate, the owner, custodian, or agent should be informed if such delegation is to occur.

9. Education: Within the limits of knowledge, ability, time, and facilities, the conservation professional is encouraged to become involved in the education of conservation personnel. The objectives and obligations of the parties shall be agreed upon mutually.

10. Consultation: Since no individual can be expert in every aspect of conservation, it may be appropriate to consult with colleagues or, in some instances, to refer the owner, custodian, or authorized agent to a professional who is more experienced or better equipped to accomplish the required work. If the owner requests a second opinion, this request must be respected.

11. Recommendations and References: The conservation professional should not provide recommendations without direct knowledge of a colleague's competence and experience. Any reference to the work of others must be based on facts and personal knowledge rather than on hearsay.

12. Adverse Commentary: A conservation professional may be required to testify in legal, regulatory, or administrative proceedings concerning allegations of unethical conduct. Testimony concerning such matters should be given at these proceedings or in connection with paragraph 13 of these Guidelines.

13. Misconduct: Allegations of unethical conduct should be reported in writing to the AIC president as described in the AIC Bylaws, section II, 12. As stated in the bylaws, all correspondence regarding alleged unethical conduct shall be held in the strictest confidence. Violations of the Code and Guidelines that constitute unethical conduct may result in disciplinary action.

14. Conflict of Interest: The conservation professional should avoid situations in which there is a potential for a conflict of interest that may affect the quality of work, lead to the dissemination of false information, or give the appearance of impropriety.

15. Related Professional Activities: The conservation professional should be especially mindful of the considerable potential for conflict of interest in activities such as authentication, appraisal, or art dealing.

Examination and Scientific Investigation

16. Justification: Careful examination of cultural property forms the basis for all future action by the conservation professional. Before undertaking any examination or tests that may cause change to cultural property, the conservation professional should establish the necessity for such procedures.

17. Sampling and Testing: Prior consent must be obtained from the owner, custodian, or agent before any material is removed from a cultural property. Only the minimum required should be removed, and a record of removal must be made. When appropriate, the material removed should be retained.

18. Interpretation: Declarations of age, origin, or authenticity should be made only when based on sound evidence.

19. Scientific Investigation: The conservation professional should follow accepted scientific standards and research protocols.

Preventative Conservation

20. Preventive Conservation: The conservation professional should recognize the critical importance of preventive conservation as the most effective means of promoting the long-term preservation of cultural property. The conservation professional should provide guidelines for continuing use and care, recommend appropriate environmental conditions for storage and exhibition, and encourage proper procedures for handling, packing, and transport.

Treatment

21. Suitability: The conservation professional performs within a continuum of care and will rarely be the last entrusted with the conservation of a cultural property. The conservation professional should only recommend or undertake treatment that is judged suitable to the preservation of the aesthetic, conceptual, and physical characteristics of the cultural property. When nonintervention best serves to promote the preservation of the cultural property, it may be appropriate to recommend that no treatment be performed.

22. Materials and Methods: The conservation professional is responsible for choosing materials and methods appropriate to the objectives of each specific treatment and consistent with currently accepted practice. The advantages of the materials and methods chosen must be balanced against their potential adverse effects on future examination, scientific investigation, treatment, and function.

23. Compensation for Loss: Any intervention to compensate for loss should be documented in treatment records and reports and should be detectable by common examination methods. Such compensation should be reversible and should not falsely modify the known aesthetic, conceptual, and physical characteristics of the cultural property, especially by removing or obscuring original material.

Documentation

24. Documentation: The conservation professional has an obligation to produce and maintain accurate, complete, and permanent records of examination, sampling, scientific investigation, and treatment. When appropriate, the records should be both written and pictorial. The kind and extent of documentation may vary according to the circumstances, the nature of the object, or whether an individual object or a collection is to be documented. The purposes of such documentation are:

- to establish the condition of cultural property;
- to aid in the care of cultural property by providing information helpful to future treatment and by adding to the profession's body of knowledge;
- to aid the owner, custodian, or authorized agent and society as a whole in the appreciation and use of cultural property by increasing understanding of an object's aesthetic, conceptual, and physical characteristics; and
- to aid the conservation professional by providing a reference that can assist in the continued development of knowledge and by supplying records that can help avoid misunderstanding and unnecessary litigation.

25. Documentation of Examination: Before any intervention, the conservation professional should make a thorough examination of the cultural property and create appropriate records. These records and the reports derived from them must identify the cultural property and include the date of examination and the name of the examiner. They also should include, as appropriate, a description of structure, materials, condition, and pertinent history.

26. Treatment Plan: Following examination and before treatment, the conservation professional should prepare a plan describing the course of treatment. This plan should also include the justification for and the objectives of treatment, alternative approaches, if feasible, and the potential risks. When appropriate, this plan should be submitted as a proposal to the owner, custodian, or authorized agent.

27. Documentation of Treatment: During treatment, the conservation professional should maintain dated documentation that includes a record or description of techniques or procedures involved, materials used and their composition, the nature and extent of all alterations, and any additional information revealed or otherwise ascertained. A report prepared from these records should summarize this information and provide, as necessary, recommendations for subsequent care.

28. Preservation of Documentation: Documentation is an invaluable part of the history of cultural property and should be produced and maintained in as permanent a manner as practicable. Copies of reports of examination and treatment must be given to the owner, custodian, or authorized agent, who should be advised of the importance of maintaining these materials with the cultural property. Documentation is also an important part of the profession's body of knowledge.

The conservation professional should strive to preserve these records and give other professionals appropriate access to them, when access does not contravene agreements regarding confidentiality.

Emergency Situations

29. Emergency Situations: Emergency situations can pose serious risks of damage to or loss of cultural property that may warrant immediate intervention on the part of the conservation professional. In an emergency that threatens cultural property, the conservation professional should take all reasonable action to preserve the cultural property, recognizing that strict adherence to the Guidelines for Practice may not be possible.

Amendments

Amendments: Proposed amendments to the Code of Ethics and Guidelines for Practice must be initiated by petition to the AIC Board of Directors from at least five members who are Fellows or Professional Associates of AIC. The board will direct the appropriate committee to prepare the amendments for vote in accordance with procedures described in Section VII of the Bylaws. Acceptance of amendments or changes must be affirmed by at least two-thirds of all AIC Fellows and Professional Associates voting.

Commentaries

Commentaries: Commentaries are prepared or amended by specialty/sub groups, task forces, and appropriate committees of AIC. A review process shall be undergone before final approval by the AIC Board of Directors.
*Revised August 1994

Glossary

Acid: Hydrogen-containing molecules or ions that are usually soluble in water and have a pH less than 7. Acids react with most metals and corrosion products.

Acid-free: Paper-based products that are processed to eliminate acids and have pH of 7 (neutral) or higher (alkaline).

Acrylic media: A thermoplastic resin made by polymerizing acrylic or methacrylate acid which is often used in paints as the vehicle or binder for the pigments.

Adhesive: A material that fills gaps between spaces physically joining surfaces together. Some of the more common adhesives are starches, resins, proteins, or cellulose ethers. Adhesives can be solvent activated, heat activated, or pressure sensitive.

Alabaster: A hard material such as gypsum or calcite, frequently used in the decorative arts, sometimes as a substitute for marble.

Albumen: Water-soluble proteins found in blood plasma, sera, and milk. In photography, the albumen print was the most popular printing medium from 1850 to 1890. The albumen was in this instance derived from egg whites.

Alkali: A soluble salt with a pH above 7. Alkali solutions can react with many metals and corrosion products and play an important role in metal chemistry.

Alloy: A solid solution composed of two or more metal elements intimately mixed, while in the molten state.

Anoxic: An environment free of oxygen.

Archaeological object: An artifact made from any material that has been recovered from an environment for which it was not originally intended and in which it spent a period of time. An archaeological object may come from an underwater location or from a burial in the ground.

Armature: (1) A skeleton or framework used by sculptors during modeling to support the modeling material (clay, wax, or plaster). (2) A support made to reinforce or articulate artifacts in an exhibit.

Backing: A material used as a support or protective cover on the reverse side of a two-dimensional object such as a print, painting, or textile. The backing may or may not be a part of the original object.

Binder: (1) A material such as a natural or synthetic resin, gum, or wax used as a vehicle for pigments or as a sort of adhesive, e.g., for consolidants. Also referred to as a medium. (2) In photography, a transparent material commonly called the emulsion that holds or binds the final image material to the support of a photograph.

Blasting: A method of mechanically cleaning sculpture that involves spraying sand, small glass beads, crushed walnut shells, or other lightly abrasive materials.

Bleaching: The use of chemical agents, artificial light, or sunlight with ultraviolet filtration to reduce discoloration and stains in works on paper and textiles.

Bloom: The formation of a loosely adhered substance on a surface that may be a result of biological activity such as mold, or of a chemical process such as metal corrosion, or of the buildup of soluble salts on masonry, creating an opaque or cloudy appearance. On a transparent film or varnish, bloom is caused by excess moisture absorbed by the film, in the paper, or the painting.

Bole: A material made of fine clay and mixed with a binder that is used to form a smooth uniform surface for gold leafing. Armenian bole is red in color.

Bronze: An alloy of copper and tin. Copper is the element of greatest proportion. Other elements may also be present, especially lead and zinc.

Bronze disease: Deterioration that occurs in bronzes as the result of the interaction of moisture, air, and chlorides with the metal, resulting in a powdery, light green corrosion product.

Buffer: A term commonly used for an alkaline salt, such as calcium carbonate, used in paper conservation treatments to counteract effects of acidity in future aging of the paper. Buffered papers are often used in storage materials to counteract the inherent acidity of wood pulp papers and acidity exposure to airborne pollutants.

Cockling: A term used in paper and book conservation referring to small puckers or planar distortion of a sheet of paper. Cockling usually occurs in response to high relative humidity and/or local restraints such as hinges or mats.

Collodion: A viscous solution of pyroxylin, with cellulose, used as a binder in many nineteenth-century photographic negatives and prints.

Compensation: Restoring aesthetic unity or structural integrity to an artifact by replacing areas that are missing or damaged.

Compo: A composite material that is shaped while moist. When dry it becomes hard and sturdy. Compo is used to make ornamental parts of picture frames. Duplicate parts are easily obtained since they are formed in a mold. Compo usually contains glue, whiting, rosin, and other materials.

Composites: Artifacts made from two or more materials. Frequently the materials have different chemical or physical properties that contribute to the utility of the object. Such objects may be difficult to treat.

Condition report: A written summary to the owner of an artifact by a conservator describing the composition and condition of an artifact. This report usually includes photographs and is written in conjuncture with the treatment proposal.

Conservation: The profession devoted to the preservation of cultural property for the future. Conservation activities include examination, documentation, treatment, and preventive care supported by research and education. (Reprinted with permission from the AIC Directory.)

Conservation treatment: The deliberate alteration of the chemical and/or physical aspects of cultural property, aimed primarily at prolonging its existence. Treatment may consist of stabilization and/or restoration.

Corrosion: The chemical or electrochemical reaction between a material, usually a metal, and its environment, that produces a deterioration of the material and its properties.

Cosmetic treatments: Actions taken to improve the appearance of an object, which may or may not contribute to its physical and chemical stability.

Crizzling: A series of very fine cracks within the body of a material, usually associated with glass and ceramic glazes.

Crazing: Microscopic cracks, which can appear on the plastic's surface or inside the plastic, often resulting in a frosted appearance. The object may or may not be "cracked," but could reach that point eventually.

Cross-linking: The joining of two or more polymer chains through a chemical bond. Cross-linking can be triggered by ultraviolet light and/or solvent evaporation. For polymer adhesives, cross-linking produces an insoluble bond.

Crystalline structure: The tendency of many molecular compounds to be arranged in a uniform and repeating geometric pattern. Often this microscopic structure manifests itself in a macroscopic manner such as quartz or the cubic structure of pyrite.

Deacidification: Conservation treatment used to describe the partial or complete removal of acids, or the neutralization of acids, from a material, especially papers, and raising of the pH to 7 or above. With respect to paper artifacts, the term may or may not imply adding an alkaline buffer to protect against future contact with an acidic environment.

Deionized water: Water that has been purified of ions by passing it through synthetic resins that have affinity for dissolved and ionized salts.

Delamination: A physical separation between layers, such as the lifting of a photograph off of a backing board or the separation of a veneer from a substrate. The term also refers to an insecure attachment of media to support.

Dichroic glass filters: A filter that transmits certain wavelengths of energy and reflects those that are not transmitted. In museum lighting, dichroic filters reflect infrared radiation (heat) through the back of the lamp or light fixture.

Disaster plan: A written plan of action in case of emergency such as fire, flood, explosion, which directs employees of an institution, business, or homeowner, whom to call and objects to be saved in order of priority. It should outline course of action, recommended location for supplies, and emergency recovery procedures.

Distilled water: Water that is purified by converting it to a gas by means of heating and then condensing the water vapor over cold coils. In the process, chemical and biological contaminants are eliminated.

Dry cleaning: (1) The cleaning of a textile by immersion and agitation in a non-aqueous solvent. (2) A surface cleaning technique using a mild abrasive, such as the cleaning of paper with grated eraser crumbs or soft brushes.

Dye: An intense colorant, usually water soluble, that is absorbed in a permanent manner to a fiber.

Efflorescing salts: Formations of white crusts or blooms on masonry and ceramic surfaces often caused by high relative humidity and/or water migration.

Electromagnetic spectrum: The characterization of all known forms of energy by wavelength measured in nanometers. Ultraviolet radiation, visible light, and infrared radiation are of greatest concern for artifact preservation. X-rays, radio waves, and microwaves are among the other forms characterized in the spectrum.

Enamel: (1) vitreous fired metal oxides. (2) a type of paint.

Encapsulation: The enclosing of an artifact within a sealed environment. Documents, for example, are often placed between two sheets of inert polyester film, which is sealed along the outside edges.

Encrustation: The formation of a hard crust around an artifact, often rendering it indistinct. Such crusts are often associated with metal or ceramic artifacts that have been buried in the ground or immersed in seawater for long periods. The term can also refer to a deposit on paper or a painting.

Epoxy: A synthetic thermosetting resin used in adhesives and coatings.

Ethnographic object: A cultural object that reflects both the idea and activities of a people, whether from prehistoric times or the present. Ethnographic objects may serve a functional purpose or have spiritual significance, or both. They are often made from natural materials found in the immediate environment, but may also incorporate less traditional materials such as aluminum, plastics, and glass. In many instances ethnographic objects are all that remains of a culture and thus the primary source of information about it. Also called, in anthropology, material culture.

Fabric: (1) A generic term for all fibrous constructions. The term is used to refer to cloth produced by the joining of fibers, such as weaving, knitting, or felting. (2) Also used to refer to an object's structure, e.g. the fabric of a building.

Fixative: Adhesive applied to drawing media such as soft graphite pencil, charcoal, or pastel to minimize smudging or detachment from the paper surface.

Fluorescent tube: A low-pressure mercury electric discharge lamp in which a fluorescing coating (phosphor) transforms some of the energy generated by the discharge into light. The light emitted from fluorescent tubes has strong intensity, including some ultraviolet radiation (UV).

Foxing: Yellow, brown, or gray circular or snowflake-shaped spots formed on a paper or textile surface by mold, or metallic impurities within the structure, that result from high humidity.

Freeze-drying: A process of sublimation used to dry out various materials such as waterlogged wood or paper and archival materials that have become wet. The materials are first frozen and then put into a chamber where the ice crystals are converted to water vapor and exhausted from the chamber. In the process, the water goes from the solid state to the gaseous state without passing through the liquid state.

Freeze-thaw cycles: The freezing, melting, and refreezing of water in architectural stone or in hollow metalwork. The physical expansion that occurs when water freezes can result in spalling or the cracking of brittle metals, such as cast iron.

Friable: A condition in which media such as charcoal or pastel, that have little binder, become dislodged. It comes from the Latin *friare,* meaning to crumble.

Fumigation: Use of a toxic gas to kill insect, pests, or mold growth.

Gesso: A ground composed of a binder and gypsum or chalk and usually used to prepare a wood or canvas surface for painting.

Gilding: The process of covering a metal surface with gold. This process may be accomplished by plating; applying an amalgam of gold and mercury to an object, and heating; or by applying thin sheets of gold and burnishing. For wooden surfaces, there are traditionally two types of gilding—water gilding and oil gilding. Oil gilding is more permanent as the mordant is less likely to be affected by moisture.

Glazing: (1) The application of a clear or tinted material to a surface to create a gloss. (2) The creation of a glaze or glass-like surface on a ceramic. (3) The covering of a framed artwork with a clear plastic or glass in order to protect it.

Gum: A natural colloidal material derived from plants and used as a paint medium. Gums are generally water-soluble. Gum arabic is one of the more common gums used by artists and is the binder for most watercolor paints.

Hardness: (1) The resistance of a substance to surface abrasion. (2) The concentration of alkaline salts in water.

Hatching: (1) A term used in painting conservation to describe techniques used to distinguish inpainting from the surrounding original paint layer. (2) A traditional miniature painting technique often found in combination with stippling and washing.

Housing (rehousing): The enclosure for an artifact or object in which that object is stored. It is important that the housing be archival, physically sturdy, and chemically compatible with the object.

Humidistat: A sensing device that controls humidification and dehumidification and can also control heating and cooling equipment to maintain a desired level of relative humidity.

HVAC system: The heating, ventilating, and air conditioning system that maintains desired environmental and air quality conditions within a building.

Hygrothermograph: A device used to measure temperature and humidity in a prescribed environment, such as storage or exhibit areas.

Illuminance: The intensity or strength of visible light striking an object. A light meter, also referred to as an illuminance meter, can be used to measure the intensity of light falling on an object. The units of measurement are lux or foot-candle.

Incandescent lamp: A light fixture containing a filament that produces light when heated to incandescence by an electric current. Tungsten is a common filament material.

Infrared light (IR): Radiant energy beyond the visible spectrum, from 770nm and 1,000,000nm. IR is most commonly perceived as heat from a light source or solar radiation.

Inherent vice: The quality of a material or an object to self-destruct or to be unusually difficult to maintain. Examples include nitrocellulose films and wood pulp papers.

Inorganic material: Generally a material that is not derived from plants or animals. Examples include metals, ceramics, stone, and glass.

Inpainting: The compensation for a loss in a painted surface by filling and/or painting over the void. Also referred to as compensation or retouching.

Japanese paper: A term referring to a wide range of papers usually produced from plants, such as gampi, mitsumata, and mulberry, using techniques native to Japan. These papers are often used in paper conservation. Kozo, kizukishi, and tengujo papers are examples. The term may be used interchangeably with tissue.

Japanned surface: A heavy lacquer surface, usually red or black in color and often on a wood substrate. The lacquered surface is built up in many layers and can be carved and decorated.

Lacquer: A resinous material derived from a tree and used as a coating for woods and as an artist's material. Today the term is applied to a wide variety of natural and synthetic coatings.

Laser technology: The amplification of electromagnetic energy to form an intense focused beam. Lasers have been used in conservation treatment, often to burn away undesirable encrustations.

Leaf casting: A technique used in paper conservation to compensate for losses. Essentially a slurry of paper pulp is prepared and deposited in holes or along missing edges, where it remains to form new paper upon drying.

Limestone: A sedimentary rock consisting mainly of calcium carbonate.

Lining: A technique associated with painting and paper conservation in which an additional support is added to the back of a degraded support. In textile conservation, the term refers to a cover on the back of a flat textile or a layer of fabric on the interior of a costume.

Marble: Limestone that has been transformed by the process of metamorphism into a harder stone. Heat and pressure beneath the earth's surface cause structural changes in the molecular structure of the stone.

Marquetry and parquetry: Inlaid work in wood or ivory.

Mechanical cleaning: A technique for cleaning a surface that is usually dry and entails some degree of rubbing, scraping, or abrading.

Medium: A binding material such as an oil, gum, gelatin, or acrylic resin that contains a pigment. The term may also be used to differentiate the design or pictorial material from the surface to which it is applied.

Metal: An element or mixtures of elements (alloys) that possess high electrical conductivity and a lustrous appearance in the solid state. Metals are usually divided into two groups—ferrous (steel and iron) and nonferrous.

Moisture content: A measure of the amount of water contained in organic materials, such as wood, paper, and animal skins, that contributes to their stability.

Mold: (1) A fine microbial organic growth such as fungi, usually on an organic substrate and often a result of high relative humidity. Mold is often visible as a fuzzy deposit on paper or other organic substrate. (2) A hollow form for the casting of metals, ceramics, or plastics.

Oil medium: Paints in which the pigment is suspended in an oil medium such as linseed oil.

Organic material: Commonly thought to be natural plant or animal substances, but also including plastics. Organic materials are formed from hydrocarbons and their derivatives. Most contain the elements carbon, hydrogen, and oxygen.

Overpainting: The process of painting over an existing surface.

Ozone: A molecular form of oxygen consisting of three oxygen atoms. Ozone is often found in polluted urban air, and because of its tendency to react with other chemical species is considered a general threat to cultural resources.

Paper: A sheet made from a liquid suspension of beaten plant fibers deposited on a wire or bamboo screen. The primary constituent is cellulose. Paper can be handmade or machine made. Its quality is dependent on the slurry additives, type of fiber, and manner of fabrication.

Paper splitting: A technique for splitting a sheet of paper in half, front and back. A support can be inserted between the two halves for structural stability, or the two halves can be backed and used for exhibit side by side. Recent mechanization of the technique has been developed.

Papier-mâché: A material consisting of paper pulp or strips mixed with glue, chalk, and sometimes fine sand. The material is easy to work when plastic and can be air-dried or baked to make it hard.

Parchment: Treated animal skins, usually sheep or goatskin, used as a writing or printing surface, painting, furniture, and other objects. Also referred to as vellum.

Pastel: An artist's chalk composed of pigment and fillers usually bound together with a little gum.

Patina: The naturally formed surface appearance of a metal sculpture resulting from corrosion due to aging or burial, or an artificial surface appearance created by the application of chemical coatings.

Pewter: An alloy consisting of tin and other elements such as copper, lead, antimony, and bismuth. There are many different alloys of pewter; some, but not all, contain lead.

pH: A measure of acidity or alkalinity of a solution or a material. A value of 7 is neutral. Values below 7 are increasingly acidic, and values above 7 are increasingly basic.

Photodegradation: Deterioration of light-sensitive material resulting from exposure to visible light and ultraviolet radiation.

Photographic Activity Test (PAT): A standard (ANSI IT 9.14) written by the American National Standards Institute that provides a way for buyers of enclosure materials for photographs to be assured what they buy will not harm their photographs. Many manufacturers and suppliers of housing materials now conduct this test on their products.

Pigment: A finely ground organic or inorganic compound used by artists to give color to a design or picture. Pigments are often bound by a medium such as oil, acrylic resin, or vegetable gum. Pigments are also used to tint waxes and adhesives.

Pith paper: A smooth white paper-like support made from peeling concentric circles of bark of certain plants. The origin is Chinese.

Planar distortions: Distortion in a two-dimensional surface, such as cockling or warping. The distortion is often a response to relative humidity, heat, or excessive restraint.

Plastic: An object composed of polymers, including natural, semisynthetic, and synthetic materials.

Plating: A very thin layer of a metal deposited on the surface of another metal.

Polish: An abrasive material used to obtain a high luster in stonework and metalwork. The term also refers to waxes used to obtain a glossy surface on wood and leather.

Pollutant: Unwanted gas or vapor that can cause deterioration to many different types of materials. Harmful pollutants include nitrogen dioxide, carbon dioxide, sulfur dioxide, and ozone.

Polyester film: A clear plastic film that provides support and flexibility, and is used for encapsulation of documents. Polyester film is inert (does not interact chemically with materials), but it does hold a static charge, so friable or easily rubbed media like pastel or graphite should not be used with it. A brand-name for polyester film is Mylar®.

Polymer: A large molecule made up of a large number of small molecules called monomers.

Porcelain: A hard, nonporous and sometimes translucent ceramic made from kaolin clay, quartz, and feldspar and fired at a high temperature.

Porosity: The quality or state of having a high percentage of voids or interstices, such as low-fired ceramics, brick, and some stone, as well as paint film, that can absorb water and promote mold growth and/or the deposition of soluble salts.

Poultice: In conservation, the application of a material saturated with a solvent, cleaning solution, or chemical compound to the surface of an artifact to clean it or to remove undesirable contaminants.

Preservation: The protection of a cultural property through activities that minimize chemical and physical deterioration. The primary goal is to prolong its existence. (Reprinted with permission from the AIC Directory.)

Preventive conservation: The mitigation of deterioration through procedures and actions other than chemical or mechanical manipulation of the artifact, such as control of environment, proper housing, and storage.

Provenance: The source or place where an object was made or where it was found. The history of ownership.

Pumice: A light, porous volcanic rock that can be used to abrade a surface and used as a polishing agent for metals and stone.

Rabbet: A channel or ledge cut into the back of a picture frame in order to support the artwork.

Radiocarbon dating: A dating technique for organic materials that measures the residual amount of carbon 14.

Red rot: A form of leather degradation characterized by a dry, powdery surface and a loss of strength.

Regilding: The removal of old gilt and the application of new. Due to the weathering properties of gold leaf on outdoor metals and sculpture, periodic regilding may be necessary and desirable.

Relative humidity: The amount of moisture in a given volume of air at a given temperature and barometric pressure expressed as a percent of the actual amount of moisture that same air could hold. To preserve both organic and inorganic materials, it is important to monitor relative humidity.

Repatination: The cleaning and chemical coloring of a bronze surface. The artifact or sculpture may be cleaned to bare metal before repatination, but often a conservator will endeavor to retain as much of the original surface as possible.

Resins: Initially the term applied to the secretions of certain plants and trees that could be used as coatings or adhesives and formed the basis of all natural varnishes. Today the term applies to a wide range of natural and synthetic materials.

Resoldering: The rejoining of metals by the use of (solders) alloys that flow at temperatures lower that the melting point of the metals being joined. Soldering is accomplished by fluxing or cleaning of the joint, often with an acid, and then melting the solder with a torch. The molten solder flows into the joint and solidifies.

Restoration: Treatment procedures intended to return cultural property to a known or assumed state through the addition of nonoriginal material. (Reprinted with permission from the AIC Directory.)

Reversibility: The capacity of material or process to be undone or removed in the future, should further conservation be necessary. A major characteristic of good conservation is the combination of reversible materials and techniques with a solution for the problem at hand.

Reweaving: Replacing missing warp or weft, or both, in a woven textile.

Rising damp: The passage of water upward through a material, such as a masonry wall.

Sandstone: A sedimentary rock usually composed of quartz sand and silica and/or calcium carbonate.

Shellac: The resinous secretion of the lac insect. Shellac used traditionally as a surface, applied and dissolved in alcohol solvent.

Sizing: A material such as a glue, varnish, or resin used to seal a porous surface such as paper, leather, or plaster.

Spalling: The separation of a masonry or stone surface due to hydrostatic pressure or freeze-thaw cycling.

Stabilization: A treatment procedure intended to maintain the integrity of cultural property and to minimize deterioration.

Steel: An alloy of iron and carbon, with a carbon content between 0.1 and 2.0 percent.

Sticky-shed syndrome: A softening of the polyurethane binder in videotape and audiotape that occurs in response to moisture. The binder, which holds the image or sound to the tape base, becomes sticky and falls off the tape base when played.

Stippling: A painting technique often used in inpainting to distinguish the treated area from the original paint surface. The paint is applied in small dots.

Stone: Lithic materials formed by sedimentation, metamorphic, or igneous processes.

Strainer: A support over which canvas is stretched in preparation for painting. The corners of this device are fixed and cannot be adjusted.

Stretcher: A support over which canvas is stretched in preparation for painting. The corners of this device are adjustable.

Support: A brace, strut, or armature used to stabilize or hold up an artifact. In painting and paper conservation, the term refers to the canvas, wood panel, or paper that has been painted on. In photographic conservation, the terms refers to the material that provides the foundation for the binder and gives physical strength to the photograph.

Surfactant: A group of chemical compounds that have an affinity for other materials such as oils. Surfactants reduce the surface tension of a solvent, like water; can emulsify a liquid otherwise not soluble in that solvent; and suspend solid particles (dirt) in solution. Surfactants are often used in detergents to latch onto dirt and oils and to keep them in suspension until they are rinsed away.

Tapa cloth: A paper-like material, traditional in the South Pacific islands, that is formed from the hand-beaten inner bark of trees.

Tarnish: The discoloration of a metal surface caused by a thin film of corrosion product, usually in reference to silver objects.

Tapestry: A weft-faced plain weave fabric with a discontinuous weft. Often the term is used to describe woven, worsted wool textiles from Europe with complex pictorial compositions. Among embroiders, the term can also refer to a type of needlework embroidery. Broadly, the term applies to any woven cloth with a pictorial image, often power-loomed in the nineteenth or early twentieth century.

Terra-cotta: A naturally occurring clay fired at a high temperature to produce utilitarian objects and architectural components such as roof and floor tiles.

Textile: A fabric or cloth made from the interlacing of warp and weft yarns.

Thermal shock: Physical damage resulting from a change in the temperature of a material.

Thermoluminescence dating (TL): A dating technique for ceramics.

Thermoplastic: Materials that can be repeatedly softened by heat and hardened when cold. Nylon, polypropylene, and polyethylene are examples of thermoplastic materials.

Thermosetting: Materials that undergo a chemical reaction by the action of heat and therefore remain in a fixed shape when heated again. Examples include epoxies, PVC, polyester, and urea formaldehyde.

Tide line: A stain or line of discoloration usually caused by the congregation of water-soluble soils or degradation products at the edge of a wetted area.

Treatment proposal: A written estimate to the owner of an artifact by a conservator describing the advised course of treatment and requesting the owner's signature of approval. Cost estimate is included, sometimes as a range, allowing for more or less time needed of the completion of the treatment.

Treatment report: A written report to the owner of an artifact by a conservator after conservation treatment is completed, summarizing the course of treatment undertaken and outlining the materials used.

Tungsten-halogen lamp: A tungsten filament lamp to which a small quantity of iodine has been added to produce a more efficient and whiter light.

Ukiyoe: Traditional Japanese woodblock prints that depict scenes of beautiful women, entertainers, landscapes, and other pleasures.

Ultraviolet radiation (UV): Any radiant energies within the wavelength range 10 to 400 nanometers. The UV band of electromagnetic energy is adjacent to the violet side of the visible light-band, as UV light waves are shorter than visible light waves. UV radiation can be particularly damaging to light-sensitive materials.

UV/IR photography: Photography using specific lights, camera filters, and photographic film in order to detect the presence of certain coatings, varnishes, or other materials on works of art and antiques that are only observed in either the presence of ultraviolet light or infrared light.

Varnish: A surface coating containing resinous matter either dissolved in hot drying oils (oil varnish) or cold solvents (spirit varnish).

Vellum: An animal skin used as a writing surface and as a support for paintings, furniture, and other objects. Vellum is usually calf, sheep, or goatskin. Also referred to as parchment.

Veneer: A thin wood laminate applied to a thicker wood substrate.

Vinegar syndrome: A deterioration of cellulose acetate in the presence of water in which acetic acid, which smells like vinegar, is formed and released. Elevated temperature and relative humidity accelerate this reaction, and the acetic acid contributes to continuing deterioration.

Visible light: Radiant energy within the wavelength range of 400 to 760 nanometers. It is termed visible because it is the energy sensed by the human eye. Visible light is considered less damaging than UV radiation, however it can cause significant damage to artifacts.

Vitrine: A glass or Plexiglas museum case.

Wash: The immersion or wetting of a textile, paper, or a three-dimensional artifact with water or a water-based solution in order to clean it. A technique used in miniature painting in which paint is flowed over a surface with a wet and fully loaded brush.

Watercolor: A pigment-colored, powdered substance mixed in a water-soluble gum, usually gum arabic, and diluted with water to create a paint used on paper or in portrait miniatures on ivory.

Weephole: A hole drilled in a sculpture or an artifact to allow the drainage of water.

Weeping glass: A condition often observed in deteriorating glass in which small droplets of water form on the surface. It is often associated with crizzling.

Weeping plastic: Liquid droplets, most often acidic, which are released from a plastic material and often appear on the surface.

Wet-cleaning: (1) Any cleaning method that involves a liquid in the form of water, solvents, or other chemicals. (2) The cleaning of a textile by immersion and agitation in water only.

Wheat starch paste: The standard adhesive used by paper conservators. Wheat starch paste is strong, non-staining, and reversible.

X-radiography: The use of short electromagnetic radiation to obtain images of the internal structure of opaque objects such as paintings or sculpture. X-ray sensitive photographic film captures the image.

Conservator Index

Index

weepholes, 84, 221
weeping glass, 21, 68, 221
weeping plastic, 108, 221
Wellman, Howard, 171
Western paintings. *See* paintings
wet-cleaning. *See* washing
wheat starch paste, 40, 221
Willman, Polly, 179
wooden objects
    conservation treatments, 92–94
    effects of environment, 90–91, 101
    insect infestations, 57, 91
    painting supports, 10, 14
    patina of, 92
    problems, 90–94
    structure, 89

technical analysis, 95
  See also ethnographic objects;
    frames; furniture

X
X-radiography, 221
  of ethnographic objects, 59
  of frames, 102
  of paintings, 13

Y
Young, Lisa, 129–30

Z
Zilius, James, 176

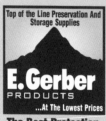

  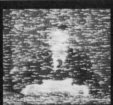 

American Institute for Conservation
of Historic and Artistic Works

Guide to Conservation Services
...the nationwide directory for conservation services

Please visit the AIC website at <u>aic.stanford.edu</u>
and click on "Selecting a Conservator"

1717 K Street, NW Suite 200
Washington, DC 20006
202/452-9545 ◆   202/452-9328 ◆   info@aic-faic.org

MEMBERSHIP FORM

_____ $25.00 ($30.00 Overseas)   _____ $15.00 (Student/Intern)

Make check payable to the Washington Conservation Guild or WCG.
Enclose your check with this form and mail to:

WASHINGTON CONSERVATION GUILD
P.O. Box 23364
Washington, D.C. 20026

Only members paid by July 1 will be included in the directory, published
in September. Only current members can vote in the May election.

_____

name

_____

address

_____

_____

_____

company

_____

IMPORTANT NUMBERS
(place an asterisk* by the number for use by clients)

_____   _____

work   *home*

_____   _____

email   *fax*

Please check no more than three professional specializations. Of those three, circle your primary specialization

_____	AM	Architectural Materials
_____	AO	Archaeological Objects
_____	BK	Books
_____	CA	Conservation Administrator
_____	CE	Conservation Educator
_____	CS	Conservation Scientist
_____	EO	Ethnographic Objects
_____	FR	Frames
_____	GO	Guilded Objects
_____	IN	Intern/Student
_____	MA	Matting and Framing
_____	OB	Objects
_____	PM	Photographic Materials
_____	PP	Paper
_____	PT	Paintings
_____	SC	Sculpture
_____	TX	Textiles
_____	WA	Wooden Artifacts
_____	OT	Other

Please indicate your availability for speaking, treatment, disaster assistance, consultations and surveys:

_____	C&S	Available for consultation and survey
_____	D	Available to assist with emergency response to disasters
_____	S	Available as speaker
_____	T	Available for treatment

QUESTIONS OR COMMENTS

E-mail:	washingtonconservationguild@hotmail.com
Website:	http//palimpsest.stanford.edu/wcg/
Address:	P.O. Box 23364
	Washington, DC 20026

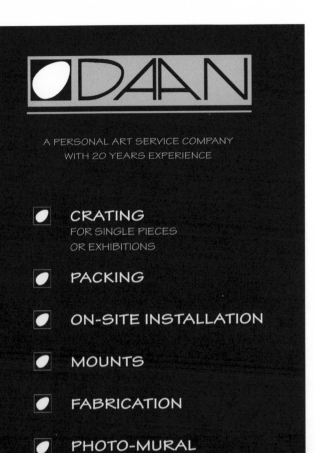

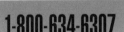

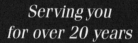
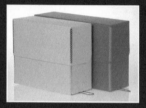